# OLNEY HYMNS:

IN

## THREE BOOKS.

I. ON SELECT TEXTS OF SCRIPTURE.

II. ON OCCASIONAL SUBJECTS.

III. ON THE PROGRESS AND CHANGES
OF THE SPIRITUAL LIFE.

WITH

## AN INTRODUCTORY ESSAY

BY

## JAMES MONTGOMERY,

AUTHOR OF 'THE WORLD BEFORE THE FLOOD,' 'SONGS OF ZION.'
'THE CHRISTIAN PSALMIST,' 'THE CHRISTIAN POET,' ETC.

SECOND EDITION.

GLASGOW:

WILLIAM COLLINS, S. FREDERICK STREET.

EDINBURGH: OLIVER & BOYD—W. WHYTE & CO.—W. OLIPHANT & SON.
DUBLIN: WILLIAM CURRY, JUNIOR, & CO.
LONDON: WHITTAKER & CO.—HAMILTON, ADAMS, & CO.—
SIMPKIN, MARSHALL, & CO.

1840.

## Printing Statement:

Due to the very old age and scarcity of this book,
many of the pages may be hard to read due to the
blurring of the original text, possible missing pages,
missing text, dark backgrounds and other issues
beyond our control.

Because this is such an important and rare work, we
believe it is best to reproduce this book regardless of
its original condition.

Thank you for your understanding.

# SELECT

# CHRISTIAN AUTHORS,

WITH

# INTRODUCTORY ESSAYS.

No. 46.

# INTRODUCTORY ESSAY.

On a small island, covered with palm-trees, lying off the western coast of Africa, visited by none but slave-ships,—in the year 1746, there lived a young man, of respectable English parentage. His mother, whose only child he was, had died during his infancy ; and his father being a mariner, much occupied abroad in the mercantile service, maintained little control over his son after the latter had once escaped from under his eye. The youth himself was headstrong and capricious, and, by his rashness or perversity, repeatedly thwarted the prudent purposes of his surviving parent to settle him honourably in his own profession. After a series of strange adventures by sea and land, during which he had escaped various perils, but fallen into many snares, and lost all sense of religion and decorum, he was impressed and carried on board of the Harwich, about to sail for the East Indies. Here, though promoted by his father's interest to the rank of midshipman, from the outset he exposed himself to the displeasure of the commander by his irregular conduct, and soon afterwards, in a fit of folly, deserted from the service, at the very time when he was appointed to watch over a boat's company, and prevent any of them from deserting. Being retaken, and brought in chains to the vessel, he was publicly flogged, and expelled from the quarter-deck. When the ship reached Madeira, he was exchanged with the captain of a merchantman for one more likely to serve his Majesty. From Madeira he was brought to the little island above-mentioned, where, quitting the vessel, he entered into the service of an English speculator in the trade of that coast—a broker in blood, buying and selling men, woman, and children, on such terms, and for such profits, as could be made in that lottery of inhuman adventure. His master, though a slave-dealer, was himself the slave, by brutal passion, of a black woman, who lived with him as his wife, and ruled over his household with a tyranny not surpassed by a native driver, with his cart-whip, in the sugar islands.

How our renegade stripling, at an age when youth and ill health might have softened the heart of the least compassionate of the gentler sex, came to be so much out of favour with his mistress, has not been told by himself, but her cruelty has, and the record will not soon be effaced from his pages, though thousands of wretches like him may have suffered as much, under similar circumstances, whose wrongs and oppressions ceased from the earth with themselves, and were written in no book but that out of which the dead as well as the living shall be judged at the last day. *His* miseries, however, have been preserved by enduring memorials,—perhaps as examples of the horrible re-action and vengeance on the spot, and in the persons of the perpetrators, which, even in this world, accompany the practice of that unexpiated crime against God and man, in which civilized nations have been engaged for more than three centuries—that crime of Christendom, which has robbed Africa of millions of her offspring, peopled the West Indies with a perishing population beyond the power of nature to renew, and brought upon Europe judgments, which may never be traced to their real source till the secret counsels of Providence shall be revealed, and the ways of God to man be justified, in the presence of all the lost, and all the saved, of heaven and earth.

The sufferings of our unhappy outcast cannot be expressed with equal force by any other words than his own. Let him, then, speak for himself—not at the time;—no, not at the time, for then he would have spoken swords and spears, and buried his complaints under the burden of execrations, which he would have poured, and often did pour out, in the bitterness of his soul, upon the female scourge under whose lash of scorpions he (the representative of guilty England, that fostered such spoilers of Guinea) was daily writhing. No, let him speak, as he spoke long afterwards, when the grace of God had reclaimed and translated him from the bondage of Satan into the kingdom of Christ. Having been left sick by his master, under the care of his mistress, he says:—

" I had sometimes not a little difficulty to procure a draught of cold water when burning with a fever. My bed was a mat spread upon a board, and a log of wood my pillow. When my fever left me, my appetite returned. I would gladly have eaten, but there was no one gave unto me. She lived in plenty herself, but hardly allowed me sufficient to sustain life, except now and then, when in the highest good humour, she would send me victuals on her own plate, after she had dined; and this (so greatly was my pride humbled) I received with thanks and eagerness, as the most needy beggar does an alms. Once I was called to receive this bounty from her own hand; but, being exceedingly weak and feeble, I dropped the plate. Those who live in plenty can hardly conceive how this loss touched me; but she had the cruelty to laugh at my disappointment; and though the table was covered with dishes, she refused to give me any more. My distress has been so great as to compel me to go by night and pull up roots in the plantation, (though at the risk of being punished as a thief,) which I have eaten raw upon the spot, for fear of discovery. The roots I speak of are very wholesome food when boiled, but as unfit to be eaten raw as a potato. The consequence of this diet—which after the first experiment I always expected and seldom missed—was the same as if I had taken tartar emetic; so that I have often returned as empty as I went; yet necessity urged me to the trial several times. I have sometimes been relieved by strangers, nay, *even by the slaves in the chain*, who secretly brought me victuals (for they durst not be seen to do it,) *from their own slender pittance.*"

His master also, instigated by her unnatural antipathy, proved as merciless as his mistress. On a coasting voyage, being suspected of theft from the stores.—" almost the only crime I could not justly be charged with," as he himself testifies, he says :—

" The charge was believed, and I was condemned without evidence. From that time he used me very hardly. Whenever he left the vessel, I was locked up on deck, with a pint of rice for my day's allowance, and if he staid longer, I had no relief till his return.—When fowls were killed for his own use, I seldom was allowed any part but the entrails, to bait my hooks with ; and at what we call *slack water*, that is, about the changing of the tides, when the current was still, I used generally to fish, (for at other times it was not practicable,) and I often succeeded. If I saw a fish on my hook, my joy was little less than any other person may have found in the accomplishment of the scheme which he had most at heart. Such a fish, hastily broiled, or rather half burned, without sauce, salt, or bread, has afforded me a delicious meal. If I caught none, I might, if I could, sleep away my hunger till the next return of slack water, and then try again. Nor did I suffer less from the inclemency of the weather and the want of clothes. The rainy season was now advancing ; my whole suit was a shirt, a pair of trowsers, a cotton handkerchief instead of a cap, and a cotton cloth about two yards long to supply the want of upper garments ; and thus accoutred I have been exposed for twenty, thirty, perhaps nearly forty hours together, in incessant rain, accompanied with strong gales of wind, without the least shelter, when my master was on shore. I feel to this day some faint returns of the violent pains I then contracted. The excessive cold and wet I endured in that voyage, and soon after I had recovered from a long sickness, quite broke my constitution and my spirits. The latter were soon restored ; but the effects of the former still remain with me, as a needful memento of the service and the wages of sin."

One circumstance more from his revolting narrative must be quoted here, to consummate the picture of his personal distresses, and to introduce the reader of this sketch to a knowledge of the far-surpassing debasement of his enslaved, abandoned, and infatuated mind. He says to his friend and correspondent, in after life,—" Had you seen me, then, go pensive and solitary, in the dead of the night, to wash my one shirt upon the rocks, and afterwards put it on wet, that it might dry upon my back while I slept ;—had you seen me so poor a figure that, when a boat's crew came to the island, shame often constrained me to hide myself in the woods, from the sight of strangers ; —especially had you known that my conduct, prin-

ciples, and heart, were still darker than my outward
condition, how little would you have imagined.... ...."
But we must break off here.

In this iron furnace, heated seven times, under a
tropical sun, amidst the pestilential atmosphere of a
low coast tangled with woods and traversed by rivers,
not rolling their healthful and fertilizing streams into
the open sea, but degenerating into shallows and
marshes—our young prodigal did *not* come to himself.
His heart, which amidst former adversities had been
hardened with pride, inflamed with rage, and brooded
with resentment, was now brought down, quenched,
and subdued. Here he lost all resolution, and almost
all reflection, sinking into that fatuity which is the
last refuge of exhausted nature in hopeless captivity.
He himself thus describes his apathy :—" I had lost
the fierceness which fired me when on board the Harwich, and which made me capable of the most despe-
rate attempts ; but I was no further changed than a
tiger tamed by hunger ;—remove the occasion, and he
will be as wild as ever."

Such was his personal and mental, but what was
his spiritual state ? It has already been intimated,
that he was the only son of his mother ; but she was
in her grave ; she could no longer plead for him at a
throne of grace ; her earnest intercession for him in
infancy seemed to have been answered no otherwise
than by her own providential removal from the evil to
come upon him. She had not been permitted to live
for him to break her heart ; and in mercy to both, *he*
was spared that sin unto death—that species of parri-
cide which it is to be feared is more frequent than
forgiving parents and rebellious children are themselves aware. His mother, before he was six years

old, had instilled into his heart such principles of
Christian faith and practice, as he never could wholly
get rid of, amidst all the dissipation of his reprobate
career. The remembrance of these early lessons had
often haunted him before the time at which we have
been contemplating his fallen character and condition.
Thrice before he became recklessly apostate from the
faith—an avowed infidel, half persuading himself that
he was altogether such ; he had tried to accommodate
his desires and projects in life to a form of godliness ;
but in each instance he had utterly miscarried ; for it
was in his own wisdom and by his own strength that
he sought to make out a righteousness to suit corrupt
nature, rather than in obedience to the gospel. In the
issue he had been so bewildered by Shaftesbury—
whose ' Characteristics ' had fallen into his hands, and
in whose paradise of fools he delighted to wander and
revel till his imagination was intoxicated—that he
cast off all reverence for revealed truth, and appeared
to others what he himself desired to be—a hardened
sceptic. In this victory over better knowledge he was
aided by the sophistry of a profligate companion
a-board the man of war, after his impressment, and
the conflict was decided by the treachery of his own
deceitful and desperately wicked heart ; for no cup of
enchantment, with whatsoever subtlety mingled, can
in any case prevail till " a man is drawn away of his
own lust, and enticed."

Here, then, on that island of despair, where he
wanted every earthly comfort, the forlorn exile was
equally destitute of heavenly consolations. God was
not in all his thoughts, though often on his tongue,
but acknowledged only in curses, and invoked in
" the swearer's prayer "—that prayer which, through
the forbearance of divine mercy, is oftener than any

other uttered in vain!—Had the gifted eye of some living contemporary been miraculously opened to look round the whole world, and select from among the millions of its most miserable inhabitants *one* supreme in wretchedness, and of whom no hope, either in this world or that which is to come, could be entertained —*that* one of whom we speak might well have been fixed upon as he—motherless, homeless, friendless—a stranger in a strange land, disinherited, for aught he knew, by his father, forsaken of God, and trampled under foot by man—experiencing in its most literal fulfilment the curse upon Canaan, (the oldest and direst next to that which accompanied expulsion from Eden) being truly " a servant of servants "—a slave's slave, for whom none prayed, and who prayed not for himself! So fallen below the lowest of his race was he at the crisis which we have described, that had the man of most practical faith then living been permitted to survey such a spectacle of mental, personal, and spiritual reprobation, and heard a voice from eternity whispering in his ear—" Behold, *he* is a chosen vessel—*this* shall be a light of the world, a star in the right hand of Him who walketh amidst the golden candlesticks—this derider of the faith shall be the angel of a church, the church of Philadelphia ; and of him shall this testimony be given, ' I know thy works ; behold I have set before thee an open door, and no man can shut it ; for thou hast a little strength, and hast kept my word, and hast not denied my name. Hold fast that which thou hast, that no man take thy crown!' "—We say, had the man of most practical faith in existence seen our prodigal in this state, and heard such a prophecy, he could only have received it as the most secret things of the eternal counsels are received—on the simple authority of Him who cannot lie—and if he had been startled into the exclamation, " How can these things be !" he would have answered himself, and silenced unbelief, by saying—" The things which are impossible with men are possible with God. '

We pass to the exhibition of another portrait, of which it may emphatically be affirmed—and he who penned the lines understood well the incommunicable bitterness of heart which they imply—

" This is a sight for Pity to peruse,
    Till she resemble faintly what she views;
    Till Sympathy contract a kindred pain,
    Pierced with the woes which she laments in vain."

One day, in the month of December, 1763, a sufferer under the most deplorable of human maladies was brought to the house of a medical practitioner, at a small town, in a midland county of England, and left under his care. The patient was little advanced in manhood, but sorrow had done the work of years on his debilitated frame and faded cheek, while something more than sorrow had wrought a sadder ruin within, where no eye could search out the cause, unless it could see into the invisible world, and discern the spirit itself within the tabernacle of clay. Reason had been overthrown, and imagination, usurping its seat, reigned as "lord of misrule," through all the region of thought, over all the faculties of the soul. He was a member of the younger branch of an illustrious house. He, too, (like the former subject of consideration,) had early lost his mother, and being a delicate child, that loss was to him in every way incalculable and irreparable. At school his spirit had been rebuked and prostrated by the tyranny of an elder boy, who exercised such fiend-like dominion over him that he was afraid to lift up his eyes higher than his tormentor's knees ; and "knew him by his shoe-buckles better than any other part of his dress." It cannot be doubted that the peace of his whole life thenceforward was disturbed by the consequences of this almost-demoniacal possession—not of his person indeed, but of his phantasy and his fears. Being destined for the bar, his relatives took the most prudent means to qualify him for his profession ; but he lacked by nature what no discipline could supply, and no learning compensate—the face to show his face, and the tongue to speak in his own hearing before a large assembly. At the age of three and thirty years, having made no progress towards eminence as a practising lawyer, and all prospect of success by his personal exertions having vanished, he was successively nominated to two parliamentary offices, of which the duties were easy and the emoluments considerable. The mere terror, however, which seized him at the idea of a public appearance before the House of Lords to qualify for his appointment threw the reluctant candidate (whom Fortune seemed to pursue with her favours, but could never overtake,) into paroxysms of despair. In the delirium that ensued, he repeatedly attempted self-destruction, and failed—not for want of the resolution which on better occasions had failed him—but because a hand of mercy, unseen though ever present, turned aside his purposes, and (as it seemed to himself) with immediate intervention, preserved a life the extraordinary issues of which were yet as unsuspected as they were undeveloped.

At the time above stated, he was placed under the superintendence of a wise and good physician, who knew not only how to treat a morbid frame and shattered nerves, with tenderness and skill, but to administer the healing balm of gospel comfort to a wounded spirit—to

> " Assuage the throbbings of the fester'd part,
> And staunch the bleedings of a broken heart."

Yet here, if ever, appeared a case beyond the reach of medicine or of counsel. Inveterate predisposition to mental derangement had been urged to agony at the existing crisis, in which was involved the failure of all the victim's plans for life, conceived in the credulity of youth and cherished with the poetry of hope. He had done nothing for himself, and he had frustrated all the efforts of his powerful connexions to serve him. To these disappointments of laudable ambition, alone sufficient to drive a fevered brain to frenzy, or plunge a self-tormenting mind in melancholy, were added, about the same time, the bereavement, by death, of a friend whom he loved as his own soul; and the loss, by something worse than death, of another object yet more beloved. In his own affecting words, he

> ......................" Mourn'd, from day to day,
> *Him*, snatch'd by fate in early youth away,
> And *her*, through tedious years of doubt and pain,
> Fix'd in her choice, and faithful, but in vain."

When this sufferer found a sanctuary under the roof of one who merited from all who knew him the appellation which St. Paul bestowed upon Luke—" the beloved physician "—the horrors which had previously exasperated his wild imagination to self-slaying rage had nearly subsided into gloomy tranquility. The direful visitation had left his mind, like the lake of Sodom after the storm of fire and brimstone had blown over, dark and motionless—a pool of death, which all the waves of Jordan, flowing into it, could not purify; which nothing, indeed, could heal but the waters of that river of life, clear as crystal, proceeding out of the throne of God and of the Lamb. Nay, if there could be imagined a spot, in the region

of human misery, which even these might never visit
—the desolation of heart in him must have seemed
that spot. The most experienced in the symptoms
of that fearful distemper under which he laboured
could not have anticipated more than the bare possi-
bility of one so lost being restored to precarious sanity
by the happiest efforts of human skill, under the blessing of God. Had Dr. Johnson—at that time the
Apollo of literature, whose oracles were both less am-
biguous and less fallible than the Pythian responses
of old—been admitted to the sight of our captive, roving, as by instinct, through the grounds that enclosed
his quiet prison—

> "Lips busy, and eyes fix'd, foot falling slow,
> Arms hanging idly down, hands clasp'd below,"

brooding over bosom-sorrows not to be told, refusing
comfort or hope from every created source, and from
religion itself deriving nothing but despair :—had Dr.
Johnson seen him thus ; and had the good angel of the
poor unknown spoken aloud in the critic's ear, and
cried, "Behold the man whose mind, by its ascen-
dance over the minds of contemporaries, shall purify
the public taste, and restore British song from its
half-century of captivity and degradation, in French
fetters, to its inherited freedom. Behold the man
who shall be the father of a new generation of bards,
worthy of their native language and their native land ;
—the man, who shall exhibit, in his uncompromising
verse, a style so pure, so simple, and severe, that intellectual excellence alone shall compel admiration,
even from those who hate the poet's themes because
they hate the gospel. The mourner, the maniac before your eyes, shall do this ; and he shall do more,
—he shall redeem the character of religious poetry
from the reproach which, in the presumption of mis-

understanding, you yourself have cast upon it."—
Had Dr. Johnson been thus addressed, what would
have been his reply?—" Though an angel from heaven declare it, I will not believe."

This "stricken deer," thus abandoned by the herd,
and thus withdrawn, " in secret shades to die alone,"
we may now bring into contact and comparison with
the former object of sympathy.

Misery more hopeless than either of these cases
once embodied is rare even in this world of sinners
and sufferers. Recovery from equal depths of moral
depravity as the one, and prostration of intellect as
the other presents, is rarer still. But that the subjects of such humiliating afflictions should be exalted,
like the first, to the summit of influential piety, and
like the second, to supremacy of commanding genius
—especially, that they should be associated during
life, and after death in their respective honours, must
be ranked with the few examples which " He that
doeth what he will among the inhabitants of the earth "
places on record, at long intervals, to teach us, that of
no human being, who once possessed reason and conscience, can it be absolutely said " there is no hope
for him in this life,—useless to himself, it is impossible
that he should ever be useful to others." These very
individuals — for the pictures here drawn are not
from imagination but from fearful realities — those
very individuals, dissimilar as they were in rank, edu-
cation, habits, and all external circumstances, in
the sequel became bosom-friends and counsellors, and
were long engaged as fellow-labourers, with heart and
hand, in the work of the Lord on earth. Nor did
they serve their transient generation only, by the exercise of their distinguished talents ; each of them has
left behind him some works which " the world will

not willingly let die." In the autumn of 1767, they met as residents in the same town ;—the impenitent prodigal of the isle of Plantanes was then "the Rev. JOHN NEWTON, Curate of Olney," and the desponding recluse of St. Alban's was " WILLIAM COWPER, Esq., of the Inner Temple," destined to be "the author of the Task," and the regenerator of English poesy, at the end of the eighteenth century.

It is not necessary here to trace the remarkable changes of life, and the greater changes of heart, which had made these two men as much to differ from what they formerly were as though they had been new creatures in every thing except personal identity. Newton's story (told by himself in letters to a friend) contains a more striking variety of "moving accidents by flood and field" than can often be found in the memoirs of a private adventurer. Fourteen times at least, on his own testimony, he was saved from imminent death, and almost as often (judging by his spiritual state,) "plucked as a brand from the fire" that "is not quenched." From his detestable thraldom on the coast of Africa he was rescued by a messenger from his father, to whom he had repeatedly written for help without receiving any answer. Even in this instance he was delivered against his will, having left the hard service of his first master and engaged with another, who allowed him such a share of the hire of iniquity in the staple traffic of the coast, that he grew savagely in love with his inhuman occupation, and so eagerly grasped at its filthy lucre, that the captain of the vessel was tempted to use falsehood to lure him away from it, under pretence that a large fortune had been bequeathed to him in Europe. The hardening, demoralizing, soul-destroying effects of evil associations which he began to feel he thus describes : " There is a significant phrase frequently used in those parts, that such a white man is grown black. It does not intend an alteration of complexion, but of disposition. I have known several in Africa who gradually became assimilated to the tempers, customs, and ceremonies of the natives so far as to prefer that country to England. They have also become dupes to all the pretended charms, necromancies, and divinations of the blinded Negroes ; and put more trust in such things than the wiser sort of natives. A part of this spirit of infatuation was growing upon me : in time perhaps I might have yielded to the whole."

Though, during his residence on that frightful coast, it could not be said that " there was found in him *any* good thing towards the Lord God of Israel ;" yet one deep, powerful, and unswerving passion, which he cherished in his heart of hearts, towards her whom he afterwards married, but whom he *then* dared not hope to call his own, seems to have happily restrained him from some excesses, into which he would otherwise have run, amidst his headlong career of licentiousness. The same tender and hallowing affection, through his saddest reverses, had sweetened his thoughts, and softened his desperation, as well when ignominiously punished and degraded on board the Harwich, as when groaning out existence in hunger, thirst, nakedness, and disease, during his bondage under the bond-woman, the negro-mistress of his worse than negro-master. Through a long series of strange vicissitudes and appalling chastisements, he experienced how hard it is for the most determined to enter into the kingdom of darkness, though they fight their way, sword in hand, to the gates of hell, through opposing judgments and surrounding mercies. *He* did so, but could not prevail, for the Lord was stronger than he, and by a succession of humbling and purifying trials, not only brought the rebel to repentance and submission, while he was for several years captain of a Guinea ship; but afterwards, while he was tide-surveyor at Liverpool, prepared him to enter the Holy of holies in the Christian temple, as a minister of the gospel.

As in providence the dealings of the Lord with this refractory subject had been at once more severe and merciful than in the usual course of a sinner's experience, so in grace also the divine discipline by which he was trained seemed no less signally sove-reign and peculiar. " The words which his mother taught him " had never been erazed from his mind, nor had they otherwise died in his heart than as good seed, to be re-quickened in due season. In full man-hood, then, while prosperously engaged in that infa-mous commerce, of which he had not yet learned the unlawfulness,—so blinding and deluding is sin of any kind,—his conscience was awakened, his fears were alarmed, and the fountains of that great deep, the natural heart of man, " deceitful above all things, and desperately wicked," were broken up; all was dark-ness, horror, and confusion within. Then "the Spirit of God moved upon the face of the waters, and God said, *Let there be light; and there was light.*" Gra-dually—as the six days' works of creation, in which, without agent or auxiliary, God wrought alone—the regenerating change went on in this new creation of a human soul; till, as " the morning stars sang toge-ther, and all the sons of God shouted for joy," when " the heavens and the earth were finished, and all the host of them,"—so may we believe that there was joy in the presence of the angels of God over this one

sinner that repented. Far from the ordinary means
of grace,—beyond the hearing of the word, without
the fellowship of Christians, and almost unaided by
the writings of divines, — having no book but the
Bible, or occasionally a religious treatise, (and these
as he says, not always the best,) John Newton, the infidel and blasphemer, was awakened, alarmed, convinced, comforted, and instructed, in such a manner
that he could rejoice in the Lord, and joy in the God
of his salvation. During the same extraordinary in-
terval he had patience and resolution to apply himself
diligently both to science and polite literature; and
he actually acquired as much knowledge of mathe-
matics, and the learned languages, as enabled him
in after life to pursue those studies till he became a
good reading scholar, if not a great proficient or an
acute critic. Thus his mind was expanded and en-
lightened as his heart was renewed and sanctified.—
And where was this twofold miracle wrought?—On
board of a slave-ship, amidst the iniquities of the
coast-traffic, the horrors of the middle passage, and
the abominations of the West Indian market. The
fact might be doubted had not a life of unwearied
labour, most exemplary piety, and pre-eminent usefulness, as a Christian minister, (hardly paralleled
among his contemporaries,) proved the reality of his
transition, amidst such hindrances, from darkness to
light, and from the power of Satan to serve the living
God. Verily and literally to his experience might
be applied the words of his friend, Cowper,

> " God moves in a mysterious way
> His wonders to perform:
> *He plants his footsteps in the sea,*
> *And rides upon the storm.*"

To his companion at Olney we return. Congeniality

of sentiment soon united Cowper and Newton in a
friendship interrupted only, during the residue of their
lives, by the mysterious visitations, from time to time,
of that constitutional malady which haunted the former.
The first tremendous access of this calamity had been
repelled by the skill of Dr. Cotton, at St. Albans.
But the good physician had not only stayed, for a
while, the plague that laid waste his intellect; he
poured the wine and oil of gospel-consolation into the
wounds of a spirit in which the arrows of the Almighty
had struck deep and remained fixed, till

" One,
Who had himself been hit by the archers,"

found him " withdrawn—to seek a tranquil death in
distant shades," and then,

" With gentle force soliciting the darts,"

had healed, and bade him live.    Hitherto the conscious transgressor had known religion only by its
terrors—" thunder and earthquake and devouring
flame :" now he partook of its delights ; occasionally
of its transports :—

"'Twas heaven, all heaven descending on the wings
Of the bright legions of the King of kings ;
'Twas more ;—'twas God diffused through every part ;
'Twas God himself triumphant in his heart."

This was indeed the time of the soul's espousals,
when the Beloved " allured her into the wilderness,
and spake comfortably to her."    The page which com-
memorates our Poet's deliverance from the fear that
hath torment, into joy unspeakable and full of glory,
is the fairest in the dark-and-bright volume of his
book of life ; and that page is written by his own hand,
in the language of his heart, when he poured forth its
fulness and sweetness, in those two hymns of the fol-
lowing Collection, which cannot be read and under-

stood without experiencing, by sympathy, a measure
of the bliss and tranquility which they breathe.—See
Book iii, Hymns 44 and 45.—"How blest thy creature is, O God!" and, "Far from the world, O Lord,
with thee."

The experience of nearly two years of humble and
uninterrupted walking with God had confirmed the
fugitive from the world in this peaceful frame of mind,
when his acquaintance with Newton commenced, under circumstances peculiarly auspicious to both. It
has often been ignorantly or insidiously said, that
Cowper's connection with the latter was unfortunate
for himself; for had he fallen under the influence of
some other person, of equal piety, but less hardihood
in holding and enforcing certain doctrinal tenets, his
own hope in the promises of the gospel might never
have failed, nor his reason on that point been utterly
perverted,—not only in the cheerless days of mental
alienation, but when on every other subject his faculties were clear, and his faith orthodox. What *might*
have been, if what *was* had not happened, it is in vain
to speculate. The contingencies of any one hypothetical event lie far beyond the reach of created intellect. The counsels of God, even in what *does* come
to pass, are in many respects unsearchable. Known
unto himself alone from the beginning are all his
works; and to justify *his* ways—for, after all, they
were God's ways, and not man's—in the particular
instance before us, it is sufficient to consider what
was the positive result of the connection between these
two remarkable men,—the one brought from a slave-
ship, and the other from a lunatic asylum, to teach
the world justice and mercy, and enlighten it with
knowledge. In the preface to the present volume,
Newton himself gives a clew to the enquiry, "The

public may be assured, that the whole number (of Hymns) were composed by two persons only. The original design would not admit of any other association."—What was that design?—" It was intended as a monument to perpetuate an intimate and endeared friendship."

Thus then, prompted by the suggestion and emboldened by the example of plain but intrepid John Newton, the diffident poet was encouraged to make trial of those pure and exquisitely precious talents which had lain like gold untouched, nay, almost undiscovered in the mine, through the greater part of that period of life during which the instinct of ambition is most restless, and its votaries are eagerly pursuing fame at every sacrifice which they can or cannot afford. No person qualified to judge impartially (the mere man of letters is *not*, for such things must be spiritually discerned) will deny that the greater number of those Hymns which bear the mark of C. in their titles bear also the impress of Cowper's genius in their style, character, and subjects. Many of them, in fact, are miniature poems, regularly planned, brilliantly adorned, and felicitously executed. It is true, that, amidst these morning dreams of his awakening muse, blackness of darkness fell upon his mind, from the malignant influence of bodily distemper acting upon it; yet will his unfinished portion remain a splendid trophy of intellectual prowess, and spiritual attainments, in one who was permitted, by the inscrutable direction of Providence, at times, to lose all command of the former, and all consciousness of the latter. When Cowper was restored to sanity the second time, this very evidence of the gift within him was considered as a pledge of what greater things might be expected from the employment of his genius in an

ampler field, on themes more complex and difficult,
—such as would call forth, if not create, in a capacity
like his, the strength to execute them. The hopes of
his friends were not too sanguine. In the course of
a few years, he produced those singularly original
poems which, though written in direct opposition to
the taste of the times, and embued with sentiments
hateful alike to the scorner and the self-righteous,
effected a greater change in the character of contemporary literature than any poetic novelty before had
done in a refined and critical age. It is not to be
questioned, that the success of Cowper, (in a degree
probably unknown even to themselves,) influenced
Southey, Wordsworth, and Coleridge, in their daring
and successful insurrection against antiquated autho-
rities, to enfranchise English verse from the drawling,
driveling imitation of French models, which two of
the mightiest masters of the art (Dryden and Pope)
had imposed upon their spiritless and imbecile suc-
cessors.

The subject is only touched upon here, to exhibit
Cowper in just proportion between his elder and his
junior brethren; as well as to give honour to whom
honour is due, by fearlessly stating the fact, that to
Newton the world owes Cowper as Cowper appears
to the world. It is not presumed, that had the latter
never fallen in with the former, he might not have
broken out from inglorious obscurity, in all the power
of irrepressible genius; but whatever other, or even
higher achievements he might have wrought under
different circumstances, those by which he will be
for ever known and honoured and endeared were all
(directly or indirectly) called from his slumbering
mind, (oppressed by a burthen more awful than Etna
and all its fires on the breast of the giant Enceladus,)

B                        46

by the awakening voice, the animating example, and
the cordial companionship of Newton. Nor is this
said in disparagement of any happy influence which
Mrs. Unwin, Lady Austen, or other inspirers of his
verse, occasionally exercised over him in the sequel.
But by enlisting Cowper, as his coadjutor, in the
Olney Hymns, Newton gave to the poet's mind both
the bias and the impulse which ever afterwards directed its course.

There are few joint-memorials of friendship and
talents, raised by kindred spirits, in polite literature.
Every other species of art may be successfully practised by "many men and many minds." In architec-
ture, sculpture, and painting, the diversified talents of
various hands may often be so harmoniously associated as to form a magnificent whole ; because the
composition, however exquisitely and intellectually
designed, consists of material parts, and is accom-
plished by manual process. But those original works
of genius, of which language is the expression, scarcely
admit of fellowship, either in conception or execution. One book must be the product of one brain,
in which, to constitute excellence, there ought to be
as strict unity of thought and diction as the ancient
critic required of time and place in dramatic action.
Now, two minds cannot think simultaneously ; nor can
one express a thought suggested by another, in terms
which shall convey it to a third with precisely the
same impression as it was felt by the first. Language
in itself being as invisible and immaterial as the ideas
which it communicates, those ideas will necessarily be
best communicated in *his* language who first conceived
them ; and though others may seize hints, and carry
them out into more perfect and beautiful exhibition
than the inventors could have done, yet the original

thoughts themselves will be as much changed (perhaps for the better) as the diction has been improved. These remarks, of course, refer principally to those more recondite and complicated imaginations and reasonings which it is the prerogative of superior minds to create or evolve in their diviner moods, when "thoughts that breathe, and words that burn," give perpetuity of youth to their mental offspring. Yet they *do* apply, more or less, to all literary productions in which fancy, feeling, or elaborate argument, are component principles, or characteristic features. There is but one splendid exception to this *usage*— not to call it *law*—of nature in our poetic annals. The plays which pass under the names of Beaumont and Fletcher were unquestionably written so consentaneously, that it is impossible now to ascertain the peculiar merits of either, by apportioning to each his share of personal contributions to the common stock, or of labour in turning that capital to the best advantage. Unhappily, however, these extraordinary emanations of twin-minds—nobly gifted, but atrociously prostituted—are so tainted with the grossness of the age in which they appeared, and which they too faithfully reflected, that they will neither bear to be read nor represented in our better and more fastidious times ; for not merely more fastidious, but positively better, in this respect, our times *are*, notwithstanding the well-founded charges of licentiousness which may yet be brought against many of the books and much of the conversation of the present day.

The volume before us is a monument of friendship and genius far otherwise directed and far more honourably employed, however short in poetical display it may fall of the former meretricious offspring of combined talents, at once the glory and the shame of

their possessors. It also belongs to a different class
of literary labours,—a class which readily admits of
joint-stock authorship, and in which the independent
contributions of any number of individuals may be associated, for the illustrations of a connected series of
subjects. These Hymns, however, (as we have seen
already,) were written by two persons only,—living
miracles of divine grace,—to perpetuate the remembrance of their fellowship in the bonds of the Gospel.
to show what great things the Lord had done for them,
and thereby to edify the church of Christ in the neighbourhood where they dwelt. This, and much more,
has been effected: the collection has become a stan-
dard-book, of its kind, among devout readers of every
evangelical denomination. Such a miscellany, with
no other means of recommendation than its own in-
trinsic worth, cannot have been a work of ordinary
character, however humble its claims, and unpretend-
ing its execution. Many a superficial book has *ob-
tained*, but not one in the annals of literature ever
*kept* popular favour for half a century, or even half
that term. Public opinion is often mistaken *before* it
is formed, but *when* formed, it is not less infallible and
irreversible than human judgment can be when there
is neither necessity nor inducement to continue in
error. By the decision of posterity—for the present
generation is posterity to the authors—this volume
may now safely abide, whatever imperfections or
offences against good taste may be found in its numerous and very unequal compositions.

Newton's portion of the work is by far the largest.
and it is no disparagement to his memory to say, that
this might be considerably reduced with advantage to
the remainder, though it would be a bold hand, and
ought to be a delicate one, that should presume to

attempt the desirable excision. Let the good man, however, speak for himself:—" My part would have been much smaller than it is, and the book would have appeared in a very different form, if the wise though mysterious providence of God had not seen fit to cross my wishes. We had not proceeded far upon our proposed plan before my dear friend was prevented, by a long and affecting indisposition, from affording me any further assistance. My grief and disappointment were great; I hung my harp upon the willows, and for some time thought myself determined to proceed no farther without him. Yet my mind was afterwards led to resume the service."—It was well for him, and well for the world, that he did so. The blessings of millions, on his memory, among the dead, the living, and the unborn, will justify his courage and perseverance in finishing, at his peril, an enterprise so auspiciously begun, and so lamentably interrupted. The suspension of Cowper's labours is the more to be regretted as the pieces which he did furnish towards the work—few (about sixty) in comparison with Newton's—were, nevertheless, sufficient to prove his own peculiar talent for this species of sacred song, and to disprove the unwarrantable canon of criticism which his friend thus lays down:— " There is a style and manner suited to the composition of hymns, which may be more successfully or at least more easily attained by a versifier than a poet. They should be *Hymns*, not *Odes*, if designed for public worship, and the use of plain people. Perspicuity, simplicity, and ease, should be chiefly attended to ; and the imagery and colouring of poetry, if admitted at all, should be indulged very sparingly, and with great judgment."—What does all this mean? Certainly *not* that mere versifiers can write hymns better than poets—which tho author intended to say, but has happily miscarried ;—it means neither more nor less than that hymn-writing, like every other kind of poetry, has a style suitable to itself. But to take it for granted, that, because this is the case, a poet, a genuine poet, a poet of the highest order, is not better qualified to excel in this branch of his own art than a free-and-easy syllable-monger, is not less gratuitous and self-contradictory than it would be to affirm, that because an artist, of surpassing skill, can contrive a time-piece, which shall show, not only the lapse of every second, minute, and hour, but also the days of the week, month, year, with all the phases of the moon, and the sun's course through the zodiac,— he is, for that very reason, less able to make a common watch than his own apprentice. The major necessarily includes the minor capacity, as great power includes less ; otherwise a child, who might lift ten pounds and no more, would do *that* better (more easily) than a porter, who could heave five hundred weight. Now, Cowper, in the very "style and manner" which his less-gifted coadjutor lays down as most "suited to this kind of composition ;" namely, "perspicuity, simplicity, and ease," combined also with grace, elegance, pathos, and energy, such as poetic inspiration alone could supply,—Cowper as much excels his less-gifted coadjutor in these requisites as in his later and loftier productions, ' The Task,' &c., he excels himself, when considered only as the Author of these humbler and holier essays, in which (again to borrow Newton's own words,) " the imagery and colouring of poetry," though admitted, are "indulged sparingly, and with great judgment." It was no discredit to Newton, to be distanced by Cowper in such a race ; he has won glory, which will

not soon pass away, by having, as he honestly says,
" done his best ;" and he had reason to be satisfied,
that, by " the mediocrity of talent" with which " it
pleased the Lord to favour him," he was admirably
" qualified for usefulness to the weak and the poor of
Christ's flock, without disgusting persons of superior
discernment."—For, not in the smallest degree to ex-
aggerate his merits, it may be said, that " persons of
superior discernment," who are, at the same time,
spiritually-minded, are those by whom his labours
will be most highly esteemed, and the value of some
of them even put into competition with the more
poetic effusions of his friend, to whom he himself so
willingly concedes the palm, in his preface to the
finished work, at a time when that friend was never
likely to claim or enjoy his superior honours.

Though Newton's pieces in this collection may be
regarded as fair models, according to his own view of
the nature of such compositions, yet it must be confessed, by his warmest admirers, that the pulpit idioms,
the bald phraseology, and the conversational cadence
of his lines, frequently lower the tone of his poetry
so much, that what would be pleasing and impressive
in prose becomes languid and wearisome in verse.
Indeed, when verse (not otherwise pretending to be
poetical) is not *much better* than prose, by the charm
of numbers alone it is *much worse.* Its artificial struc-
ture is *then* a decided disadvantage, and no reader *can*
even if he would, (though many try to persuade
themselves that they do,) like a sentence better for the
clanking of a chain of syllables. " The day that
makes a man a slave takes half his worth away," says
the old poet ; and language enslaved in metre loses
half its power, unless the loss of natural freedom be
abundantly compensated by the grace of accent, and
the melody of rhythm.

This volume is divided into three Books. The
first consists of Hymns on select portions of the Old
and New Testaments. No experiments in verse can
be more hopeless and thankless than such. The difficulty consists partly in the *ease* with which scriptural
passages may be shaped into measured lines, to the
satisfaction of the paraphrast himself, and the indif-
ference with which the reader receives the most successful performances of the kind, from their inevitable
inferiority to (what are to him) the *originals* in his native tongue. With these he has been so familiarized
from infancy, that no new collocation of words—even
in prose, much less in rhyme—can ever be so pleasing
to his ear, or convey to his mind so ineffable an impression of the meaning of the sacred oracles. In plain
truth, scripture language, whether historical, poetic,
or doctrinal, is so comprehensive, that in anywise to
alter is to impair it ; if you add you encumber ; if
you diminish you maim the sense ; to paraphrase is
to enfeeble everlasting strength ; to imitate is to im-
poverish inexhaustible riches ; and to translate into
verse is necessarily to do one, or the other, or both
of these, in nearly every line. For example—I pur-
posely choose what may be called an extreme case, to
make the illustration more palpable,—Ps. xix, 7, 8,
" The law of the Lord is perfect, converting the soul:
the testimony of the Lord is sure, making wise the
simple :—The statutes of the Lord are right, rejoicing
the heart ; the commandment of the Lord is pure, en-
lightening the eyes."—The literal terms here are so
perfect a vehicle of pure thought, that any metrical
reading must render them less so, because words
equally few and simple cannot be found in the English
tongue which would express these plain sentiments
in rhymes and numbers. The failure of all who have

attempted this passage has proved that it is the cross of versifiers; and he who could carry it, without being put to shame, need not despair of accomplishing what must still be considered as a desideratum—a version of the Psalms, which shall not (on the whole) disappoint every reader. That such is all but impossible may be inferred from one case.—The 137th Psalm is one of the most poetical in imagery and diction; therefore one of the fittest for metrical arrangement. Now this has been oftener essayed than any other, by poets of the highest talents, from Lord Surrey, in the sixteenth century, downwards; yet all have laboured in vain, and spent their strength for nought; as may be seen by turning over the multitudinous volumes of Chambers's British Poets, as well as the countless collections of Psalms and Hymns and Spiritual Songs by versifiers of all ranks.

The prime cause of miscarriage in every attempt to paraphrase scripture passages appears to be, that, in order to bring them within the rules of rhyme and metre, all that the poet introduces of his own becomes alloy, which debases the standard of the original. On the contrary, when he adorns a train of his private thoughts with scripture images and ideas, or interweaves with his own language, scripture phrases, that fall without straining into his verse, the latter is illustrated and enriched by the alliance or the amalgamation. In a word, divine themes are necessarily degraded by human interpolations; while human compositions are necessarily exalted by the felicitous introduction of sacred allusions. This is a secret of which few that have meddled with the perilous and . delicate subject have been aware. A single verse, in each way, will probably make the point clear.

Olney Hymns, Book ii, Hymn 74.

" But could I bear to hear him say,
—' Depart, accursed, far away !
With Satan in the lowest hell
Thou art for ever doom'd to dwell !' "

How impotent is this, compared with the terrible words—" Depart from me, ye cursed, into everlasting fire, prepared for the devil and his angels." Here the divine theme is degraded by human interpolation and omission *both*.

Book iii, Hymn 28.

" Perhaps some golden wedge supprest,
Some secret sin offends my God ;
Perhaps that Babylonish vest,
Self-righteousness, provokes the rod."

Here the poet adorns the train of his private thoughts with scripture images ; and oh with what force and conviction are " the wedge of gold," and " Babylonish vest," brought in ! The reader, from previous knowledge, needs no other hint to recollect the whole history,—yea, and to make him tremble too, as though he felt himself in the tent of Achan at the moment when his sin was discovered. Who does not instinctively recoil, and look with horror towards that dark corner of his own heart, in which " the accursed thing " was once found, or *is there still?*

Of the scriptural hymns before us, Newton's are not so often feeble paraphrases of the text, as suitable meditations on the respective subjects, and not seldom appear to be little skeletons of sermons, which he may have actually preached. Among these " Cain and Abel," Book i, Hymn 2, may be quoted as an average specimen of plain narrative, easy to be understood, but having little grace or elevation besides.— Book i, Hymn 19, is a good sample of his spiritualizing manner, and indeed is of a superior order.

Book i, Hymn 31, is excellent. The author is wakening up his heart to prayer. Indeed, this collection contains so many beautiful and exhilarating views of the privilege and happiness connected with that duty, as show the writers to have been themselves men of prayer. Book ii, Hymn 60, Book iii, Hymns 12 and 19, may be specially adduced.—These hymns are often *retrospective* also, alluding to the real circumstances under which the individual (whether Cowper or Newton) was found by divine grace, and delivered from sin. See Book i, Hymns 41, 43, and 70, Book ii, Hymn 57.—For a cheerful strain of thanksgiving, Book i, Hymn 57, may be named.—Book i, Hymn 119, affectingly describes some of the finer internal conflicts which exercise the faith, the patience, and the love of God's people. Book i, Hymn 130, furnishes a lesson of close self-examination. A preceding hymn (126) in the same book well describes the warfare between sin and grace in the believer's heart. 'Jonah's Gourd,' Hymn 75, in the same Book, is pathetically applied to the writer's Christian trial, on losing the delight of his eyes and the desire of his heart.

A question too comprehensive to be discussed here may be touched upon, since it arises out of the character of the pieces of this First Book, and likewise peculiarly affects the experimental hymns in the other two. Are such compositions fit to be sung in great congregations, consisting of all classes of saints and sinners?—It must be frankly answered, with respect to the far greater proportion—*No!*—except upon the principle, that whatever may be *read* by such an assembly may also be *sung*. On no ground can either the reading or chaunting of the Psalms from the Common Prayer-Book of the Church of England, or the singing of authorised versions of the same, be justified except on *this*—namely, that these are subjects to be impressed upon the minds and memories of the people, for individual application by themselves (when they can be persuaded to make it ;) but generally, for instruction, warning, reproof, correction, and example,—in reality as means of grace. The part which a congregation of professing Christians can personally take in the routine of Divine service—in reading, praying, responding, or singing—is a subject (considering what is the real usage,) almost too awful to think upon in any other view than the foregoing. Confining himself to this point of justification alone, the writer of these remarks ventures to add, that, whereas singing is only one of the forms of utterance which God has given to man—not which man has invented any otherwise than as he may be said to have invented speech, by the faculty which God gave him to do so—whatever a man may, without sin, *recite* with his lips, in the house of God, he may also *sing*, when the same subjects or sentiments are modeled verse, or set forth in numerous prose, like the translated Psalms, and other poetical parts of Holy Writ, suitable for chaunting. After all, let every man be persuaded in his own mind, and do that in the house of God which he can do to edification.

The Second Book contains pieces on occasional subjects, and these, for the most part, were on actual, not imagined or hypothetical occasions, though capable also of extensive application under similar circumstances—local, temporal, and providential. Thus there are hymns not only for *any New* Years or *Old* Years, but which were expressly written, and used as devotional exercises on the commencement and departure of *particular* years, long ago numbered with those beyond the flood,—years that came and went

over millions to whom time is now no longer, but
whose everlasting destinies are at this moment affect-
ed by their respective employment, for good or for
evil, of those very portions of time thus given and
taken away. Others, who were then children, may
yet be living, and living, at this day, under the effects
of the influence which these individual hymns may
have then had upon their tender and susceptible
minds.—The same may be predicated of the dead,
and presumed of the living, with respect to the follow-
ing hymns for the various ' Seasons' of years, which
had their spring, summer, autumn, and winter, in
turn,—their flowers and buds, their fruits, their
breezes and their storms, not otherwise recorded than
in these humble strains ; but yet to some of those who
then lived—to some who may still be alive—those
seasons had days of the Son of Man on earth—days
to be remembered through eternity.—The hymns also
under the head of ' Ordinances,' were composed to
celebrate special Sabbaths, Sacraments, and Anniver-
saries, &c., though they may generally be used, on
corresponding opportunities, to the end of time.

The hymns on ' Providences,' in the same Book,
are very striking, as commemorating national, local,
and personal judgments, visitations, and deliverances.
Of those on the commencement of hostilities with the
American Colonies, the Fast day in 1776, the earthquake in 1775, it may be said, in justice to each,
" that strain was of an higher mood." The stanzas
' On the Fire at Olney, 1777,' contain incidental
glimpses into the dark and fearful condition (spiritually considered) in which Christian society exists,
even in places where the Gospel is most faithfully
preached, and where it seems to bring forth much
fruit. They show us in what a perilous state of un-

preparedness the majority of our fellow-creatures
every night lie down to sleep,—though liable to be
awakened at any hour, by a cry of fire, by the shock
of an earthquake, or by the last trumpet itself, for
aught they can foresee. How picturesque and terrible are these two verses :—

> " The shout of fire, a dreadful cry,
>   Impress'd each heart with deep dismay,
>   While the fierce blaze and reddening sky
>   Made midnight wear the face of day.
>
> " The throng and terror who can speak ?
>   The various sounds that fill'd the air—
>   The infant's wail, the mother's shriek,
>   *The voice of blasphemy and prayer !*"

The compositions in the latter part of this Second
Book are on the works of creation and the phenomena
of nature, which belong rather to poetry than devotion ; and these being written more generally by
Newton than Cowper, are less interesting than most
others in the volume : feeble, though not unpleasing,
they are evidently on themes chosen for the purpose
of versifying and spiritualizing them—not forced upon
the writer's attention by the impulses of his heart, the
reveries of his mind, or the duties of his station. The
last hymn, however, in this Book, is a more poetical
example of Newton's skill in allegorizing than any of
the former. It is rather remarkable, that one who
had such " visions of the night," and instruction
sealed upon his mind, even in youth, as his dream in
the Mediterranean implies, should have succeeded so
indifferently as he often does in his fancy-pieces and
moral fictions. From this flight of imagination, the
appearance of a second Bunyan might have been au-
gured ; but Newton, though in many other respects
much resembling the author of the ' Pilgrim's Progress,' was far behind him " in similitudes." The

dream alluded to is one of the most perfect specimens
on record of a real yet consistent dream, having a re-
gular plot, a well-connected progress, and moral close.
Newton himself, in his waking hours, never beheld
such a vision of awe and glory. The incident of his
looking from ship-board at the very instant after the
loss of the ring, and seeing the range of Alps along
the midnight horizon, bursting out into volcanic con-
flagration, presents an image of consummate terror
and sublimity.*

* " The scene presented to my imagination was the harbour
of Venice, where we had lately been. I thought it was night,
and my watch upon the deck ; and that, as I was walking to and
fro by myself, a person came to me, (I do not remember from
whence,) and brought me a ring, with an express charge to keep
it carefully ; assuring me, that while I preserved that ring I
should be happy and successful ; but if I lost or parted with it,
I must expect nothing but trouble and misery. I accepted the
present and the terms willingly, not in the least doubting my
own care to preserve it, and highly satisfied to have my happiness in my own keeping. I was engaged in these thoughts,
when a second person came to me, and, observing the ring on
my finger, took occasion to ask me some questions concerning
it. I readily told him its virtues ; and his answer expressed a
surprise at my weakness in expecting such effects from a ring.
I think he reasoned with me some time, upon the impossibility
of the thing, and at length urged me, in direct terms, to throw
it away. At first I was shocked at the proposal ; but his in-
sinuations prevailed. I began to reason and doubt ; and at last
plucked it off my finger, and dropped it over the ship's side into
the water, which it had no sooner touched, than I saw at the
same instant, a terrible fire burst out from a range of mountains (a part of the Alps) which appeared at some distance behind the city of Venice. I saw the hills as distinct as if awake,
and that they were all in flames. I perceived, too late, my
folly ; and my tempter, with an air of insult, informed me, that
all the mercy God had in reserve for me was comprised in that
ring, which I had wilfully thrown away. I understood, that I
must now go with him to the burning mountains, and that all
the flames I saw were kindled on my account. I trembled and
was in a great agony ; so that it was surprising I did not then
awake ; but my dream continued, and when I thought myself
upon the point of a constrained departure, and stood self-con-

The hymns in the Third Book are very miscellaneous, embracing the most solemn, affecting, delightful,
and splendid, as well as the most important and practical themes of religion—warnings and exhortations
to repentance ; confession of sin, contrition, seeking,
pleading, and hoping for salvation ; reasonings and
trials, temptations within and without ; devotion, self-
denial, and surrender of all the ransomed powers of
mind and body : and finally, songs of praise and
thanksgiving. These are frequently in a higher tone
of poetry, with deeper pathos and more ardent expression, than the average strain of pieces in the foregoing Books. The best wine has been reserved to the
last. Book iii. Hymn 10, is very earnest in prayer
and faith and hope : the two concluding stanzas, in

demned, without plea or hope, suddenly either a third person,
or the same who brought the ring at first (I am not certain
which), came to me, and demanded the cause of my grief. I
told him the plain case, confessing that I had ruined myself
wilfully, and deserved no pity. He blamed my rashness, and
asked if I should be wiser, supposing I had my ring again. I
could hardly answer to this ; for I thought it was gone beyond
recall. I believe, indeed, I had not time to answer, before I
saw this unexpected friend go down under the water, just in
the spot where I had dropped it ; and he soon returned, bringing the ring with him. The moment he came on board, the
flames in the mountains were extinguished, and my seducer left
me. Then was 'the prey taken from the hand of the mighty,
and the lawful captive delivered.' My fears were at an end ;
and with joy and gratitude I approached my kind deliverer to
receive the ring again ; but he refused to return it, and spoke
to this effect :—' If you should be entrusted with this ring
again, you would very soon bring yourself into the same distress : you are not able to keep it ; but I will preserve it for
you, and whenever it is needful will produce it in your behalf.'
Upon this I awoke, in a state of mind not to be described : I
could hardly eat or sleep, or transact my necessary business
for two or three days ; but the impression soon wore off, and
in a little time I totally forgot it ; and I think it hardly oc-
curred to my mind again till several years afterwards."

particular, may be often used by the Christian reader in reference to himself, in his own time of need, but not of despondency. The 22nd Hymn in this Book is very faithful in describing a species of temptation which often pursues the suppliant to the very throne of grace, and in the form of Satan among the sons of God, accuses the self-condemned sinner, who, yet clinging to the footstool, and not to be moved, pleads the promises, and cries for the blessing, which never was *so* sought in vain. Book iii, Hymn 58—' Home in View,' is one of the most consolatory in the volume, and may make the drooping yet reviving heart home-sick for heaven, in prospect, for the last time, before he reaches it for ever. In Hymn 60, Book iii, Newton very strikingly alludes to his former and his latter state ; his change from nature unto grace, and the fruits that followed.

On the whole, though it must be acknowledged that Newton was a poet of very humble order, yet he has produced, in this collection, proofs of great versatility in exercising the one talent of this kind entrusted to him. He has also turned it to the best account, by rendering it wholly subservient to the best purposes in the service of God and man. With this sanction, all his deficiencies as a technical versifier will be forgiven and forgotten by those who have the religious feeling which can appreciate the far higher excellencies of these plain, practical, and often lively, fervent, and sincere effusions of a heart full to overflowing of the love of God, and labouring with indefatigable zeal to promote the kingdom of Christ upon earth.

Of Cowper's share in this work little need be said. Those may disparage the poetry of his hymns who hate or despise the doctrines of the Gospel. They are worthy of him, and honourable to his Christian

profession. These first-fruits of his Muse, after she
had been baptised,—but we must drop the fictitious
being, and say rather, after *he* had been baptised
"with the Holy Ghost and with fire," will ever be
precious (independent of their other merits,) as the
transcripts of his happiest feelings, the memorials of
his walk with God, and his daily experience (amidst
conflicts and discouragements,) of the consoling power
of that religion in which he had *found* peace, and often
*enjoyed* peace to a degree that passed understanding.
On the other hand, it is a heart-withering reflection,
that his mightier efforts of genius—the poems by
which he commands universal admiration—though
they breathe the soul of purest, humblest, holiest
piety, and might have been written amidst the clear
shining of the Sun of Righteousness arisen on him
with healing in his wings—were yet composed under
darkness like that of the valley of the shadow of death.
While the tempted poet sang the privileges, the duties,
and the blessedness of the Christian, he had himself
lost all except the remembrance that he once possessed it, and the bitter, insane, and invincible conviction,
that for him there was no hope, "either in this life or
that which is to come." Under this frightful delu
sion, in its last effect, for several years, even his intellectual being was absorpt, till the disordered body fell
into dust, and the soul returned to God who gave it.
Oh! when that veil of horror, with the veil of flesh,
was taken away, and the enfranchised captive emerged
in the invisible world,—may we not hope, that, like
dying Stephen on *this* side of eternity, he on the *other*
saw heaven opened, with Jesus standing at the right
hand of God,—may we not believe that he could *then*
and *there* exclaim, with that first triumphant martyr,
—"Lord Jesus, receive my spirit!"

In conclusion, this volume of Olney Hymns ought
to be for ever dear to the Christian public, as an un-
precedented memorial, in respect to its authors, of
the power of Divine grace, which called one of them
from the negro-slave market, on the coast of Africa, to
be a burning and a shining light in the church of God
at home,—and raised the head of the other, when he
was a companion of lunatics, to make him, (by a most
mysterious dispensation of gifts,) a poet of the highest
intellectuality, and in his song an unshaken, uncompromising confessor of the purest doctrines of the Gospel,
even when he himself had lost sight of its consolations.

J. M.

SHEFFIELD, January, 1829.

# PREFACE.

COPIES of a few of these Hymns have already appeared in periodical publications and in some recent collections. I have observed one or two of them attributed to persons who certainly had no concern in them but as transcribers. All that have been at different times parted with in manuscript are included in the present volume; and (if the information were of any great importance) the public may be assured, that the whole number were composed by two persons only. The original design would not admit of any other association. A desire of promoting the faith and comfort of sincere Christians, though the principal, was not the only motive to this undertaking. It was likewise intended as a monument, to perpetuate the remembrance of an intimate and endeared friendship. With this pleasing view I entered upon my part, which would have been smaller than it is, and the book would have appeared much sooner, and in a very different form, if the wise though mysterious providence of God had not seen fit to cross my wishes. We had not proceeded far upon our proposed plan before my dear friend was prevented, by a long and affecting indisposition, from affording me any further assistance. My grief and disappointment were great; I hung my harp upon the willows, and for some time thought myself determined to proceed no farther without him. Yet my mind was afterwards led to resume the service. My progress in it, amidst a variety of other engagements, has been slow; yet, in a course of years, the Hymns amounted to a considerable number; and my deference to the judgment and desires of others has at length overcome the reluctance I long felt to see them in print, while I had so few of my friend's* Hymns to insert in the collection. Though it is possible a good judge of composition might be able to distinguish those which are his. I have thought it proper to preclude misapplication, by prefixing the letter C. to each of them. For the rest I must be responsible.

There is a style and manner suited to the composition of hymns, which may be more successfully, or at least more easily attained by a versifier than by a poet. They should be *Hymns*, not *Odes*, if designed for public worship, and for the use of plain people. Perspicuity, simplicity, and ease, should be chiefly attended to : and the imagery and colouring of poetry, if admitted at all, should be indulged very sparingly, and with great judgment. The late Dr. Watts, many of whose hymns are admirable patterns in this species of writing, might, as a poet, have a right to say, That it cost him labour to restrain his fire, and to accommodate himself to the capacities of common readers. But it would not become me to make such a declaration. It behoved me do my best. But though I would not offend readers of taste by a wilful coarseness and negligence, I do not write professedly for them. If the Lord, whom i serve, has been pleased to favour me with that mediocrity of talent, which may qualify me for usefulness to the weak and the poor of his flock, without quite disgusting persons of superior discernment, I have reason to be satisfied.

As the workings of the heart of man, and of the Spirit of God, are in general the same in all who are the subjects of grace, I hope most of these hymns, being the fruit and expression of my own experience, will coincide with the views of real Christians of all denominations. But I cannot expect that every sentiment I have advanced will be universally approved. However, I am not conscious of having written a single line with an intention either to flatter or to offend any party or person upon earth. I have simply declared my own views and feelings, as I might have done if I had composed hymns in some of the newly discovered islands in the South sea, where no person

* Cowper, Author of the Task, &c.

had any knowledge of the name of Jesus but myself.
I am a friend of peace; and being deeply convinced
that no one can profitably understand the great truths
and doctrines of the Gospel any further than he is
taught of God, I have not a wish to obtrude my own
tenets upon others in a way of controversy; yet I do
not think myself bound to conceal them. Many gracious persons (for many such I am persuaded there
are) who differ from me, more or less, in those points
which are called Calvinistic, appeared desirous that
the Calvinists should, for their sakes, studiously avoid
every expression which they cannot approve. Yet
few of them, I believe, impose a like restraint upon
themselves, but think the importance of what they
deem to be truth justifies them in speaking their
sentiments plainly and strongly. May I not plead
for an equal liberty? The views I have received of
the doctrines of grace are essential to my peace; I
could not live comfortably a day or an hour without
them. I likewise believe, yea, so far as my poor attainments warrant me to speak, I know them to be
friendly to holiness, and to have a direct influence in
producing and maintaining a gospel conversation; and
therefore I must not be ashamed of them.

The Hymns are distributed into three Books. In
the first I have classed those which are formed upon
select passages of Scripture, and placed them in the
order of the Books of the Old and New Testament.
The second contains occasional Hymns, suited to
particular seasons, or suggested by particular events
or subjects. The third book is miscellaneous, com-
prising a variety of subjects relative to a life of faith
in the Son of God, which have no express reference
either to a single text of Scripture, or to any deter-
minate season or incident. These are further subdi-
vided into distinct heads. This arrangement is not
so accurate but that several of the hymns might have
been differently disposed. Some attention to method
may be found convenient, though a logical exactness
was hardly practicable. As some subjects in the
several books are nearly coincident, I have, under
the divisions in the third book, pointed out those

which are similar in the two former. And I have likewise here and there, in the first and second, made a reference to hymns of a like import in the third.

This publication, which, with my humble prayer to the Lord for his blessing upon it, I offer to the service and acceptance of all who love the Lord Jesus Christ in sincerity, of every name and in every place, into whose hands it may come, I more particularly dedicate to my dear friends in the parish and neighbourhood of Olney, for whose use the hymns were originally composed, as a testimony of the sincere love I bear them, and as a token of my gratitude to the Lord and to them, for the comfort and satisfaction with which the discharge of my ministry among them has been attended.

The hour is approaching, and at my time of life cannot be very distant, when my heart, my pen, and my tongue, will no longer be able to move in their service. But I trust while my heart continues to beat, it will feel a warm desire for the prosperity of their souls; and while my hand can write, and my tongue speak, it will be the business and the pleasure of my life, to aim at promoting their growth and establishment in the grace of our God and Saviour. To this precious grace I commend them, and earnestly entreat them, and all who love his name, to strive mightily with their prayers to God for me, that I may be preserved faithful to the end, and enabled at last to finish my course with joy.

JOHN NEWTON.

Olney, Bucks,
February 15, 1779.

# TABLE OF FIRST LINES.

C                               46

44

# OLNEY HYMNS.

## 1.

*Adam.*—Gen. iii.

1 ON man, in his own image made,
　　How much did God bestow!
　The whole creation homage paid,
　　And own'd him lord below.

2 He dwelt in Eden's garden, stored
　　With sweets for every sense;
　And there, with his descending Lord,
　　He walk'd in confidence.

3 But, oh by sin how quickly changed—
　　His honour forfeited—
　His heart from God and truth estranged—
　　His conscience fill'd with dread!

4 Now from his Maker's voice he flees,
　　Which was before his joy,
　And thinks to hide amidst the trees
　　From an all-seeing eye.

5 Compell'd to answer to his name,
　　With stubbornness and pride,
　He cast on God himself the blame,
　　Nor once for mercy cried.

6 But grace, unask'd, his heart subdued,
　　And all his guilt forgave ;
　By faith the promised Seed he view'd,
　　And felt His power to save.

7 Thus we ourselves would justify,
　　Though we the law transgress,—
　Like him, unable to deny,
　　Unwilling to confess.

8 But when by faith the sinner sees
　　A pardon bought with blood,
　Then he forsakes his foolish pleas
　　And gladly turns to God.


## 2

*Cain and Abel.*—Gen. iv, 3—8.

1 WHEN Adam fell he quickly lost
　God's image, which he once possess'd :
　See *all* our nature since could boast,
　In Cain, his first-born son, express'd !

2 The sacrifice the Lord ordain'd
　In type of the Redeemer's blood
　Self-righteous reasoning Cain disdain'd,
　And thought his own first-fruits as good.

3 Yet rage and envy fill'd his mind
　When, with a sullen downcast look,
　He saw his brother favour find,
　Who God's appointed method took.

4 By Cain's own hand good Abel died,
　Because the Lord approved his faith ;
　And, when his blood for vengeance cried,
　He vainly thought to hide his death.

5 Such was the wicked murderer Cain,
　And such by nature still are we—
　Untill by grace we're born again,
　Malicious, blind, and proud as he.

6 Like him the way of grace we slight,
　And in our own devices trust ;

Call evil good, and darkness light,
And hate and persecute the just.

7 The saints in every age and place
Have found his history fulfill'd :
The numbers all our thoughts surpass
Of Abels whom the Cains have kill'd !

8 Thus Jesus fell ; but, oh ! his blood
Far better things than Abel's cries,—
Obtains his murderers' peace with God,
And gains them mansions in the skies.

### 3

*Walking with God.*—Gen. v, 24.    C.

1 Oh for a closer walk with God,
A calm and heavenly frame,
A light to shine upon the road
That leads me to the Lamb !

2 Where is the blessedness I knew
When first I saw the Lord ?
Where is the soul-refreshing view
Of Jesus and his word ?

3 What peaceful hours I once enjoy'd !
How sweet their mem'ry still !
But they have left an aching void
The world can never fill.

4 Return, O holy Dove ! return,
Sweet messenger of rest ;
I hate the sins that made thee mourn,
And drove thee from my breast.

5 The dearest idol I have known,
Whate'er that idol be,
Help me to tear it from thy throne,
And worship only thee.

6 So shall my walk be close with God,
Calm and serene my frame ;
So purer light shall mark the road
That leads me to the Lamb.

## 4

### *Another.*

1 By faith in Christ I walk with God,
　With heaven, my journey's end, in view ;
　Supported by his staff and rod,
　My road is safe and pleasant too.

2 I travel through a desert wide,
　Where many round me blindly stray :
　But he vouchsafes to be my guide,
　And will not let me miss my way.

3 Though snares and dangers throng my path,
　And earth and hell my course withstand,
　I triumph over all by faith,
　Guarded by his almighty hand.

4 The wilderness affords no food,
　But God for my support prepares,—
　Provides me every needful good,
　And frees my soul from wants and cares.

5 With him sweet converse I maintain :
　Great as he is, I dare be free ;
　I tell him all my grief and pain,
　And he reveals his love to me.

6 Some cordial from his word he brings
　Whene'er my feeble spirit faints,—
　At once my soul revives and sings,
　And yields no more to sad complaints.

7 I pity all that worldlings talk
　Of pleasures that will quickly end:
　Be this my choice, O Lord, to walk
　With thee, my Guide, my Guard, my Friend.

## 5

### *Lot in Sodom.*—Gen. xiii, 10.

1 How hurtful was the choice of Lot,
　　Who took up his abode
　(Because it was a fruitful spot)
　　With them who fear'd not God!

2 A pris'ner he was quickly made,
   Bereaved of all his store ;
And but for Abra'm's timely aid
   He had return'd no more.

3 Yet still he seem'd resolved to stay,
   As if it were his rest,
Although their sins from day to day
   His righteous soul distress'd.

4 Awhile he stay'd, with anxious mind,
   Exposed to scorn and strife ;
At last he left his all behind,
   And fled to save his life.

5 In vain his sons-in-law he warn'd ;
   They thought he told his dreams ;
His daughters too of them had learn'd,
   And perish'd in the flames.

6 His wife escaped a little way,
   But died for looking back :
Does not her case to pilgrims say,
   " Beware of growing slack " ?

7 Yea, Lot himself could ling'ring stand
   Though vengeance was in view ;
'Twas Mercy pluck'd him by the hand
   Or he had perish'd too.

8 The doom of Sodom will be ours
   If to the earth we cleave :
Lord, quicken all our drowsy powers
   To flee to thee and live.

### 6.

*Jehovah-Jireh—The Lord will Provide.—*
       Gen. xxii, 14.  C.

1 THE saints should never be dismay'd,
   Nor sink in hopeless fear ;
For, when they least expect his aid,
   The Saviour will appear.

2 This Abra'm found : he raised the knife,
   God saw, and said, " Forbear !

Yon ram shall yield his meaner life—
  Behold the victim there.''

3 Once David seem'd Saul's certain prey;
  But hark! the foe's at hand;
Saul turns his arms another way,
  To save th' invaded land.

4 When Jonah sunk beneath the wave
  He thought to rise no more;
But God prepared a fish to save
  And bear him to the shore.

5 Bless'd proofs of power and grace divine
  That meet us in his word!
May every deep-felt care of mine
  Be trusted with the Lord!

6 Wait for his seasonable aid,
  And though it tarry, wait:
The promise may be long delay'd.
  But cannot come too late.

## 7.

### *The Lord will Provide.*

1 THOUGH troubles assail,
  And dangers affright,
Though friends should all fail,
  And foes all unite;
Yet one thing secures us,
  Whatever betide,
The Scripture assures us
  The Lord will provide.

2 The birds without barn
  Or storehouse are fed;
From them let us learn
  To trust for our bread:
His saints what is fitting
  Shall ne'er be denied,
So long as 'tis written,
  The Lord will provide.

3 We may, like the ships,
 By tempests be tost
 On perilous deeps,
 But cannot be lost:
 Though Satan enrages
 The wind and the tide,
 The promise engages
 The Lord will provide.

4 His call we obey,
 Like Abr'am of old,
 Not knowing our way,
 But faith makes us bold:
 For though we are strangers,
 We have a good guide,
 And trust, in all dangers,
 The Lord will provide.

5 When Satan appears,
 To stop up our path
 And fill us with fears,
 We triumph by faith;
 He cannot take from us,
 Though oft he has tried,
 This heart-cheering promise,
 The Lord will provide.

6 He tells us we're weak,
 Our hope is in vain,
 The good that we seek
 We ne'er shall obtain;
 But when such suggestions
 Our spirits have plied,
 This answers all questions,
 The Lord will provide.

7 No strength of our own
 Or goodness we claim;
 Yet since we have known
 The Saviour's great name,
 In this our strong tower
 For safety we hide,
 The Lord is our power,
 The Lord will provide.

8 When life sinks apace,
And death is in view,
This word of his grace
Shall comfort us through :
No fearing or doubting
With Christ on our side,——
We hope to die shouting,
The Lord will provide.

## 8.

*Esau.*—Gen. xxv ; Heb. xii, 16.

1 Poor Esau repented too late
That once he his birthright despised,
And sold, for a morsel of meat,
What could not too highly be prized :
How great was his anguish when told,
The *blessing* he sought to obtain
Was gone with the *birthright* he sold,
And none could recall it again !

2 He stands as a warning to all
Wherever the gospel shall come ;
O hasten and yield to the call
While yet for repentance there's room !
Your season will quickly be past ;
Then hear and obey it to-day,
Lest, when you seek mercy at last,
The Saviour should frown you away.

3 What is it the world can propose ?
A morsel of meat at the best !
For this are you willing to lose
A share in the joys of the bless'd ?
Its pleasures will speedily end,
Its favour and praise are but breath :
And what can its profits befriend
Your soul in the moments of death ?

4 If Jesus for these you despise.
And sin to the Saviour prefer,
In vain your entreaties and cries
When summon'd to stand at his bar :

How will you his presence abide?
What anguish will torture your heart!
The saints all enthroned by his side,
And you be compell'd to depart.

5 Too often, dear Saviour, have I
Preferr'd some poor trifle to thee ;
How is it thou dost not deny
The blessing and birthright to me ?
No better than Esau I am,
Though pardon and heaven be mine ;
To me belongs nothing but shame—
The praise and the glory be thine.

## 9.

*Jacob's Ladder.*—Gen. xxviii, 12.

1 If the Lord our leader be,
We may follow without fear ;
East or west, by land or sea,
Home with him is every where.
When from Esau Jacob fled,
Though his pillow was a stone,
And the ground his humble bed,
Yet he was not left alone.

2 Kings are often waking kept,
Rack'd with cares on beds of state :
Never king like Jacob slept,
For he lay at heaven's gate.
Lo ! he saw a ladder rear'd,
Reaching to the heavenly throne ;
At the top the Lord appear'd,
Spake, and claim'd him for his own :—

3 " Fear not, Jacob, thou art mine,
And my presence with thee goes ;
On thy heart my love shall shine,
And my arm subdue thy foes :
From my promise comfort take,
For my help in trouble call ;
Never will I thee forsake
Till I have accomplish'd all."

4 Well does Jacob's ladder suit
　To the gospel throne of grace ;
　We are at the ladder's foot,
　Every hour, in every place.
　By assuming flesh and blood,
　Jesus heaven and earth unites :
　We by faith ascend to God,
　God to dwell with us delights.

5 They who know the Saviour's name
　Are for all events prepared ;
　What can changes do to them,
　Who have such a guide and guard ?
　Should they traverse earth around,
　To the ladder still they come :
　Every spot is holy ground,—
　God is there, and he's their home.

## 10.

*My Name is Jacob.*—Gen. xxxii, 27.

1 NAY, I cannot let thee go
　Till a blessing thou bestow :
　Do not turn away thy face,
　Mine's an urgent, pressing case.

2 Dost thou ask me who I am ?
　Ah, my Lord, thou know'st my name !
　Yet the question gives a plea
　To support my suit with thee.

3 Thou didst once a wretch behold,
　In rebellion blindly bold,
　Scorn thy grace, thy power defy,
　That poor rebel, Lord, was I.

4 Once a sinner near despair
　Sought thy mercy-seat by prayer ;
　Mercy heard and set him free—
　Lord, that mercy came to me.

5 Many years have pass'd since then,
　Many changes I have seen,

Yet have been upheld till now ;
Who could hold me up but thou ?

6 Thou hast help'd in every need,
This emboldens me to plead ;
After so much mercy past,
Canst thou let me sink at last ?

7 No—I must maintain my hold ;
'Tis thy goodness makes me bold ;
I can no denial take,
When I plead for Jesu's sake.

## 11.

*Plenty in the Time of Dearth.*—Gen. xli, 56.

1 My soul once had its plenteous years,
And throve, with peace and comfort fill'd,
Like the fat kine and ripen'd ears
Which Pharaoh in his dream beheld.

2 With pleasing frames and grace received,
With means and ordinances fed,
How happy for a while I lived,
And little fear'd the want of bread!

3 But famine came, and left no sign
Of all the plenty I had seen ;
Like the dry ears and half-starved kine,
I then look'd wither'd, faint, and lean.

4 To Joseph the Egyptians went ;
To Jesus I made known my case :
He, when my little stock was spent,
Open'd *his* magazine of grace.

5 For he the time of dearth foresaw,
And made provision long before ;
That famish'd souls, like me, might draw
Supplies from his unbounded store.

6 Now on his bounty I depend,
And live from fear of dearth secure :
Maintain'd by such a mighty friend,
I cannot want till he is poor.

7 O sinners, hear his gracious call !
  His mercy's door stands open wide :
  He has enough to feed you all,
  And none who come shall be denied.

## 12.

*Joseph made known to his Brethren.*—Gen. xlv, 3, 4.

1 WHEN Joseph his brethren beheld
  Afflicted and trembling with fear,
  His heart with compassion was fill'd ;
  From weeping he could not forbear.
  Awhile his behaviour was rough,
  To bring their past sins to their mind :
  But when they were humbled enough,
  He hasted to show himself kind.

2 How little they thought it was he
  Whom they had ill-treated and sold !
  How great their confusion must be,
  As soon as his name he had told !
  " I am Joseph, your brother," he said,
  "And still to my heart you are dear ;
  You sold me, and thought I was dead,
  But God for your sakes sent me here."

3 Though greatly distressed before,
  When charged with purloining the cup,
  They now were confounded much more,—
  Not one of them dared to look up.
  " Can Joseph, whom we would have slain,
  Forgive us the evil we did ?
  And will he our households maintain ?
  O this is a brother indeed !"

4 Thus dragg'd by my conscience I came,
  And laden with guilt, to the Lord,
  Surrounded with terror and shame,
  Unable to utter a word.
  At first he look'd stern and severe,
  What anguish then pierced my heart !
  Expecting each moment to hear
  The sentence, " Thou cursed, depart!"

5 But, O what surprise when he spoke,
  While tenderness beam'd in his face!
My heart then to pieces was broke,
  O'erwhelm'd and confounded by grace:
"Poor sinner, I know thee full well,
  By thee I was sold and was slain;
But I died to redeem thee from hell,
  And raise thee in glory to reign.

6 "I am Jesus, whom thou hast blasphemed,
  And crucified often afresh;
But let me henceforth be esteem'd
  Thy brother, thy bone, and thy flesh:
My pardon I freely bestow,
  Thy wants I will fully supply;
I'll guide thee and guard thee below,
  And soon will remove thee on high.

7 "Go, publish to sinners around,
  That they may be willing to come,
The mercy which now you have found,
  And tell them that yet there is room."
O sinners, the message obey!
  No more vain excuses pretend;
But come without further delay,
  To Jesus, our brother and friend.

## 13.

*The Bitter Waters.*—Exod. xv, 23—25.

1 BITTER indeed the waters are
    Which in this desert flow;
Though to the eye they promise fair,
    They taste of sin and woe.

2 Of pleasing draughts I once could dream;
    But now, awake, I find
That sin has poison'd every stream,
    And left a curse behind.

3 But there's a wonder-working wood,
    I've heard believers say,
Can make these bitter waters good,
    And take the curse away.

4 The virtues of this healing tree
   Are known and prized by few :
Reveal the secret, Lord, to me,
   That I may prize it too.

5 The cross on which the Saviour died
   And conquer'd for his saints,
This is the tree by faith applied,
   Which sweetens all complaints.

6 Thousands have found the bless'd effect,
   Nor longer mourn their lot ;
While on his sorrows they reflect,
   Their own are all forgot.

7 When they, by faith, behold the cross,
   Though many griefs they meet,
They draw a gain from every loss,
   And find the bitter sweet.

## 14.

*Jehovah-Rophi—I am the Lord that healeth thee.—*
Exod. xv.   C.

1 HEAL us, Emmanuel ; here we are,
   Waiting to feel thy touch :
Deep-wounded souls to thee repair,
   And, Saviour, we are such.

2 Our faith is feeble, we confess,—
   We faintly trust thy word ;
But wilt thou pity us the less ?
   Be that far from thee, Lord !

3 Remember him who once applied
   With trembling for relief ;
" Lord, I believe," with tears he cried.
   " O help my unbelief !"

4 She too who touch'd thee in the press,
   And healing virtue stole,
Was answer'd, " Daughter, go in peace :
   Thy faith hath made thee whole."

5 Conceal'd amid the gathering throng,
   She would have shunn'd thy view.

And if her faith was firm and strong—
    Had strong misgivings too.

6 Like her, with hopes and fears we come,
    To touch thee if we may ;
Oh! send us not despairing home,
    Send none unheal'd away.

## 15.

*Manna.*—Exod. xvi, 18.

1 MANNA to Israel well supplied
    The want of other bread ;
While God is able to provide,
    His people shall be fed.

2 (Thus though the corn and wine should fail,
    And creature-streams be dry,
The prayer of faith will still prevail
    For blessings from on high.)

3 Of his kind care how sweet a proof ;
    It suited every taste :
Who gather'd most had just enough—
    Enough who gather'd least.

4 'Tis thus our gracious Lord provides
    Our comforts and our cares ;
His own unerring hand divides,
    And gives us each our shares.

5 He knows how much the weak can bear,
    And helps them when they cry ;
The strongest have no strength to spare,
    For such he'll strongly try.

6 Daily they saw the manna come
    And cover all the ground :
But what they tried to keep at home
    Corrupted soon was found.

7 Vain their attempt to store it up,
    This was to tempt the Lord :
Israel must live by faith and hope,
    And not upon a hoard.

## 16.

*Manna hoarded.*—Exod. xvi, 20.

1 THE manna, favour'd Israel's meat,
   Was gather'd day by day ;
When all the host was served, the heat
   Melted the rest away.

2 In vain to hoard it up they tried
   Against to-morrow came ;
It then bred worms and putrified,
   And proved their sin and shame.

3 'Twas daily bread, and would not keep,
   But must be still renewed ;
Faith should not want a hoard or heap.
   But trust the Lord for food.

4 The truths by which the soul is fed
   Must thus be had afresh ;
For notions resting in the head
   Will only feed the flesh:

5 However true, they have no life
   Or unction to impart ;
They breed the worms of pride and strife,
   But cannot cheer the heart.

6 Nor can the best experience past
   The life of faith maintain ;
The brightest hope will faint at last
   Unless supplied again.

7 Dear Lord, while we in prayer are found,
   Do thou the manna give ;
Oh let it fall on all around,
   That we may eat and live !

## 17.

*Jehovah-Nissi—The Lord my Banner.*—
Exod. xvii, 15.   C.

1 By whom was David taught
   To aim the dreadful blow,

When he Goliath fought,
And laid the Gittite low?
No sword nor spear the stripling took,
But chose a peeble from the brook.

2   'Twas Israel's God and King
Who sent him to the fight,—
Who gave him strength to sling,
And skill to aim aright.
Ye feeble saints, your strength endures,
Because young David's God is yours.

3   Who order'd Gideon forth
To storm th' invader's camp,
With arms of little worth—
A pitcher and a lamp?
The trumpets made his coming known,
And all the host was overthrown.

4   Oh! I have seen the day
When, with a single word,
God helping me to say,
My trust is in the Lord,
My soul has quell'd a thousand foes,
Fearless of all that could oppose.

5   But unbelief, self-will,
Self-righteousness, and pride,
How often do they steal
My weapon from my side!
Yet David's Lord and Gideon's friend
Will help his servant to the end.


## 18.

*The Golden Calf.*—Exod. xxxii, 4, 31.

1  WHEN Israel heard the fiery law
From Sinai's top proclaim'd,
Their hearts seem'd full of holy awe,
Their stubborn spirits tamed:

2  Yet, as forgetting all they knew,
Ere forty days were past,

D                              46

With blazing Sinai still in view,
   A molten calf they cast.

3 Yea, Aaron, God's anointed priest,
   Who on the mount had been,
He durst prepare the idol-beast,
   And lead them on to sin!

4 Lord, what is man, and what are we,
   To recompense thee thus?
In their offence our own we see—
   Their story points at us.

5 From Mount Sinai we heard thee speak,
   And from Mount Calv'ry too;
And yet to idols oft we seek,
   While thou art in our view.

6 Some golden calf, or golden dream,
   Some fancied creature-good,
Presumes to share the heart with Him
   Who bought the whole with blood.

7 Lord, save us from our golden calves,
   Our sin with grief we own;
We would no more be thine by halves,
   But live to thee alone.

## 19.

*The True Aaron.*—Levit. viii, 7—9.

1 SEE Aaron, God's anointed priest,
   Within the veil appear,
In robes of mystic meaning dress'd,
   Presenting Isr'el's pray'r.

2 The plate of gold which crowns his brows
   His holiness describes;
His breast displays, in shining rows,
   The names of all the tribes.

3 With the atoning blood he stands
   Before the mercy-seat;
And clouds of incense from his hands
   Arise with odour sweet.

4 Urim and Thummim near his heart,
   In rich engravings worn,
The sacred light of truth impart,
   To teach and to adorn.

5 Through him the eye of faith descries
   A greater Priest than he :—
Thus Jesus pleads above the skies
   For you, my friends, and me.

6 He bears the names of all his saints
   Deep on his heart engraved,
Attentive to the state and wants
   Of all his love has saved.

7 In him a holiness complete—
   Light and perfections shine,
And wisdom, grace, and glory meet ;—
   A Saviour all divine.

8 The blood which as a Priest he bears
   For sinners is his own ;
The incense of his prayers and tears
   Perfumes the holy throne.

9 In him my weary soul has rest,
   Though I am weak and vile ;
I read my name upon his breast,
   And see the Father smile.

## 20.

*Balaam's Wish.*\*—Numb. xxiii, 10.

1   How bless'd the righteous are
    When they resign their breath !
No wonder Balaam wish'd to share
    In such a happy death.

2   "Oh! let me die," said he,
    "The death the righteous do,—
When life is ended, let me be
    Found with the faithful few."

* Book iii, Hymn 71.

3   The force of truth, how great!
      When enemies confess,
    None but the righteous, whom they hate,
      A solid hope possess.

4   But Balaam's wish was vain,
      His heart was insincere;
    He thirsted for unrighteous gain,
      And sought a portion here.

5   He seem'd the Lord to know,
      And to offend him loath;
    But Mammon proved his overthrow,
      For none can serve them both.

6   May you, my friends, and I,
      Warning from hence receive,
    If like the righteous we would die,
      To choose the life they live.

## 21.

*Gibeon.*—Joshua, x, 6.

1   WHEN Joshua, by God's command,
    Invaded Canaan's guilty land,
    Gibeon, unlike the nations round,
    Submission made, and mercy found.

2   Their stubborn neighbours who, enraged,
    United war against them waged,
    By Joshua soon were overthrown,
    For Gibeon's cause was now his own.

3   He from whose arm they ruin fear'd
    Their leader and ally appear'd;
    An emblem of the Saviour's grace
    To those who humbly seek his face.

4   The men of Gibeon wore disguise,
    And gain'd their peace by framing lies:
    For Joshua had no power to spare,
    If he had known from whence they were.

5   But Jesus invitations sends,
    Treating with rebels as his friends:

And holds the promise forth in view
To all who for his mercy sue.

6 Too long his goodness I disdain'd,
Yet went at last and peace obtain'd ;
But soon the noise of war I heard,
And former friends in arms appear'd.

7 Weak in myself, for help I cried,
Lord, I am press'd on every side ;
The cause is thine, they fight with me,
But every blow is aim'd at thee.

8 With speed to my relief he came,
And put my enemies to shame :
Thus saved by grace, I live to sing
The love and triumphs of my King.

## 22.

*Jehovah-Shalem——The Lord send Peace.——*
*Judges, vi, 24.   C.*

1 JESUS, whose blood so freely stream'd
To satisfy the law's demand,
By thee from guilt and wrath redeem'd,
Before the Father's face I stand.

2 To reconcile offending man,
Made Justice drop her angry rod ;
What creature could have form'd the plan,
Or who fulfill it but a God ?

3 No drop remains of all the curse
For wretches who deserved the whole ;
No arrows dipp'd in wrath to pierce
The guilty but returning soul.

4 Peace by such means, so dearly bought,
What rebel could have hoped to see ?
Peace, by his injured Sovereign wrought,
His Sovereign fasten'd to the tree!

5 Now, Lord, thy feeble worm prepare ;
For strife with earth and hell begins ;
Confirm and gird me for the war ;
They hate the soul that hates his sins.

6 Let them in horrid league agree!
  They may assault, they may distress,
  But cannot quench thy love to me,
  Nor rob me of the Lord my peace.

### 23.

*Gideon's Fleece.*—Judges, vi, 37—40.

1 THE signs which God to Gideon gave
  His holy sovereignty made known,
  That he alone has power to save,
  And claims the glory as his own.

2 The dew which first the fleece had fill'd,
  When all the earth was dry around,
  Was from it afterwards withheld,
  And only fell upon the ground.

3 To Isr'el thus the heav'nly dew
  Of saving truth was long restrain'd;
  Of which the Gentiles nothing knew,
  But dry and desolate remain'd.

4 But now the Gentiles have received
  The balmy dew of gospel peace;
  And Isr'el, who his Spirit grieved,
  Is left a dry and empty fleece.

5 This dew still falls at his command,
  To keep his chosen plants alive;
  They shall, though in a thirsty land,
  Like willows by the waters thrive.

6 But chiefly when his people meet,
  To hear his word and seek his face,
  The gentle dew, with influence sweet,
  Descends and nourishes their grace.

7 But ah! what numbers still are dead,
  Though under means of grace they lie,—
  The dew still falling round their head,
  And yet their heart untouch'd and dry.

8 Dear Saviour, hear us when we call:
  To wrestling prayer an answer give:

Pour down thy dew upon us all,
That all may feel and all may live.

## 24.

*Samson's Lion.*—Judges, xiv, 8.

1 The lion that on Samson roar'd,
   And thirsted for his blood,
With honey afterwards was stored,
   And furnish'd him with food.

2 Believers as they pass along
   With many lions meet,
But gather sweetness from the strong,
   And from the eater meat.

3 The lions rage and roar in vain,
   For Jesus is their shield :
Their losses prove a certain gain,
   Their troubles comfort yield.

4 The world and Satan join their strength,
   To fill their souls with fears ;
But crops of joy they reap at length
   From what they sow in tears.

5 Afflictions make them love the word,
   Stir up their hearts to prayer,
And many precious proofs afford
   Of their Redeemer's care.

6 The lions roar but cannot kill ;
   Then fear them not, my friends ;
They bring us, though against their will,
   The honey Jesus sends.

## 25.

*Hannah ; or, the Throne of Grace.*—1 Sam. i, 18.

1 When Hannah, press'd with grief,
      Pour'd forth her soul in pray'r ;
   She quickly found relief,
      And left her burden there :
   Like her, in every trying case
   Let us approach the throne of grace.

2　When she began to pray,
　　　Her heart was pain'd and sad ;
　　　But ere she went away
　　　Was comforted and glad.
　In trouble what a resting-place
　Have they who know the throne of grace !

3　Though men and devils rage,
　　　And threaten to devour,
　　　The saints from age to age
　　　Are safe from all their power ;
　Fresh strength they gain to run their race
　By waiting at the throne of grace.

4　Eli her case mistook ;
　　　How was her spirit moved
　　　By his unkind rebuke !
　　　But God her cause approved.
　We need not fear a creature's face
　While welcome at the throne of grace.

5　She was not fill'd with wine,
　　　As Eli rashly thought,
　　　But with a faith divine,
　　　And found the help she sought.
　Though men despise and call us base,
　Still let us ply the throne of grace.

6　Men have not power or skill
　　　With troubled souls to bear ;
　　　Though they express good-will,
　　　Poor comforters they are :
　But swelling sorrows sink apace
　When we approach the throne of grace.

7　Numbers before have tried,
　　　And found the promise true ;
　　　Nor yet one been denied,
　　　Then why should I or you ?
　Let us by faith their footsteps trace,
　And hasten to the throne of grace.

8　As fogs obscure the light,
　　　And taint the morning air,

But soon are put to flight
If the bright sun appear,
Thus Jesus will our troubles chase,
By shining from the throne of grace.*

### 26.

*Dagon before the Ark.*—1 Sam. v, 4, 5.

1 WHEN first, to make my heart his own,
   The Lord reveal'd his mighty grace,
   Self reign'd, like Dagon, on the throne,
   But could not long maintain its place.

2 It fell, and own'd the power divine,
   (Grace can with ease the victory gain,)
   But soon this wretched heart of mine
   Contrived to set it up again.

3 Again the Lord his name proclaim'd,
   And brought the hateful idol low ;
   Then self, like Dagon, broken, maim'd,
   Seem'd to receive a mortal blow:

4 Yet self is not of life bereft,
   Nor ceases to oppose his will ;
   Though but a maimed stump be left,
   'Tis Dagon—'tis an idol still.

5 Lord! must I always guilty prove,
   And idols in my heart have room ?
   Oh! let the fire of heavenly love
   The very stump of self consume.

### 27.

*The Milch Kine drawing the Ark: Faith's Surrender
of all.*—1 Sam. vi, 12.

1 THE kine unguided went
   By the directest road,
   When the Philistines homeward sent
   The ark of Israel's God.

2 Lowing they pass'd along
   And left their calves shut up ;

* Book ii, Hymn 61.

They felt an instinct for their young,
   But would not turn or stop.

3   Shall brutes, devoid of thought,
    Their Maker's will obey;
And we, who by his grace are taught,
    More stubborn prove than they?

4   He shed his precious blood,
    To make us his alone:
If wash'd in that atoning flood,
    We are no more our own.

5   If he his will reveal,
    Let us obey his call:
And think, whate'er the flesh may feel,
    His love deserves our all.

6   We should maintain in view
    His glory as our end;
Too much we cannot bear or do
    For such a matchless Friend.

7   His saints should stand prepared
    In duty's path to run;
Nor count their greatest trials hard
    So that his will be done.

8   With Jesus for our guide,
    The path is safe, though rough,
The promise says, " I will provide:"
    And faith replies, " Enough!"

### 28.

*Saul's Armour.*—1 Sam. xvii, 38—40.

1  WHEN first my soul enlisted
    My Saviour's foes to fight,
Mistaken friends insisted
    I was not arm'd aright:
So Saul advised David
    He certainly would fail,
Nor could his life be saved
    Without a coat of mail.

2 But David, though he yielded
    To put the armour on,
Soon found he could not wield it,
    And ventured forth with none.
With only sling and pebble
    He fought the fight of faith:
The weapons seem'd but feeble,
    Yet proved Goliath's death.

3 Had I by him been guided,
    And quickly thrown away
The armour men provided,
    I might have gain'd the day:.
But arm'd as they advised me,
    My expectations fail'd;
My enemy surprised me,
    And had almost prevail'd.

4 Furnish'd with books and notions,
    And arguments and pride,
I practised all my motions,
    And Satan's power defied:
But soon perceived with trouble
    That these would do no good;
Iron to him is stubble,
    And brass like rotten wood.

5 I triumph'd at a distance,
    While he was out of sight;
But faint was my resistance
    When forced to join in fight:
He broke my sword in shivers,
    And pierced my boasted shield;
Laugh'd at my vain endeavours,
    And drove me from the field.

6 Satan will not be braved
    By such a worm as I;
Then let me learn with David
    To trust in the Most High,—
To plead the name of Jesus,
    And use the sling of prayer:
Thus arm'd, when Satan sees us
    He'll tremble and despair.

## 29.

*David's Fall.*—2 Sam. xi, 27.

1 How David, when by sin deceived,
    From bad to worse went on !
For when the Holy Spirit's grieved,
    Our strength and guard are gone.

2 His eyes, on Bathsheba once fix'd,
    With poison fill'd his soul ;
He ventured on adult'ry next,
    And murder crown'd the whole.

3 So from a spark of fire at first,
    That has not been descried,
A dreadful flame has often burst,
    And ravaged far and wide.

4 When sin deceives it hardens too :
    For though he vainly sought
To hide his crimes from public view,
    Of God he little thought.

5 He neither would nor could repent.
    No true compunction felt,
Till God in mercy Nathan sent.
    His stubborn heart to melt.

6 The parable held forth a fact,
    Design'd his case to show;
But though the picture was exact,
    Himself he did not know.

7 " Thou art the man," the prophet said :
    That word his slumber broke ;
And when he own'd his sin and pray'd.
    The Lord forgiveness spoke.

8 Let those who think they stand, beware,
    For David stood before :
Nor let the fallen soul despair,
    For Mercy can restore.

## 30.

*Is this thy kindness to thy Friend?*—2 Sam. xvi, 17.

1 Poor, weak, and worthless, though I am,
　I have a rich, almighty Friend;
　Jesus, the Saviour, is his name,
　He freely loves, and without end.

2 He ransom'd me from hell with blood,
　And by his power my foes control'd;
　He found me wand'ring far from God,
　And brought me to his chosen fold.

3 He cheers my heart, my want supplies,
　And says that I shall shortly be
　Enthroned with him above the skies:
　O what a Friend is Christ to me!

4 But ah! my inmost spirit mourns,
　And well my eyes with tears may swim,
　To think of my perverse returns;
　I've been a faithless friend to him.

5 Often my gracious Friend I grieve,
　Neglect, distrust, and disobey;
　And often Satan's lies believe
　Sooner than all my Friend can say.

6 He bids me always freely come,
　And promises whate'er I ask;
　But I am straiten'd, cold, and dumb,
　And count my privilege a task.

7 Before the world, that hates his cause,
　My treach'rous heart has throbb'd with shame;
　Loath to forego the world's applause,
　I hardly dare avow his name.

8 Sure, were not I most vile and base,
　I could not thus my Friend requite!
　And were not he the God of grace
　He'd frown, and spurn me from his sight.

## 31

*Ask what I shall give Thee.*—1 Kings, iii, 5.

1 COME, my soul, thy suit prepare,—
Jesus loves to answer prayer;
He himself has bid thee pray,
Therefore will not say thee nay.

2 Thou art coming to a King,
Large petitions with thee bring;
For his grace and power are such
None can ever ask too much.

3 With my burden I begin,—
Lord, remove this load of sin!
Let thy blood, for sinners spilt,
Set my conscience free from guilt.

4 Lord! I come to thee for rest,—
Take possession of my breast;
There thy blood-bought right maintain,
And without a rival reign.

5 As the image in the glass
Answers the beholder's face,
Thus unto my heart appear,
Print thine own resemblance there.

6 While I am a pilgrim here
Let thy love my spirit cheer;
As my Guide, my Guard, my Friend,
Lead me to my journey's end:

7 Show me what I have to do;
Every hour my strength renew;
Let me live a life of faith,
Let me die thy people's death.

## 32.

### *Another.*

1 IF Solomon for wisdom pray'd,
The Lord before had made him wise;
Else he another choice had made,
And ask'd for what the worldings prize.

2 Thus he invites his people still,—
  He first instructs them how to choose,
  Then bids them ask whate'er they will,
  Assured that he will not refuse.

3 Our wishes would our ruin prove,
  Could we our wretched choice obtain,—
  Before we feel the Saviour's love
  Kindle our love to him again :

4 But when our hearts perceive his worth,
  Desires, till then unknown, take place ;
  Our spirits cleave no more to earth,
  But pant for holiness and grace.

5 And dost thou say, " Ask what thou wilt " ?
  Lord, I would seize the golden hour,—
  I pray to be released from guilt,
  And freed from sin and Satan's power.

6 More of thy presence, Lord, impart ;
  More of thy image let me bear ;
  Erect thy throne within my heart,
  And reign without a rival there.

7 Give me to read my pardon seal'd,
  And from thy joy to draw my strength,—
  To have thy boundless love reveal'd
  In all its height and breadth and length.

8 Grant these requests,—I ask no more,
  But to thy care the rest resign ;
  Sick or in health, or rich or poor,
  All shall be well if thou art mine.

### 33.

*Another.*

1   Behold the throne of grace !
    The promise calls me near ;
  There Jesus shows a smiling face,
    And waits to answer pray'r.

2   That rich atoning blood
    Which sprinkled round I see

Provides for those who come to God
　　An all-prevailing plea.

3　My soul, ask what thou wilt,——
　　Thou canst not be too bold;
Since his own blood for thee he spilt,
　　What else can he withhold?

4　Beyond thy utmost wants
　　His love and power can bless:
To praying souls he always grants
　　More than they can express.

5　Since 'tis the Lord's command,
　　My mouth I open wide;
Lord, open thou thy bounteous hand,
　　That I may be supplied.

6　Thine image, Lord, bestow,
　　Thy presence and thy love;
I ask to serve thee here below,
　　And reign with thee above.

7　Teach me to live by faith,
　　Conform my will to thine;
Let me victorious be in death,
　　And then in glory shine.

8　If thou these blessings give,
　　And wilt my portion be,
Cheerful the world's poor toys I leave
　　To them who know not thee.

## 34.

*Queen of Sheba.*—1 Kings, x, 1—9.

1　FROM Sheba a distant report
　　Of Solomon's glory and fame
Invited the queen to his court,
　　But all was outdone when she came:
She cried with a pleasing surprise,
　　When first she before him appear'd,
" How much what I see with my eyes
　　Surpasses the rumour I heard!"

2 When once to Jerusalem come
   The treasure and train she had brought,
   The wealth she possessed at home
   No longer had place in her thought :
   *His* house, *his* attendants, *his* throne,
   All struck her with wonder and awe ;
   The glory of Solomon shone
   In every object she saw.

3 But Solomon most she admired,
   Whose spirit conducted the whole,—
   His wisdom, which God had inspired,
   His bounty, and greatness of soul.
   Of all the hard questions she put
   A ready solution he show'd,—
   Exceeded her wish and her suit,
   And more than she ask'd him bestow'd.

4 Thus I, when the gospel proclaim'd
   The Saviour's great name in my ears,
   The wisdom for which he is famed,
   The love which to sinners he bears,
   I long'd, and I was not denied,
   That I in his presence might bow ;
   I saw, and transported I cried,
   " A greater than Solomon thou !"

5 My conscience no comfort could find,
   By doubt and hard questions opposed ;
   But he restored peace to my mind,
   And answer'd each doubt I proposed.
   Beholding me poor and distress'd,
   His bounty supplied all my wants ;
   My pray'r could have never express'd
   So much as this Solomon grants.

6 I heard and was slow to believe,
   But now with my eyes I behold
   Much more than my heart could conceive,
   Or language could ever have told.
   How happy thy servants must be
   Who always before thee appear !
   Vouchsafe, Lord, this blessing to me,
   I find it is good to be here.

## 35.

*Elijah fed by Ravens.* *—1 Kings, xvii, 6.

1 ELIJAH's example declares,
  Whatever distress may betide,
  The saints may commit all their cares
  To Him who will surely provide :
  When rain long withheld from the earth
  Occasion'd a famine of bread,
  The prophet, secured from the dearth,
  By ravens was constantly fed.

2 More likely to rob than to feed
  Were ravens, who live upon prey;
  But when the Lord's people have need,
  His goodness will find out a way.
  This instance to those may be strange
  Who know not how faith can prevail;
  But sooner all nature shall change
  Than one of God's promises fail.

3 Nor is it a singular case
  The wonder is often renew'd:
  And many can say to his praise,
  He sends them by ravens their food.
  Thus worldlings, though ravens indeed,
  Though greedy and selfish their mind,
  If God has a servant to feed,
  Against their own wills can be kind.

4 Thus Satan, that raven unclean,
  Who croaks in the ears of the saints,
  Compell'd by a Power unseen,
  Administers oft to their wants:
  God teaches them how to find food
  From all the temptations they feel;
  This raven, who thirsts for my blood,
  Has help'd me to many a meal.

5 How safe and how happy are they
  Who on the good Shepherd rely!

          * Book iii, Hymn 47.

He gives them out strength for their day,
Their wants he will surely supply:
He ravens and lions can tame,——
All creatures obey his command;
Then let me rejoice in his name,
And leave all my cares in his hand.

### 36.

*The Meal and Cruse of Oil.*——1 Kings, xvii, 16.

1 By the poor widow's oil and meal
    Elijah was sustain'd;
  Though small the stock, it lasted well,
    For God the store maintain'd.

2 It seem'd as if from day to day
    They were to eat and die;
  But still, though in a secret way,
    He sent a fresh supply.

3 Thus to his poor He still will give
    Just for the present hour;
  But for to-morrow they must live
    Upon his word and power.

4 No barn or storehouse they possess
    On which they can depend;
  Yet have no cause to fear distress,
    For Jesus is their Friend,

5 Then let not doubts your mind assail;
    Remember God has said,
  "The cruse and barrel shall not fail,——
    My people shall be fed."

6 And thus, though faint it often seems,
    He keeps their grace alive;
  Supplied by his refreshing streams,
    Their dying hopes revive.

7 Though in ourselves we have no stock,
    The Lord is nigh to save;
  His door flies open when we knock,
    And 'tis but ask and have.

## 37.

*Jericho; or, The Waters healed.*—2 Kings, ii, 19—22.

1 Though Jericho pleasantly stood,
  And look'd like a promising soil,
  The harvest produced little food,
  To answer the husbandman's toil.
  The water some property had
  Which poisonous proved to the ground,
  The springs were corrupted and bad,
  The streams spread a barrenness round.

2 But soon by the cruse and the salt
  Prepared by Elisha's command
  The water was cured of its fault,
  And plenty enriched the land.
  An emblem sure this of the grace
  On fruitless dead sinners bestow'd;
  For man is in Jericho's case
  Till cured by the mercy of God.

3 How noble a creature he seems!
  What knowledge, invention, and skill!
  How large and extensive his schemes!
  How much can he do if he will!
  His zeal to be learned and wise
  Will yield to no limits or bars;
  He measures the earth and the skies,
  And numbers and marshals the stars.

4 Yet still he is barren of good;
  In vain are his talents and art;
  For sin has infected his blood,
  And poison'd the streams of his heart.
  Though cockatrice' eggs he can hatch,
  Or, spider-like, cobwebs can weave,
  'Tis madness to labour and watch
  For what will destroy and deceive.

5 But grace, like the salt in the cruse,
  When cast in the spring of the soul,
  A wonderful change will produce,
  Diffusing new life through the whole:

The wilderness blooms like a rose,
The heart which was vile and abhorr'd
Now fruitful and beautiful grows—
The garden and joy of the Lord.

### 38.

*Naaman.—2 Kings, v, 14.*

1　BEFORE Elisha's gate
　　The Syrian leper stood ;
　　But could not brook to wait,—
　　He deem'd himself too good :
He thought the prophet would attend,
And not *to him* a message send.

2　" Have I this journey come,
　　And will he not be seen ?
　　I were as well at home
　　Would washing make me clean ;
Why must I wash in Jordan's flood ?
Damascus' rivers are as good."

3　Thus, by his foolish pride,
　　He almost miss'd a cure ;
　　Howe'er at length he tried,
　　And found the method sure :
Soon as the pride was brought to yield
The leprosy was quickly heal'd.

4　Leprous and proud as he,
　　To Jesus thus I came,
　　From sin to set me free,
　　When first I heard his fame :
Surely, thought I, my pompous train
Of vows and tears will notice gain.

5　My heart devised the way
　　Which I supposed he'd take ;
　　And when I found delay,
　　Was ready to go back :
Had he some painful task enjoin'd,
I to performance seem'd inclined.

6　When by his word he spake,
　　" That fountain open'd see ;

'Twas open'd for thy sake,—
" Go wash, and thou art free ;"
Oh! how did my proud heart gainsay,—
I fear'd to trust his simple way.

7    At length I trial made,
      When I had much endured ;
      The message I obey'd,—
      I wash'd, and I was cured.
Sinners, this healing fountain try,
Which cleansed a wretch so vile as I.

## 39.

*The borrowed Axe.*—2 Kings, vi, 5, 6.

1 THE prophets' sons in times of old,
      Though to appearance poor,
   Were rich without possessing gold,
      And honour'd though obscure.

2 In peace their daily bread they eat,
      By honest labour earn'd ;
   While daily at Elisha's feet
      They grace and wisdom learn'd.

3 The prophet's presence cheer'd their toil,
      They watch'd the words he spoke,
   Whether they turn'd the furrow'd soil,
      Or fell'd the spreading oak.

4 Once as they listen'd to his theme
      Their conference was stopp'd ;
   For one beneath the yielding stream
      A borrow'd axe had dropp'd.

5 " Alas! it was not mine," he said;
      " How shall I make it good ?"
   Elisha heard, and when he pray'd,
      The iron swam like wood.

6 If God in such a small affair
      A miracle performs,
   It shows his condescending care
      Of poor unworthy worms.

7 Though kings and nations in his view
  Are but as motes and dust,
  His eyes and ear are fix'd on you
  Who in his mercy trust.

8 Not one concern of ours is small
  If we belong to him.
  To teach us this, the Lord of all
  Once made the iron swim.

## 40.

*More with us than with them.*—2 Kings, vi, 16.

1 ALAS! Elisha's servant cried,
  When he the Syrian army spied ;
  But he was soon released from care,
  In answer to the prophet's prayer.

2 Straightway he saw, with other eyes,
  A greater army from the skies,—
  A fiery guard around the hill ;
  Thus are the saints preserved still.

3 When Satan and his host appear,
  Like him of old, I faint and fear ;
  Like him, by faith, with joy I see
  A greater host engaged for me.

4 The saints espouse my cause by pray'r,
  The angels make my soul their care ;
  Mine is the promise seal'd with blood,
  And Jesus lives to make it good.

## 41.

*Faith's Review and Expectation.*—1 Chron. xvii, 16, 17.

1 AMAZING grace! (how sweet the sound!)
  That saved a wretch like me !
  I once was lost, but now am found,—
  Was blind, but now I see.

2 'Twas grace that taught my heart to fear,
  And grace my fears relieved ;
  How precious did that grace appear
  The hour I first believed !

3 Through many dangers, toils, and snares.
 I have already come ;
'Tis grace has brought me safe thus far,
 And grace will lead me home.

4 The Lord has promised good to me,——
 His word my hope secures ;
He will my shield and portion be
 As long as life endures.

5 Yes, when this flesh and heart shall fail,
 And mortal life shall cease,
I shall possess, within the veil,
 A life of joy and peace.

6 The earth shall soon dissolve like snow,
 The sun forbear to shine ;
But God, who call'd me here below,
 Will be for ever mine.

## 42.

*The Joy of the Lord is your Strength.——*
*Neh. viii, 10.*

1 Joy is a fruit that will not grow
 In Nature's barren soil ;
All we can boast till Christ we know
 Is vanity and toil.

2 But where the Lord has planted grace,
 And made his glories known,
There fruits of heavenly joy and peace
 Are found, and there alone.

3 A bleeding Saviour seen by faith,
 A sense of pard'ning love,
A hope that triumphs over death,
 Give joys like those above.

4 To take a glimpse within the veil,
 To know that God is mine,
Are springs of joy that never fail,
 Unspeakable ! divine !

5 These are the joys which satisfy
 And sanctify the mind ;

Which make the spirit mount on high,
And leave the world behind.

3 No more, believers, mourn your lot,
But if you are the Lord's,
Resign to them that know him not
Such joys as earth affords.

### 43.

*Oh that I were as in Months past !——*
Job, xxix, 2.

1 Sweet was the time when first I felt
The Saviour's pard'ning blood
Applied, to cleanse my soul from guilt,
And bring me home to God.

2 Soon as the morn the light reveal'd,
His praises tuned my tongue ;
And when the evening shades prevail'd,
His love was all my song :

3 In vain the tempter spread his wiles,
The world no more could charm ;
I lived upon my Saviour's smiles,
And lean'd upon his arm.

4 In pray'r my soul drew near the Lord,
And saw his glory shine ;
And when I read his holy word
I call'd each promise mine.

5 Then to his saints I often spoke
Of what his love hath done :
But now my heart is almost broke,
For all my joys are gone.

6 Now when the evening shade prevails,
My soul in darkness mourns ;
And when the morn the light reveals,
No light to me returns.

7 My pray'rs are now a chatt'ring noise,
For Jesus hides his face ;
I read, the promise meets my eyes,
But will not reach my case.

8 Now Satan threatens to prevail,
    And make my soul his prey;
  Yet, Lord, thy mercies cannot fail:
    O come without delay!

## 44.

### *The Change.**

1 SAVIOUR, shine, and cheer my soul:
  Bid my dying hopes revive;
  Make my wounded spirit whole;
  Far away the tempter drive;
  Speak the word, and set me free:
  Let me live alone to thee.

2 Shall I sigh and pray in vain,
  Wilt thou still refuse to hear;
  Wilt thou not return again;
  Must I yield to black despair?
  Thou hast taught my heart to pray.
  Canst thou turn thy face away?

3 Once I thought my mountain strong.
  Firmly fix'd, no more to move;
  Then thy grace was all my song,
  Then my soul was fill'd with love:
  Those were happy golden days,
  Sweetly spent in pray'r and praise.

4 When my friends have said, "Beware.
  Soon or late you'll find a change,"
  I could see no cause for fear,
  Vain their caution seem'd and strange:
  Not a cloud obscured my sky.
  Could I think a tempest nigh?

5 Little then myself I knew.
  Little thought of Satan's power;
  Now I find their words were true,
  Now I feel the stormy hour!
  Sin has put my joys to flight,
  Sin has changed my day to night.

* Book ii, Hymn 34; and Book iii, Hymn 86.

6 Satan asks, and mocks my woe,
" Boaster, where is now your God?"
Silence, Lord, this cruel foe ;
Let him know I'm bought with blood ;
Tell him, since I know thy name,
Though I change, thou art the same.

## 45.

*Pleading for Mercy.*—Psalm vi.

1 In mercy, not in wrath, rebuke
Thy feeble worm, my God!
My spirit dreads thy angry look,
And trembles at thy rod.

2 Have mercy, Lord, for I am weak;
Regard my heavy groans ;
O let thy voice of comfort speak,
And heal my broken bones!

3 By day, my busy beating head
Is fill'd with anxious fears ;
By night, upon my restless bed,
I weep a flood of tears.

4 Thus I sit desolate and mourn,
Mine eyes grow dull with grief ;
How long, my Lord, ere thou return,
And bring my soul relief?

5 O come and show thy power to save,
And spare my fainting breath ;
For who can praise thee in the grave,
Or sing thy name in death?

6 Satan, my cruel envious foe,
Insults me in my pain ;
He smiles to see me brought so low,
And tells me hope is vain.

7 But hence, thou enemy, depart!
Nor tempt me to despair ;
My Saviour comes to cheer my heart,
The Lord has heard my prayer.

## 46.

*None upon earth I desire besides Thee.—*
Psalm lxxiii, 25.

1  How tedious and tasteless the hours
   When Jesus no longer I see;
   Sweet prospects, sweet birds, and sweet
          flowers,
   Have all lost their sweetness with me:
   The midsummer sun shines but dim,
   The fields strive in vain to look gay,
   But when I am happy in him,
   December's as pleasant as May.

2  His name yields the richest perfume,
   And sweeter than music his voice,
   His presence disperses my gloom,
   And makes all within me rejoice;
   I should, were he always so nigh,
   Have nothing to wish or to fear:
   No mortal so happy as I,
   My summer would last all the year.

3  Content with beholding his face,
   My all to his pleasure resign'd,
   No changes of season or place
   Would make any change in my mind:
   While bless'd with a sense of his love,
   A palace a toy would appear;
   And prisons would palaces prove
   If Jesus would dwell with me there.

4  Dear Lord, if indeed I am thine,
   If thou art my sun and my song,
   Say, why do I languish and pine,
   And why are my winters so long?
   O drive these dark clouds from my sky,
   Thy soul-cheering presence restore:
   Or take me unto thee on high,
   Where winter and clouds are no more.

## 47.

*The Believer's Safety.*—Psalm xci.

1 INCARNATE God! the soul that knows
   Thy name's mysterious power
Shall dwell in undisturb'd repose,
   Nor fear the trying hour.

2 Thy wisdom, faithfulness, and love,
   To feeble, helpless worms,
A buckler and a refuge prove
   From enemies and storms.

3 In vain the fowler spreads his net,
   To draw them from thy care;
Thy timely call instructs their feet
   To shun the artful snare.

4 When, like a baneful pestilence,
   Sin mows its thousands down,
On every side, without defence,
   Thy grace secures thine own.

5 No midnight terrors haunt their bed,
   No arrow wounds by day;
Unhurt on serpents they shall tread,
   If found in duty's way.

6 Angels, unseen, attend the saints,
   And bear them in their arms,
To cheer the spirit when it faints,
   And guard their life from harms.

7 The angels' Lord himself is nigh
   To them that love his name,—
Ready to save them when they cry,
   And put their foes to shame.

8 Crosses and changes are their lot
   Long as they sojourn here;
But since their Saviour changes not,
   What have the saints to fear?

## 48.

### *Another.*

1 THAT man no guard or weapons needs
  Whose heart the blood of Jesus knows;
  But safe may pass, if duty leads,
  Through burning sands or mountain snows.

2 Released from guilt, he feels no fear;
  Redemption is his shield and tower;
  He sees his Saviour always near
  To help in every trying hour.

3 Though I am weak, and Satan strong,
  And often to assault me tries,
  When Jesus is my shield and song,
  Abash'd the wolf before me flies.

4 His love possessing, I am blest,
  Secure whatever change may come:
  Whether I go to east or west,
  With him I still shall be at home.

5 If placed beneath the northern pole,
  Though winter reigns with rigour there,
  His gracious beams would cheer my soul,
  And make a spring throughout the year.

6 Or if the desert's sun-burnt soil
  My lonely dwelling e'er should prove,
  His presence would support my toil,
  Whose smile is life—whose voice is love.

## 49.

### *He led them by a right Way.*—Psalm cvii, 7.

1 WHEN Israel was from Egypt freed,
  The Lord, who brought them out,
  Help'd them in every time of need,
  But led them round about.

2 To enter Canaan soon they hoped;
  But quickly changed their mind,
  When the Red sea their passage stopp'd,
  And Pharaoh march'd behind.

3 The desert fill'd them with alarms
  For water and for food;
And Amalek, by force of arms,
  To check their progress stood.

4 They often murmur'd by the way,
  Because they judged by sight;
But were at length constrain'd to say,
  The Lord had led them right.

5 In the Red sea, that stopp'd them first,
  Their enemies were drown'd;
The rocks gave water for their thirst,
  And manna spread the ground.

6 By fire and cloud their way was shown
  Across the pathless sands;
And Amalek was overthrown
  By Moses' lifted hands.

7 The way was right their hearts to prove,
  To make God's glory known,
And show his wisdom, pow'r, and love,
  Engaged to save his own.

8 Just so the true believer's path
  Through many dangers lies;
Though dark to sense, 'tis light to faith,
  And leads us to the skies.

## 50.

*What shall I render?* *—Psalm cxvi, 12, 13.

1 FOR mercies, countless as the sands,
  Which daily I receive
From Jesus my Redeemer's hands,
  My soul, what canst thou give?

2 Alas! from such a heart as mine
  What can I bring him forth?
My best is stain'd and dyed with sin,
  My all is nothing worth.

  ▲ Book iii, Hymn 67.

3 Yet this acknowledgment I'll make
　　For all he has bestow'd—
Salvation's sacred cup I'll take,
　　And call upon my God.

4 The best returns for one like me,
　　So wretched and so poor,
Is from his gifts to draw a plea,
　　And ask him still for more.

5 I cannot serve him as I ought,
　　No works have I to boast;
Yet would I glory in the thought
　　That I should owe him most.

## 51.

*Dwelling in Mesech.*—Psalm cxx, 5—7.

1 WHAT a mournful life is mine,
　　Fill'd with crosses, pains, and cares!
Every work defiled with sin,
　　Every step beset with snares.

2 If alone I pensive sit,
　　I myself can hardly bear;
If I pass along the street,
　　Sin and riot triumph there.

3 Jesus! how my heart is pain'd,
　　How it mourns for souls deceived,—
When I hear thy name profaned,
　　When I see thy Spirit grieved!

4 When thy children's griefs I view,
　　Their distress becomes my own:
All I hear or see or do
　　Makes me tremble, weep, and groan.

5 Mourning thus I long had been
　　When I heard my Saviour's voice:
" Thou hast cause to mourn for sin,
　　But in me thou may'st rejoice."

6 This kind word dispell'd my grief,
　　Put to silence my complaints:

Though of sinners I am chief,
He has rank'd me with his saints.

7 Though constrain'd to dwell a while
Where the wicked strive and brawl,
Let them frown,—so he but smile,
Heav'n will make amends for all.

8 There, believers, we shall rest,
Free from sorrow, sin, and fears;
Nothing there our peace molest
Through eternal rounds of years.

9 Let us then the fight endure.—
See our Captain looking down:
He will make the conquest sure,
And bestow the promised crown.


## 52.

*Wisdom.*—Prov. vii, 22—31.　C.

1 Ere God had built the mountains,
　Or raised the fruitful hills,
Before he fill'd the fountains
　That feed the running rills,
In me, from everlasting,
　The wonderful I AM
Found pleasures never wasting,
　And Wisdom is my name.

2 When, like a tent to dwell in,
　He spread the skies abroad,
And swathed about the swelling
　Of ocean's mighty flood,
He wrought by weight and measure;
　And I was with him then;—
Myself the Father's pleasure,
　And mine the sons of men.

3 Thus Wisdom's words discover
　Thy glory and thy grace,
Thou everlasting lover
　Of our unworthy race!

E 2

Thy gracious eye survey'd us
    Ere stars were seen above :
In wisdom thou hast made us,
    And died for us in love.

4 And couldst thou be delighted
    With creatures such as we!
Who, when we saw thee slighted
    And nail'd thee to a tree!
Unfathomable wonder,
    And mystery divine,
The voice that speaks in thunder,
    Says, " Sinner, I am thine!"

## 53.

*A Friend that sticketh closer than a Brother.—*
Prov. xviii, 24.

1 One there is, above all others,
    Well deserves the name of Friend!
His is love beyond a brother's,
    Costly, free, and knows no end :
    They who once his kindness prove,
    find it everlasting love!

2 Which of all our friends, to save us,
    Could or would have shed their blood?
But our Jesus died to have us
    Reconciled in him to God :
    This was boundless love indeed!
    Jesus is a Friend in need.

3 Men, when raised to lofty stations,
    Often know their friends no more;
Slight and scorn their poor relations,
    Though they valued them before :
    But our Saviour always owns
    Those whom he redeem'd with groans.

4 When he lived on earth abased,
    Friend of sinners was his name;
Now above all glory raised,
    He rejoices in the same :

Still he calls them brethren, friends,
And to all their wants attends.

5 Could we bear from one another
What he daily bears from us?
Yet this glorious Friend and Brother
Loves us though we treat him thus:
    Though for good we render ill,
    He accounts us brethren still.

6 O for grace our hearts to soften!
Teach us, Lord, at length to love;
We, alas! forget too often
What a Friend we have above:
    But when home our souls are brought,
    We will love thee as we ought.

## 54.

### Vanity of Life.*—Eccles. i, 2.

1 THE evils that beset our path,
    Who can prevent or cure?
We stand upon the brink of death
    When most we seem secure.

2 If we to-day sweet peace possess,
    It soon may be withdrawn;
Some change may plunge us in distress
    Before to-morrow's dawn.

3 Disease and pain invade our health,
    And find an easy prey;
And oft, when least expected, wealth
    Takes wings and flies away.

4 A fever or a blow can shake
    Our wisdom's boasted rule,
And of the brightest genius make
    A madman or a fool.

5 The gourds from which we look for fruit
    Produce us only pain;

* Book ii, Hymn 6.

A worm unseen attacks the root,
　　And all our hopes are vain.

6　I pity those who seek no more
　　　Than such a world can give;
　　Wretched they are and blind and poor,
　　　And dying while they live.

7　Since sin has fill'd the earth with woe,
　　　And creatures fade and die,
　　Lord, wean our hearts from things below,
　　　And fix our hopes on high.

### 55.

#### *Vanity of the World.*　C.

1　God gives his mercies to be spent;
　　Your hoard will do your soul no good:
　　Gold is a blessing only lent,
　　Repaid by giving others food.

2　The world's esteem is but a bribe:
　　To buy their peace you sell your own,
　　The slave of a vain-glorious tribe,
　　Who hate you while they make you known.

3　The joy that vain amusements give,
　　Oh, sad conclusion that it brings!
　　The honey of a crowded hive,
　　Defended by a thousand stings.

4　'Tis thus the world rewards the fools
　　That live upon her treach'rous smiles:
　　She leads them blindfold by her rules,
　　And ruins all whom she beguiles.

5　God knows the thousands who go down
　　From pleasure into endless woe,
　　And with a long despairing groan
　　Blaspheme their Maker as they go.

6　O fearful thought! be timely wise;
　　Delight but in a Saviour's charms,
　　And God shall take you to the skies,
　　Embraced in everlasting arms.

## 56.

*Vanity of the Creature Sanctified.*

1 Honey though the bee prepares,
An envenom'd sting he wears ;
Piercing thorns a guard compose
Round the fragrant blooming rose.

2 Where we think to find a sweet,
Oft a painful sting we meet ;
When the rose invites our eye,
We forget the thorn is nigh.

3 Why are thus our hopes beguiled ?
Why are all our pleasures spoil'd ?
Why do agony and woe
From our choicest comforts grow ?

4 Sin has been the cause of all !
'Twas not thus before the fall :
What but pain and thorn and sting
From the root of sin can spring ?

5 Now with every good we find
Vanity and grief entwined ;
What we feel or what we fear
All our joys embitter here.

6 Yet, through the Redeemer's love,
These afflictions blessings prove ;
He the wounding stings and thorns
Into healing med'cines turns.

7 From the earth our hearts they wean,
Teach us on his arm to lean ;
Urge us to a throne of grace ;
Make us seek a resting-place.

8 In the mansions of our King
Sweets abound without a sting ;
Thornless there the roses blow,
And the joys unmingled flow,

## 57.

*The Name of Jesus.*—Cant. i, 3.

1 How sweet the name of Jesus sounds
 In a believer's ear!
It soothes his sorrows, heals his wounds,
 And drives away his fear.

2 It makes the wounded spirit whole,
 And calms the troubl'd breast:
'Tis manna to the hungry soul,
 And to the weary rest.

3 Dear name! the rock on which I build,
 My shield and hiding-place;
My never-failing treas'ry, fill'd
 With boundless stores of grace.

4 By thee my pray'rs acceptance gain,
 Although with sin defiled;
Satan accuses me in vain,
 And I am own'd a child.

5 Jesus! my Shepherd, Husband, Friend,
 My Prophet, Priest, and King;
My Lord, my life, my way, my end,
 Accept the praise I bring.

6 Weak is the effort of my heart,
 And cold my warmest thought;
But when I see thee as thou art
 I'll praise thee as I ought.

7 Till then I would thy love proclaim
 With every fleeting breath;
And may the music of thy name
 Refresh my soul in death.

## 58.

*O Lord, I will praise thee.*—Isa. xii. C.

1 I WILL praise thee every day,
 Now thine anger's turn'd away!
Comfortable thoughts arise
From the bleeding sacrifice.

2 Here, in the fair gospel field,
    Wells of free salvation yield
    Streams of life, a plenteous store,
    And my soul shall thirst no more.

3 Jesus is become at length
    My salvation and my strength;
    And his praises shall prolong,
    While I live, my pleasant song.

4 Praise ye then his glorious name,
    Publish his exalted fame!
    Still his worth your praise exceeds,
    Excellent are all his deeds.

5 Raise again the joyful sound,
    Let the nations roll it round!
    Zion, shout, for this is he,
    God the Saviour dwells in thee.

## 59.

*The Refuge, River, and Rock of the Church.—*
*Isa. xxxii, 2.*

1 He who on earth as man was known,
    And bore our sins and pains,
Now, seated on the eternal throne,
    The God of glory reigns.

2 His hands the wheels of nature guide
    With an unerring skill;
And countless worlds extended wide
    Obey his sovereign will.

3 While harps unnumber'd sound his praise
    In yonder world above,
His saints on earth admire his ways,
    And glory in his love.

4 His righteousness to faith reveal'd,
    Wrought out for guilty worms,
Affords a hiding-place and shield
    From enemies and storms.

5 This land, through which his pilgrims go,
    Is desolate and dry;

But streams of grace from him o'erflow,
  Their thirst to satisfy.

6 When troubles, like a burning sun,
  Beat heavy on their head,
To this almighty Rock they run,
  And find a pleasing shade.

7 How glorious he! how happy they
  In such a glorious Friend!
Whose love secures them all the way,
  And crowns them at the end.

## 60.

*Zion; or the City of God.*\*—Isa. xxxiii, 20, 21.

1 GLORIOUS things of thee are spoken,
  Zion, city of our God!
He, whose word cannot be broken,
  Form'd thee for his own abode:
On the Rock of ages founded,
  What can shake thy sure repose?
With salvation's walls surrounded,
  Thou may'st smile at all thy foes.

2 See! the streams of living waters
  Springing from eternal love,
Well supply thy sons and daughters,
  And all fear of want remove:
Who can faint while such a river
  Ever flows their thirst t' assuage?
Grace, which, like the Lord, the giver,
  Never fails from age to age.

3 Round each habitation hov'ring,
  See the cloud and fire appear!
For a glory and a cov'ring,
  Showing that the Lord is near:
Thus deriving from their banner
  Light by night, and shade by day;
Safe they feed upon the manna
  Which he gives them when they pray.

\* Book ii, Hymn 24.

4 Bless'd inhabitants of Zion,
  Wash'd in the Redeemer's blood!
  Jesus, whom their souls rely on,
  Makes them kings and priests to God ;
  'Tis his love his people raises
  Over self to reign as kings,
  And as priests his solemn praises
  Each for a thank-off'ring brings.

5 Saviour, if of Zion's city
  I through grace a member am,
  Let the world deride or pity—
  I will glory in thy name :
  Fading is the worldling's pleasure,—
  All his boasted pomp and show ;
  Solid joys and lasting treasure
  None but Zion's children know.

## 61.

*Look unto me, and be ye saved.*—Isa. xlv, 22.

1 As the serpent raised by Moses
  Heal'd the burning serpent's bite,
  Jesus thus himself discloses
  To the wounded sinner's sight :
  Hear his gracious invitation,
  " I have life and peace to give,—
  I have wrought out full salvation ;
  Sinner, look to me and live.

2 " Pore upon your sins no longer,
  Well I know their mighty guilt ;
  But my love than death is stronger,
  I my blood have freely spilt :
  Though your heart has long been harden'd,
  Look on me—it soft shall grow ;
  Past transgressions shall be pardon'd,
  And I'll wash you white as snow.

3 " I have seen what you were doing,
  Though you little thought of me ;
  You were madly bent on ruin,
  But I said—It shall not be :

You had been for ever wretched ;
Had I not espoused your part ;
Now behold my arms outstretched
To receive you to my heart.

4 " Well may shame and joy and wonder
All your inward passions move ;
I could crush thee with my thunder,
But I speak to thee in love :
See! your sins are all forgiven,——
I have paid the countless sum!
Now my death has open'd heaven,
Thither you shall shortly come."

5 Dearest Saviour, we adore thee
For thy precious life and death ;
Melt each stubborn heart before thee,
Give us all the eye of faith :
From the law's condemning sentence,
To thy mercy we appeal ;
Thou alone canst give repentance,
Thou alone our souls canst heal.

## 62

### *The good Physician.*

1 How lost was my condition
Till Jesus made me whole!
There is but one Physician
Can cure a sin-sick soul!
Next door to death he found me,
And snatch'd me from the grave
To tell to all around me
His wondrous power to save.

2 The worst of all diseases
Is light compared with sin ;
On every part it seizes,
But rages most within :
'Tis palsy, dropsy, fever,
And madness—all combined ;
And none but a believer
The least relief can find.

3 From men great skill professing
I thought a cure to gain;
But this proved more distressing,
And added to my pain:
Some said that nothing ail'd me,
Some gave me up for lost;
Thus every refuge fail'd me,
And all my hopes were cross'd.

4 At length this great Physician,
How matchless is his grace!
Accepted my petition,
And undertook my case;
First gave me sight to view him,
For sin my sight had seal'd,
Then bid me look unto him,—
I look'd, and I was heal'd.

5 A dying, risen Jesus,
Seen by the eye of faith,
At once from anguish frees us,
And saves the soul from death:
Come then to this Physician,
His help he'll freely give,
He makes no hard condition,
'Tis only—look and live.

## 63.

*To the Afflicted, tossed with Tempests, and not Comforted.*
Isa. liv, 5—11.

1 Pensive, doubting, fearful heart,
Hear what Christ the Saviour says;
Every word should joy impart,
Change thy mourning into praise:
Yes, he speaks, and speaks to thee,
May he help thee to believe!
Then thou presently wilt see,
Thou hast little cause to grieve.

2 " Fear thou not, nor be ashamed,
All thy sorrows soon shall end:
I who heaven and earth have framed
Am thy Husband and thy Friend:

I the High and Holy One,
Isr'el's God by all adored,
As thy Saviour will be known,
Thy Redeemer and thy Lord.

3 For a moment I withdrew,
And thy heart was fill'd with pain:
But my mercies I'll renew,—
Thou shalt soon rejoice again :
Though I seem to hide my face,
Yery soon my wrath shall cease ;
'Tis but for a moment's space,
Ending in eternal peace.

4 When my peaceful bow appears,
Painted on the wat'ry cloud :
'Tis to dissipate thy fears,
Lest the earth should be o'erflow'd :
'Tis an emblem too of grace,
Of my cov'nant love a sign ;
Though the mountains leave their place,
Thou shalt be for ever mine.

5 Though afflicted, tempest-toss'd,
Comfortless awhile thou art,
Do not think thou canst be lost,
Thou art graven on my heart :
All thy wastes I will repair,
Thou shalt be rebuilt anew;
And in thee it shall appear
What a God of love can do.

## 64.

*The contrite Heart.*—Isa. lvii, 15.   C.

1 THE Lord will happiness divine
    On contrite hearts bestow :
Then tell me, gracious God, is mine
    A contrite heart or no ?

2 I hear, but seem to hear in vain,
    Insensible as steel ;
If aught is felt, 'tis only pain
    To find I cannot feel.

3 I sometimes think myself inclined
   To love thee, if I could ;
But often feel another mind,
   Averse to all that's good.

4 My best desires are faint and few,
   I fain would strive for more ;
But when I cry, " My strength renew,"
   Seem weaker than before.

5 Thy saints are comforted, I know,
   And love thy house of prayer ;
I therefore go where others go,
   But find no comfort there.

6 O make this heart rejoice or ache,
   Decide this doubt for me ;
And if it be not broken break,
   And heal it if it be.

### 65.

*The future Peace and Glory of the Church.*
Isa. lx, 15—20.   C.

1 HEAR what God the Lord hath spoken :
   " O my people, faint and few,
Comfortless, afflicted, broken,
   Fair abodes I build for you ;
Thorns of heart-felt tribulation
   Shall no more perplex your ways ;
You shall name your walls Salvation,
   And your gates shall all be Praise.

2 There, like streams that feed the garden,
   Pleasures without end shall flow ;
For the Lord, your faith rewarding,
   All his bounty shall bestow :
Still in undisturb'd possession
   Peace and righteousness shall reign ;
Never shall you feel oppression,—
   Hear the voice of war again.

3 Ye no more your suns descending,
   Waning moons no more shall see ;

But, your griefs for ever ending,
   Find eternal noon in me :
God shall rise, and shining o'er you,
Change to day the gloom of night ;
He the Lord, shall be your glory,
God your everlasting light."

## 66.

*The Trust of the Wicked and the Righteous compared.*
Jer. xvii, 5—8.

1 As parched in the barren sands.
   Beneath a burning sky,
The worthless bramble with'ring stands.
   And only grows to die ;

2 Such is the sinner's awful case.
   Who makes the world his trust.
And dares his confidence to place
   In vanity and dust.

3 A secret curse destroys his root.
   And dries his moisture up ;
He lives awhile, but bears no fruit,
   Then dies without a hope.

4 But happy he whose hopes depend
   Upon the Lord alone ;
The soul that trusts in such a Friend
   Can ne'er be overthrown.

5 Though gourds should wither, cisterns break.
   And creature-comforts die,
No change his solid hope can shake,
   Or stop his sure supply.

6 So thrives and blooms the tree whose roots
   By constant streams are fed ;
Array'd in green, and rich in fruits.
   It rears its branching head.

7 It thrives though rain should be denied.
   And drought around prevail ;
'Tis planted by a river side
   Whose waters cannot fail.

## 67.

*Jehovah our Righteousness.*—Jer. xxiii, 6.   C.

1 My God, how perfect are thy ways!
   But mine polluted are ;
Sin twines itself about my praise,
   And slides into my prayer.

2 When I would speak what thou hast done
   To save me from my sin,
I cannot make thy mercies known
   But self-applause creeps in.

3 Divine desire, that holy flame,
   Thy grace creates in me ;
Alas! impatience is its name
   When it returns to thee.

4 This heart, a fountain of vile thoughts,
   How does it overflow !
While self upon the surface floats,
   Still bubbling from below.

5 Let others in the gaudy dress
   Of fancied merits shine,
The Lord shall be my righteousness,
   The Lord for ever mine.

## 68.

*Ephrain Repenting.*—Jer. xxxi, 18—20.   C.

1 My God, till I received thy stroke,
   How like a beast was I!
So unaccustom'd to the yoke,
   So backward to comply.

2 With grief my just reproach I bear,
   Shame fills me at the thought :
How frequent my rebellions were !
   What wickedness I wrought !

3 Thy merciful restraint I scorn'd,
   And left the pleasant road ;
Yet turn me, and I shall be turn'd :
   Thou art the Lord my God.

4 Is Ephraim banish'd from my thoughts,
  Or vile in my esteem?
 No, saith the Lord, with all his faults
  I still remember him.

5 Is he a dear and pleasant child?
  Yes, dear and pleasant still:
 Though sin his foolish heart beguiled,
  And he withstood my will.

6 My sharp rebuke has laid him low.
  He seeks my face again;
 My pity kindles at his woe,
  He shall not seek in vain.

## 69.

*The Lord is my Portion.*—Lam. iii, 24.

1 FROM pole to pole let others roam,
  And search in vain for bliss;
 My soul is satisfied at home,
  The Lord my portion is.

2 Jesus, who on his glorious throne,
  Rules heaven and earth and sea.
 Is pleased to claim me for his own,
  And give himself to me.

3 His person fixes all my love,
  His blood removes my fear;
 And while he pleads for me above,
  His arm preserves me here.

4 His word of promise is my food,
  His Spirit is my guide;
 Thus daily is my strength renew'd,
  And all my wants supplied.*

5 For him I count as gain each loss,
  Disgrace for him renown;
 Well may I glory in his cross,
  While he prepares my crown!

    * Book iii, Hymn 59.

6 Let worldlings then indulge their boast,
　　How much they gain or spend;
　　Their joys must soon give up the ghost,
　　But mine shall know no end.

## 70.

*Humbled and silenced by Mercy.*—Ezek. xvi, 63.

1 ONCE perishing in blood I lay;
　　Creatures no help could give;
　　But Jesus pass'd me in the way,
　　He saw, and bade me live.

2 Though Satan still his rule maintain'd,
　　And all his arts employ'd;
　　That mighty word his rage restrain'd,
　　I could not be destroy'd.

3 At length the time of love arrived,
　　When I my Lord should know;
　　Then Satan, of his power deprived,
　　Was forced to let me go.

4 O can I e'er that day forget,
　　When Jesus kindly spoke!
　" Poor soul, my blood has paid thy debt,
　　And now I break thy yoke.

5 " Henceforth I take thee for my own,
　　And give myself to thee;
　　Forsake the idols thou hast known,
　　And yield thy heart to me."

6 Ah, worthless heart! it promised fair,
　　And said it would be thine;
　　I little thought it e'er would dare
　　Again with idols join.

7 Lord, dost thou such backslidings heal,
　　And pardon all that's past?
　　Sure, if I am not made of steel,
　　Thou hast prevail'd at last.

8 My tongue, which rashly spoke before,
　　This mercy will restrain;

F                                    46

Surely I now shall boast no more,
Nor censure, nor complain.

## 71.

*The Covenant.*—Ezek. xxxvi, 25—28.   C.

1 THE Lord proclaims his grace abroad!
" Behold, I change your hearts of stone:
Each shall renounce his idol-god,
And serve, henceforth, the Lord alone.

2 " My grace, a flowing stream, proceeds
To wash your filthiness away;
Ye shall abhor your former deeds,
And learn my statutes to obey.

3 " My truth the great design ensures,
I give myself away to you;
You shall be mine, I will be yours,
Your God unalterably true.

4 " Yet not unsought or unimplored
The plenteous grace shall I confer;
No—your whole hearts shall seek the Lord,
I'll put a praying spirit there.

5 " From the first breath of life divine,
Down to the last expiring hour,
The gracious work shall all be mine,
Begun and ended in my power."

## 72.

*Jehovah-Shammah.*—Ezek. xlviii, 35.   C.

1 As birds their infant brood protect,
And spread their wings to shelter them:
Thus saith the Lord to his elect,
" So will I guard Jerusalem."

2 And what then is Jerusalem—
This darling object of his care?
Where is its worth in God's esteem?
Who built it? who inhabits there?

3 Jehovah founded it in blood,
The blood of his incarnate Son;

There dwell the saints, once foes to God—
The sinners whom he calls his own.

4 There, though besieged on every side,
Yet much beloved and guarded well,
From age to age they have defied
The utmost force of earth and hell.

5 Let earth repent and hell despair,
This city has a sure defence;
Her name is call'd " The Lord is there,"
And who has power to drive him thence?

### 73.

*The Power and Triumph of Faith.*—Dan. iii, 6.

1 SUPPORTED by the word,
Though in himself a worm,
The servant of the Lord
Can wondrous acts perform :
Without dismay he boldly treads
Where'er the path of duty leads.

2 The haughty king in vain,
With fury on his brow,
Believers would constrain
To golden gods to bow:
The furnace could not make them fear,
Because they knew the Lord was near.

3 As vain was the decree
Which charged them not to pray:
Daniel still bow'd his knee,
And worshipp'd thrice a day.
Trusting in God, he fear'd not men,
Though threaten'd with the lions' den.

4 Secure they might refuse
Compliance with such laws;
For what had they to lose
When God espoused their cause?
He made the hungry lions crouch;
Nor durst the fire *his* children touch.

5   The Lord is still the same,
      A mighty shield and tower,
    And they who trust his name
      Are guarded by his power;
    He can the rage of lions tame,
    And bear them harmless through the flame.

6   Yet we too often shrink
      When trials are in view,
    Expecting we must sink,
      And never can get through:
    But could we once believe indeed,
    From all these fears we should be freed.

## 74.

*Belshazzar.*—Dan. v. 5, 6.

1  Poor sinners! little do they think
      With whom they have to do!
    But stand securely on the brink
      Of everlasting woe.

2  Belshazzar thus, profanely bold,
      The Lord of hosts defied;
    But vengeance soon his boasts control'd,
      And humbled all his pride.

3  He saw a hand upon the wall
      (And trembled on his throne),
    Which wrote his sudden dreadful fall
      In characters unknown.

4  Why should he tremble at the view
      Of what he could not read?
    Foreboding conscience quickly knew
      His ruin was decreed.

5  See him o'erwhelm'd with deep distress;
      His eyes with anguish roll;
    His looks and loosen'd joints express
      The terrors of his soul.

6  His pomp and music, guests and wine,
      No more delight afford:
    O sinner, ere this case be thine,
      Begin to seek the Lord.

7 The law like this hand-writing stands,
   And speaks the wrath of God;
But Jesus answers its demands,
   And cancels it with blood.

## 75.

*The Gourd.*—Jonah, iv, 6—8.

1 As once for Jonah, so the Lord,
   To sooth and cheer my mournful hours,
Prepared for me a pleasing gourd,
   Cool was its shade, and sweet its flowers.

2 To prize this gift was surely right;
   But through the folly of my heart,
It hid the Giver from my sight,
   And soon my joy was changed to smart.

3 While I admired its beauteous form,
   Its pleasant shade and grateful fruit,
The Lord, displeased, sent forth a worm,
   Unseen to prey upon the root.

4 I trembled when I saw it fade,
   But guilt restrain'd the murm'ring word;
My folly I confess'd, and pray'd—
   Forgive my sin, and spare my gourd.

5 His wondrous love can ne'er be told,—
   He heard me and relieved my pain;
His word the threat'ning worm control'd,
   And bid my gourd revive again.

6 Now, Lord, my gourd is mine no more,
   'Tis thine, who only couldst it raise;
The idol of my heart before
   Henceforth shall flourish to thy praise.

## 76.

*Prayer for the Lord's promised Presence.*—Zech. ii, 10.

1 Son of God, thy people shield!
Must we still thine absence mourn?

Let thy promise be fulfill'd,
Thou hast said, "I will return!"

2 Gracious leader, now appear,
Shine upon us with thy light!
Like the spring, when thou art near,
Days and suns are doubly bright.

3 As a mother counts the days
Till her absent son she see,
Longs and watches, weeps and prays,
So our spirits long for thee.

4 Come and let us feel thee nigh,
Then thy sheep shall feed in peace;
Plenty bless us from on high,
Evil from amongst us cease.

5 With thy love and voice and aid,
Thou canst every care assuage;
Then we shall not be afraid,
Though the world and Satan rage.

6 Thus each day for thee we'll spend,
While our callings we pursue;
And the thoughts of such a friend
Shall each night our joy renew.

7 Let thy light be ne'er withdrawn,
Golden days afford us long!
Thus we pray at early dawn,
This shall be our evening song.

## 77.

*A Brand plucked out of the Fire.*—Zech. iii, 1—5.

1 WITH Satan, my accuser, near,
My spirit trembled when I saw
The Lord in majesty appear,
And heard the language of his law.

2 In vain I wish'd and strove to hide
The tatter'd filthy rags I wore:
While my fierce foe insulting cried,
"See what you trusted in before!"

3 Struck dumb, and left without a plea,
  I heard my gracious Saviour say,
  " Know, Satan, I this sinner free,—
  I died to take his sins away.

4 " This is a brand which I in love
  To save from wrath and sin design;
  In vain thy accusations prove;
  I answer all, and claim him mine."

5 At this rebuke the tempter fled;
  Then He removed my filthy dress;
  " Poor sinner, take this robe," He said,
  " It is thy Saviour's righteousness.

6 " And see a crown of life prepared!
  That I might thus thy head adorn;
  I thought no shame of suff'ring hard,
  But wore for thee a crown of thorn."

7 O, how I heard these gracious words!
  They broke and heal'd my heart at once;
  Constrain'd me to become the Lord's,
  And all my idol-gods renounce.

8 Now, Satan, thou hast lost thy aim :
  Against this brand thy threats are vain;
  Jesus has pluck'd it from the flame,
  And who shall put it in again ?

## 78.

*On one Stone shall be seven Eyes.*—Zech. iii, 9.

1 Jesus Christ, the Lord's Anointed,
    Who his blood for sinners spilt,
  Is the Stone by God appointed,
    And the church is on him built:
He delivers all who trust him from their guilt.

2 Many eyes at once are fix'd
    On a person so divine ;
  Love, with awful justice mix'd,
    In his great redemption shine:
Mighty Jesus! give me leave to call thee mine.

3 By the Father's eye approved,
   Lo, a voice is heard from heaven,
" Sinners, this is my Beloved,
   For your ransom freely given :
All offences for his sake shall be forgiven."

4 Angels with their eyes pursued him
   When he left his glorious throne ;
With astonishment they view'd him
   Put the form of servant on ;
Angels worshipp'd Him who was on earth unknown.

5 Satan and his host, amazed,
   Saw this Stone in Zion laid ;
Jesus, though to death abased,
   Bruised the subtle Serpent's head
When, to save us, on the cross his blood he shed.

6 When a guilty sinner sees him,
   While he looks his soul is heal'd ;
Soon this sight from anguish frees him,
   And imparts a pardon seal'd :
May this Saviour be to all our hearts reveal'd !

7 With desire and admiration,
   All his blood-bought flock behold
Him who wrought out their salvation,
   And enclosed them in his fold :
Yet their warmest love and praises are too cold.

8 By the eye of carnal reason
   Many view him with disdain ;
How will they abide the season
   When he comes with all his train ?
To escape him then they'll wish, but wish in vain.

9 How their hearts will melt and tremble
   When they hear his awful voice
But his saints he'll then assemble,
   As his portion and his choice,
And receive them to his everlasting joys.

## 79.

*Praise for the Fountain opened.*—Zech. xiii, 1.   C.

1 THERE is a fountain fill'd with blood
   Drawn from Emmanuel's veins ;
And sinners plunged beneath that flood
   Lose all their guilty stains.

2 The dying thief rejoiced to see
   That fountain in his day ;
And there have I, as vile as he,
   Wash'd all my sins away.

3 Dear dying Lamb, thy precious blood
   Shall never lose its power
Till all the ransom'd church of God
   Be saved, to sin no more.

4 E'er since, by faith, I saw the stream
   Thy flowing wounds supply,
Redeeming love has been my theme,
   And shall be till I die.

5 Then in a nobler, sweeter song,
   I'll sing thy power to save,—
When this poor lisping stamm'ring tongue
   Lies silent in the grave.

6 Lord, I believe thou hast prepared
   (Unworthy though I be,)
For me a blood-bought free reward,
   A golden harp for me !

7 'Tis strung, and tuned for endless years,
   And form'd by power divine ;
To sound in God the Father's ears
   No other name but thine.

## 80.

*They shall be mine, saith the Lord.*—Mal. iii, 16—18.

1 WHEN sinners utter boasting words,
   And glory in their shame,
The Lord, well pleased, an ear affords,
   To those who fear his name.

2  They often met to seek his face ;
      And what they do or say
   Is noted in his book of grace
      Against another day.

3  For they, by faith, a day descry,
      And joyfully expect,
   When he, descending from the sky,
      His jewels will collect.

4  Unnoticed now, because unknown,
      A poor and suff'ring few ;
   He comes to claim them for his own,
      And bring them forth to view.

5  With transport then their Saviour's care
      And favour they shall prove ;
   As tender parents guard and spare
      The children of their love.

6  Assembled worlds will then discern
      The saints alone are blest,
   When wrath shall like an oven burn,
      And vengeance strike the rest.

## 81.

*The Beggar.*—Matt. vii, 7, 8.

1  ENCOURAGED by thy word
      Of promise to the poor,
   Behold a beggar, Lord,
      Waits at thy mercy's door !
   No hand, no heart, O Lord, but thine.
   Can help or pity wants like mine.

2  The beggar's usual plea,
      Relief from men to gain,
   If offer'd unto thee,
      I know thou wouldst disdain ;
   And pleas which move thy gracious ear
   Are such as men would scorn to hear.

3  I have no right to say,
      That though I now am poor,

Yet once there was a day
When I possessed more :
Thou know'st that from my very birth
I've been the poorest wretch on earth.

4  Nor can I dare profess,
    As beggars often do,
    Though great is my distress,
    My faults have been but few :
If thou shouldst leave my soul to starve,
It would be what I well deserve.

5  'Twere folly to pretend
    I never begg'd before ;
    Or if thou now befriend,
    I'll trouble thee no more ;
Thou often hast relieved my pain,
And often I must come again.

6  Though crumbs are much too good
    For such a dog as I,
    No less than children's food
    My soul can satisfy.
O do not frown and bid me go,—
I must have all thou canst bestow !

7  Nor can I willing be
    Thy bounty to conceal
    From others who, like me,
    Their wants and hunger feel :
I'll tell them of thy mercy's store,
And try to send a thousand more.

8  Thy thoughts, thou Only Wise,
    Our thoughts and ways transcend,
    Far as the arched skies
    Above the earth extend :
Such pleas as mine men would not bear,
But God receives a beggar's pray'r.

## 82.

*The Leper.*—Matt. viii, 2, 3.

1 OFT as the leper's case I read,
   My own described I feel:
Sin is a leprosy indeed
   Which none but Christ can heal.

2 Awhile I would have pass'd for well,
   And strove my spots to hide,
Till it broke out incurable,
   Too plain to be denied.

3 Then from the saints I sought to flee,
   And dreaded to be seen;
I thought they all would point at me,
   And cry, "Unclean, unclean!"

4 What anguish did my soul endure
   Till hope and patience ceased!
The more I strove myself to cure,
   The more the plague increased.

5 While thus I lay distress'd, I saw
   The Saviour passing by;
To him, though fill'd with shame and awe,
   I raised my mournful cry.

6 Lord, thou canst heal me if thou wilt,
   For thou canst all things do;
O cleanse my leprous soul from guilt,
   My filthy heart renew.

7 He heard, and with a gracious look
   Pronounced the healing word;
" I will—be clean," and while he spoke
   I felt my health restored.

8 Come, lepers, seize the present hour,
   The Saviour's grace to prove;
He *can* relieve, for he is power—
   He *will*, for he is love.

## 83.

*A sick Soul.*—Matt. ix, 12.

1 PHYSICIAN of my sin-sick soul,
　　To thee I bring my case;
My raging malady control,
　　And heal me by thy grace.

2 Pity the anguish I endure,
　　See how I mourn and pine;
For never can I hope a cure
　　From any hand but thine.

3 I would disclose my whole complaint,
　　But where shall I begin?
No words of mine can fully paint
　　That worst distemper, sin.

4 It lies not in a single part,
　　But through my frame is spread;
A burning fever in my heart,
　　A palsy in my head.

5 It makes me deaf and dumb and blind,
　　And impotent and lame;
It overclouds and fills my mind
　　With folly, fear, and shame.

6 A thousand evil thoughts intrude
　　Tumultuous in my breast;
Which indispose me for my food,
　　And rob me of my rest.

7 Lord, I am sick, regard my cry,
　　And set my spirit free:
Say, canst thou let a sinner die,
　　Who longs to live to thee?

## 84.

*Satan returning.*—Matt. xii, 43—45.

1 WHEN Jesus claims the sinner's heart,
　　Where Satan ruled before,
The evil spirit must depart,
　　And dares return no more.

2 But when he goes without constraint,
  And wanders from his home,
  Although withdrawn, 'tis but a feint,—
  He means again to come.

3 Some outward change perhaps is seen
  If Satan quit the place;
  But though the house seem swept and clean,
  'Tis destitute of grace.

4 Except the Saviour dwell and reign
  Within the sinner's mind,
  Satan, when he returns again,
  Will easy entrance find.

5 With rage and malice sevenfold
  He then resumes his sway;
  No more by checks to be control'd,
  No more to go away.

6 The sinner's former state was bad,
  But worse the latter far;
  He lives possessed, blind, and mad,
  And dies in dark despair.

7 Lord, save me from this dreadful end!
  And from this heart of mine
  O drive and keep away the fiend
  Who fears no voice but thine.

## 85.

*The Sower.*—Matt. xiii, 3.   C.

1 Ye sons of earth, prepare the plough,
  Break up your fallow ground!
  The sower is gone forth to sow,
  And scatter blessings round.

2 The seed that finds a stony soil
  Shoots forth a hasty blade;
  But ill repays the sower's toil,—
  Soon wither'd, scorch'd, and dead.

3 The thorny ground is sure to baulk
  All hopes of harvest there;

    We find a tall and sickly stalk,
      But not the fruitful ear.

4 The beaten path and highway-side
      Receive the trust in vain;
  The watchful birds the spoil divide,
      And pick up all the grain.

5 But where the Lord of grace and power
      Has bless'd the happy field,
  How plenteous is the golden store
      The deep-wrought furrows yield!

6 Father of mercies, we have need
      Of thy preparing grace;
  Let the same hand that gives the seed
      Provide a fruitful place.

## 86.

*The Wheat and Tares.*—Matt. xiii, 37—42.

1 Though in the outward church below
  The wheat and tares together grow,
  Jesus ere long will weed the crop,
  And pluck the tares in anger up.

2 Will it relieve their horrors there
  To recollect their stations here—
  How much they heard, how much they knew,
  How long amongst the wheat they grew?

3 Oh! this will aggravate their case;
  They perish'd under means of grace;
  To them the word of life and faith
  Became an instrument of death.

4 We seem alike when thus we meet,
  Strangers might think we all are wheat;
  But to the Lord's all-searching eyes
  Each heart appears without disguise.

5 The tares are spared for various ends;
  Some for the sake of praying friends,
  Others the Lord, against their will,
  Employs his counsels to fulfill.

6 But though they grow so tall and strong,
  His plan will not require them long;
In harvest, when he saves his own,
  The tares shall into hell be thrown.

## 87.

*Peter Walking upon the Water.*—Matt. xiv. 28—31.

1 A WORD from Jesus calms the sea,
  The stormy wind controls,
And gives repose and liberty
  To tempest-tossed souls.

2 To Peter on the waves he came,
  And gave him instant peace;
Thus he to me reveal'd his name,
  And bade my sorrows cease.

3 Then fill'd with wonder, joy, and love,
  Peter's request was mine;
Lord, call me down, I long to prove
  That I am wholly thine.

4 Unmoved at all I have to meet
  On life's tempestuous sea,
Hard shall be easy, bitter sweet,
  So I may follow thee.

5 He heard and smiled, and bade me try;
  I eagerly obey'd;
But when from him I turn'd my eye,
  How was my soul dismay'd!

6 The storm increased on every side,
  I felt my spirit shrink!
And soon, with Peter, loud I cried,
  " Lord, save me, or I sink."

7 Kindly he caught me by the hand,
  And said, " Why dost thou fear
Since thou art come at my command,
  And I am always near?

8 " Upon my promise rest thy hope,
  And keep my love in view;

I stand engaged to hold thee up,
  And guide thee safely through."

## 88.

*The Woman of Canaan.*—Matt. xv, 22—28.

1 PRAYER an answer will obtain,
  Though the Lord awhile delay;
  None shall seek his face in vain,
  None be empty sent away.

2 When the woman came from Tyre,
  And for help to Jesus sought,
  Though he granted her desire,
  Yet at first he answer'd not.

3 Could she guess at his intent
  When he to his foll'wers said,
  " I to Israel's sheep am sent;
  Dogs must not have children's bread " ?

4 She was not of Israel's seed,
  But of Canaan's wretched race;
  Thought herself a dog indeed;
  Was not this a hopeless case?

5 Yet although from Canaan sprung,
  Though a dog herself she styled,
  She had Israel's faith and tongue,
  And was own'd for Abram's child.

6 From His word she draws a plea:
  " Though unworthy children's bread,
  'Tis enough for one like me
  If with crumbs I may be fed."

7 Jesus then his heart reveal'd:
  " Woman, canst thou thus believe ?
  I to thy petition yield,
  All that thou canst wish receive."

8 'Tis a pattern set for us,
  How we ought to wait and pray;
  None who plead and wrestle thus
  Shall be empty sent away.

## 89.

*What think ye of Christ?*—Matt. xxii, 42.

1 WHAT think you of Christ is the test
   To try both your state and your scheme;
   You cannot be right in the rest
   Unless you think rightly of him.
   As Jesus appears in your view,
   As he is beloved or not,
   So God is disposed to you,
   And mercy or wrath are your lot.

2 Some take him a creature to be,
   A man, or an angel at most:
   Sure these have not feelings like me,
   Nor know themselves wretched and lost.
   So guilty, so helpless am I,
   I durst not confide in his blood,
   Nor on his protection rely,
   Unless I were sure he is God.

3 Some call him a Saviour in word,
   But mix their own works with his plan;
   And hope he his help will afford,
   When they have done all that they can:
   If doings prove rather too light,
   (A little, they own, they may fail,)
   They purpose to make up full weight,
   By casting his name in the scale.

4. Some style him the pearl of great price,
   And say he's the fountain of joys;
   Yet feed upon folly and vice,
   And cleave to the world and its toys;
   Like Judas, the Saviour they kiss,
   And while they salute him, betray;
   Ah! what will profession like this
   Avail in his terrible day?

5 If ask'd what of Jesus I think,—
   Though still my best thoughts are but poor,
   I say he's my meat and my drink,
   My life and my strength and my store;

My Shepherd, my Husband, my Friend,
My Saviour from sin and from thrall,
My hope from beginning to end,
My portion, my Lord, and my all.

## 90.

*The foolish Virgins.*\*—Matt. xxv, 1.

1 WHEN descending from the sky
    The Bridegroom shall appear,
And the solemn midnight cry
    Shall call professors near,
How the sound our hearts will damp—
How will shame o'erspread each face
If we only have a lamp
    Without the oil of grace !

2 Foolish virgins then will wake
    And seek for a supply ;
But in vain the pains they take
    To borrow or to buy :
Then with those they now despise
Earnestly they'll wish to share ;
But the best among the wise
    Will have no oil to spare.

3 Wise are they, and truly blest,
    Who then shall ready be !
But despair will seize the rest, ·
    And dreadful misery :
Once, they'll cry, we scorn'd to doubt,
Though in lies our trust we put ;
Now our lamp of hope is out—
    The door of mercy shut.

4 If they then presume to plead,
    " Lord, open to us now ;
We on earth have heard and pray'd,
    And with thy saints did bow:"

* Book iii, Hymn 72.

He will answer from his throne——
"Though you with my people mix'd,
Yet to me you ne'er were known ;
  Depart, your doom is fix'd."

5 Oh that none who worship here
  May hear that word, depart !
Lord, impress a godly fear
  On each professor's heart :
Help us, Lord, to search the camp,
Let us not ourselves beguile,
Trusting to a dying lamp,
  Without a stock of oil.

## 91.

*Peter sinning and repenting.*——Matt. xxvi, 73.

1 When Peter boasted, soon he fell,
  Yet was by grace restored;
His case should be regarded well
  By all who fear the Lord.

2 A voice it has, and helping hand,
  Backsliders to recall ;
And cautions those who think they stand,
  Lest suddenly they fall.

3 He said, " Whatever others do,
  With Jesus I'll abide ;"
Yet soon amidst a murd'rous crew
  His suff'ring Lord denied.

4 He who had been so bold before
  Now trembled like a leaf,——
Not only lied, but cursed and swore,
  To gain the more belief.

5 While he blasphemed he heard the cock,
  And Jesus look'd in love ;
At once, as if by lightning struck,
  His tongue forebore to move.

6 Deliver'd thus from Satan's snare,
  He starts, as from a sleep ;

His Saviour's look he could not bear,
　　But hasted forth to weep.

7 But sure the faithful cock had crow'd
　　A hundred times in vain
　Had not the Lord that look bestow'd
　　The meaning to explain.

8 As I, like Peter, vows have made,
　　Yet acted Peter's part ;
　So conscience, like the cock, upbraids
　　My base ungrateful heart.

9 Lord Jesus, hear a sinner's cry,
　　My broken peace renew ;
　And grant one pitying look, that I
　　May weep with Peter too.

## 92.

*The Legion dispossessed.*—Mark, v, 18, 19.

1 LEGION was my name by nature,
　Satan raged within my breast,
　Never misery was greater,
　Never sinner more possess'd :
　Mischievous to all around me,
　To myself the greatest foe ;
　Thus I was when Jesus found me,
　Fill'd with madness, sin, and woe.

3 Yet in this forlorn condition,
　When he came to see me free,
　I replied to my Physician,
　" What have I to do with thee ?"
　But he would not be prevented,
　Rescued me against my will :
　Had he staid till I consented
　I had been a captive still.

3 " Satan, though thou fain wouldst have it,
　Know this soul is none of thine ;
　I have shed my blood to save it,
　Now I challenge it for mine ;*
　　　　* Book iii, Hymn 54.

Though it long has thee resembled,
Henceforth it shall me obey :
Thus He spoke, while Satan trembled,
Gnash'd his teeth, and fled away.

4 Thus my frantic soul He heal'd,
Bid my sins and sorrows cease :
" Take," said he, " my pardon sealed,
I have saved thee,——go in peace."
Rather take me, Lord, to heaven,
Now thy love and grace I know ;
Since thou hast my sins forgiven,
Why should I remain below ?

5 " Love," he said, " will sweeten labours :
Thou hast something yet to do ;
Go and tell your friends and neighbours
What my love has done for you ;
Live to manifest my glory,
Wait for heaven a little space :
Sinners, when they hear thy story,
Will repent and seek my face."

## 93.

*The Ruler's Daughter raised.*——Mark, v, 39——42.

1 COULD the creatures help or ease us
Seldom should we think of prayer ;
Few, if any, come to Jesus
Till reduced to self-despair :
Long we either slight or doubt him ;
But when all the means we try
Prove we cannot do without him,
Then at last to him we cry.

2 Thus the ruler, when his daughter
Suffer'd much, though Christ was nigh,
Still deferr'd it till he thought her
At the very point to die :
Though he mourn'd for her condition,
He did not entreat the Lord
Till he found that no physician
But himself could help afford.

3 Jesus did not once upbraid him,
   That he had no sooner come ;
But a gracious answer made him,
   And went straightway with him home :
Yet his faith was put to trial
   When his servants came, and said,
" Though he gave thee no denial,
   'Tis too late,—the child is dead."

4 Jesus, to prevent his grieving,
   Kindly spoke, and eased his pain ;
" Be not fearful, but believing,—
   Thou shalt see her live again."
When he found the people weeping,
   " Cease," he said, " no longer mourn ;
For she is not dead, but sleeping :"
   Then they laughed him to scorn.

5 O thou meek and lowly Saviour,
   How determined is thy love !
Not this rude unkind behaviour
   Could thy gracious purpose move.
Soon as he the room had enter'd,
   Spoke, and took her by the hand,
Death at once his prey surrender'd,
   And she lived at his command.

6 Fear not then, distress'd believer,
   Venture on his mighty name ;
He is able to deliver,
   And his love is still the same :
Can his pity or his power
   Suffer thee to pray in vain ?
Wait but his appointed hour,
   And thy suit thou shalt obtain.

## 94.

*But one Loaf.\**—Mark, viii, 14.

1 WHEN the disciples cross'd the lake
   With but one loaf on board,
How strangely did their hearts mistake
   The caution of their Lord !

\* Book iii, Hymn 57.

2  " The leaven of the Pharisees
    Beware," the Saviour said ;
  They thought, It is because he sees
    We have forgotten bread.

3  It seems they had forgotten too
    What their own eyes had view'd—
  How, with what scarce sufficed for few,
    He fed a multitude.

4  If five small loaves, by his command,
    Could many thousands serve,
  Might they not trust his gracious hand,
    That they should never starve ?

5  They oft his power and love had known,
    And doubtless were to blame ;
  But we have reason good to own
    That we are just the same.

6  How often has he brought relief,
    And every want supplied !
  Yet soon, again, our unbelief
    Says, " Can the Lord provide ?"

7  Be thankful for one loaf to-day,
    Though that be all your store :
  To-morrow, if you trust and pray,
    Shall timely bring you more.

## 95.

*Bartimeus.*—Mark, x, 47, 48.

1  " MERCY, O thou son of David !"
  Thus blind Bartimeus pray'd ;
  " Others by thy word are saved,
  Now to me afford thine aid."
  Many for his crying chid him,
  But he call'd the louder still,
  Till the gracious Saviour bid him
  " Come, and ask me what you will."

2  Money was not what he wanted,
  Though by begging used to live ;

But he ask'd, and Jesus granted
Alms which none but he could give:
" Lord, remove this grievous blindness,
Let my eyes behold the day;"
Straight he saw and, won by kindness,
Follow'd Jesus in the way.

3 Oh! methinks I hear him praising,
Publishing to all around,
" Friends, is not my case amazing?
What a Saviour I have found!
Oh! that all the blind but knew him,
And would be advised by me;
Surely they would hasten to him,
He would cause them all to see."

## 96.

*The House of Prayer.*—Mark, xi, 17.   C.

1 THY mansion is the Christian's heart,
O Lord, thy dwelling-place secure!
Bid the unruly throng depart,
And leave the consecrated door.

2 Devoted as it is to thee,
A thievish swarm frequents the place;
They steal away my joys from me,
And rob my Saviour of his praise.

3 There too a sharp designing trade,
Sin, Satan, and the world maintain;
Nor cease to press me, and persuade,
To part with ease and purchase pain.

4 I know them, and I hate their din,
Am weary of the bustling crowd;
But while their voice is heard within
I cannot serve thee as I would.

5 Oh! for the joy thy presence gives,—
What peace shall reign when thou art here!
Thy presence makes this den of thieves
A calm delightful house of prayer.

6 And if thou make thy temple shine,
  Yet, self-abased, will I adore;
  The gold and silver are not mine,—
  I give thee what was thine before.


## 97.

*The Blasted Fig-tree.*—Mark, xi, 20.

1 ONE awful word which Jesus spoke
  Against the tree which bore no fruit,
  More piercing than the lightning's stroke,
  Blasted and dried it to the root.

2 But could a tree the Lord offend,
  To make him show his anger thus?
  He surely had a further end—
  To be a warning word to us.

3 The fig-tree by its leaves was known;
  But having not a fig to show,
  It brought a heavy sentence down—
  " Let none hereafter on thee grow."

4 Too many, who the gospel hear,
  Whom Satan blinds and sin deceives,
  We to this fig-tree may compare,
  They yield no fruit, but only leaves.

5 Knowledge and zeal and gifts and talk,
  Unless combined with faith and love,
  And witness'd by a gospel-walk,
  Will not a true profession prove.

6 Without the fruit the Lord expects,
  Knowledge will make our state the worse;
  The barren trees he still rejects,
  And soon will blast them with his curse.

7 O Lord, unite our hearts in prayer!
  On each of us thy Spirit send,
  That we the fruits of grace may bear,
  And find acceptance in the end.

## 98.

*The Two Debtors.*—Luke, vii, 47.

1 ONCE a woman silent stood
 While Jesus sat at meat;
From her eyes she pour'd a flood,
 To wash his sacred feet:
Shame and wonder, joy and love,
All at once possess'd her mind,
That she e'er so vile could prove,
 Yet now forgiveness find.

2 " How came this vile woman here?
 Will Jesus notice such?
Sure, if he a prophet were,
 He would disdain her touch!"
Simon thus, with scornful heart,
Slighted one whom Jesus loved;
But her Saviour took her part,
 And thus his pride reproved:

3 " If two men in debt were bound,
 One less, the other more,
Fifty, or five hundred pound,
 And both alike were poor;
Should the lender both forgive
When he saw them both distress'd,
Which of them would you believe
 Engaged to love him best?

4 " Surely he who most did owe,"
 The Pharisee replied:
Then our Lord, " By judging so,
 Thou dost for her decide:
Simon, if like her you knew
How much you forgiveness need,
You like her had acted too,
 And welcomed me indeed.

5 " When the load of sin is felt,
 And much forgiveness known
Then the heart of course will melt,
 Though hard before as stone:

Blame not then her love and tears,
   Greatly she in debt has been;
But I have removed her fears,
   And pardon'd all her sin."

6 When I read this woman's case,
   Her love and humble zeal,
I confess, with shame of face,
   My heart is made of steel.
Much has been forgiven to me,
Jesus paid my heavy score;
What a creature must I be,
   That I can love no more!

## 99.

*The Good Samaritan.*    Luke, x, 33—35.

1 How kind the good Samaritan
   To him who fell among the thieves!
Thus Jesus pities fallen man,
   And heals the wounds the soul receives.

2 Oh! I remember well the day
   When, sorely wounded, nearly slain,
Like that poor man, I bleeding lay,
   And groan'd for help, but groan'd in vain.

3 Men saw me in this helpless case,
   And pass'd without compassion by;
Each neighbour turn'd away his face,
   Unmoved by my mournful cry.

4 But He whose name had been my scorn
   (As Jews Samaritans despise)
Came, when he saw me thus forlorn,
   With love and pity in his eyes.

5 Gently he raised me from the ground,
   Press'd me to lean upon his arm,
And into every gaping wound
   He pour'd his own all-healing balm.

6 Unto his church my steps he led,
   The house prepared for sinners lost,

Gave charge I should be clothed and fed,
And took upon him all the cost.

7 Thus saved from death, from want secured,
I wait till he again shall come
(When I shall be completely cured,)
And take me to his heavenly home.

8 There, through eternal, boundless days,
When Nature's wheel no longer rolls,
How shall I love, adore, and praise
This good Samaritan to souls!

### 100.

*Martha and Mary.*—Luke, x, 38—42.

1 MARTHA her love and joy express'd
By care to entertain her guest;
While Mary sat to hear her Lord,
And could not bear to lose a word.

2 The principle, in both the same,
Produced in each a different aim;
The one to feast the Lord was led,
The other waited to be fed.

3 But Mary chose the better part,
Her Saviour's words refresh'd her heart,
While busy Martha angry grew,
And lost her time and temper too.

4 With warmth she to her sister spoke,
But brought upon herself rebuke:
"One thing is needful, and but one,
Why do thy thoughts on many run?"

5 How oft are we like Martha vex'd,
Encumber'd, hurried, and perplex'd,
While trifles so engross our thought
The one thing needful is forgot!

6 Lord, teach us this one thing to choose,
Which they who gain can never lose,—
Sufficient in itself alone,
And needful, were the world our own.

7  Let grov'ling hearts the world admire,—
      Thy love is all that I require!
   Gladly I may the rest resign,
      If the one needful thing be mine!

## 101.

*The Heart taken.*—Luke, xi, 21, 22.

1  THE castle of the human heart,
      Strong in its native sin,
   Is guarded well in every part
      By him who dwells within.

2  For Satan there in arms resides,
      And calls the place his own,—
   With care against assaults provides,
      And rules as on a throne.

3  Each traitor thought on him, as chief,
      In blind obedience waits;
   And pride, self-will, and unbelief,
      Are posted at the gates.

4  Thus Satan for a season reigns,
      And keeps his goods in peace:
   The soul is pleased to wear his chains
      Nor wishes a release.

5  But Jesus, stronger far than he,
      In his appointed hour
   Appears, to set his people free
      From the usurper's power.

6  "This heart I bought with blood," he says,
      "And now it shall be mine;"
   His voice the strong one arm'd dismays,—
      He knows he must resign.

7  In spite of unbelief and pride,
      And self, and Satan's art,
   The gates of brass fly open wide,
      And Jesus wins the heart.

8  The rebel soul that once withstood
      The Saviour's kindest call,

Rejoices now, by grace subdued,
  To serve him with her all.

## 102.

*The Worldling.*—Luke, xii, 16—21.

1 " My barns are full, my stores increase,
    And now, for many years,
  Soul, eat and drink, and take thine ease,
    Secure from wants and fears."

2 Thus while a worldling boasted once,
    As many now presume,
  He heard the Lord himself pronounce
    His sudden awful doom.

3 " This night, vain fool, thy soul must pass
    Into a world unknown ;
  And who shall then the stores possess
    Which thou hast call'd thine own ?"

4 Thus blinded mortals fondly scheme
    For happiness below,
  Till death disturbs the pleasing dream,
    And they awake to woe.

5 Ah ! who can speak the vast dismay
    That fills the sinner's mind,
  When, torn by Death's strong hand away,
    He leaves his all behind.

6 Wretches, who cleave to earthly things,
    But are not rich to God,
  Their dying hour is full of stings,
    And hell their dark abode.

7 Dear Saviour, make us timely wise
    Thy gospel to attend,
  That we may live above the skies
    When this poor life shall end.

## 103.

*The Barren Fig-Tree.*—Luke, xiii, 6—9.

  1   THE church a garden is,
        In which believers stand

Like ornamental trees
Planted by God's own hand!
His Spirit waters all their roots,
And every branch abounds with fruits.

2    But other trees there are
In this enclosure grow,
Which, though they promise fair,
Have only leaves to show:
No fruits of grace are on them found,
They stand but cumberers of the ground.

3    The under gardener grieves,
In vain his strength he spends,
For heaps of useless leaves
Afford him small amends:
He hears the Lord his will make known,
To cut the barren fig-trees down.

4    How difficult his post,
What pangs his bowels move,
To find his wishes cross'd,
His labours useless prove!
His last relief is earnest prayer,
"Lord, spare them yet another year.

5    " Spare them, and let me try
What further means may do;
I'll fresh manure apply,
My digging I'll renew:
Who knows but yet they fruit may yield?
If not—'tis just, they must be fell'd."

6    If under means of grace
No gracious fruits appear,
It is a dreadful case,
Though God may long forbear:
At length he'll strike the threaten'd blow,*
And lay the barren fig-tree low.

* Book ii, Hymn 26.

## 104.

*The Prodigal Son.*—Luke, xv, 11—24.

1 AFFLICTIONS, though they seem severe,
   In mercy oft are sent ;
They stopp'd the prodigal's career,
   And forced him to repent.

2 Although he no relentings felt
   Till he had spent his store,
His stubborn heart began to melt
   When famine pinch'd him sore.

3 " What have I gain'd by sin," he said,
   " But hunger, shame, and fear ?
My father's house abounds with bread
   While I am starving here.

4 I'll go and tell him all I've done,
   And fall before his face ;
Unworthy to be call'd his son,
   I'll seek a servant's place."

5 His father saw him coming back,
   He saw and ran and smiled,
And threw his arms around the neck
   Of his rebellious child.

6 " Father, I've sinn'd—but O forgive !"
   " I've heard enough," he said ;
" Rejoice, my house,—my son's alive
   For whom I mourn'd as dead.

7 " Now let the fatted calf be slain,
   And spread the news around :
My son was dead, but lives again,—
   Was lost, but now is found."

8 'Tis thus the Lord his love reveals
   To call poor sinners home ;
More than a father's love he feels,
   And welcomes all that come.

G 2

## 105.

*The rich Man and Lazarus.*—Luke, xvi, 19—25.

1 A WORLDLING spent each day
In luxury and state,
While a believer lay
A beggar at his gate.
Think not the Lord's appointment strange,
Death made a great and lasting change.

2 Death brought the saint release
From want, disease, and scorn;
And to the land of peace
His soul, by angels borne,
In Abraham's bosom safely placed,
Enjoys an everlasting feast.

3 The rich man also died,
And in a moment fell
From all his pomp and pride
Into the flames of hell:
The beggar's bliss, from far beheld,
His soul with double anguish fill'd.

4 "O, Abra'm, send," he cries,
(But his request was vain,)
"The beggar from the skies
To mitigate my pain!
One drop of water I entreat,
To sooth my tongue's tormenting heat."

5 Let all who worldly pelf
And worldly spirits have
Observe, each for himself,
The answer Abra'm gave:
"Remember thou wast fill'd with good,
While the poor beggar pined for good.

6 "Neglected at thy door,
With tears he begg'd his bread;
But now he weeps no more—
His griefs and pains are fled:
His joys eternally will flow,
While thine expire in endless woe."

7   Lord, make us truly wise,
      To choose thy people's lot,
  And earthly joys despise,
      Which soon will be forgot :
The greatest evil we can fear,
Is to possess our portion here !

## 106.

*The importunate Widow.*\*—Luke, xviii, 1—7.

1   OUR Lord, who knows full well
      The heart of every saint,
Invites us, by a parable,
      To pray and never faint.

2   He bows his gracious ear,
      We never plead in vain ;
Yet we must wait till he appear,
      And pray, and pray again.

3   Though unbelief suggest,
      Why should we longer wait ?
He bids us never give him rest,
      But be importunate.

4   'Twas thus a widow poor,
      Without support or friend,
Beset the unjust judge's door,
      And gain'd, at last, her end.

5   For her he little cared,
      As little for the laws ;
Nor god nor man did he regard,
      Yet he espoused her cause.

6   She urged him day and night,
      Would no denial take ;
At length he said, " I'll do her right,
      For my own quiet's sake."

7   And shall not Jesus hear
      His chosen when they cry ?

            Book ii, Hymn 60.

Yes, though he may a while forbear,
　　He'll help them from on high.

8　His nature, truth, and love,
　　Engage him on their side ;
　When they are grieved, his bowels move,
　　And can they be denied ?

9　Then let us earnest be,
　　And never faint in prayer ;
　He loves our importunity,
　　And makes our cause his care.

## 107.

*Zaccheus.*—Luke, xix, 1—6.

1　ZACCHEUS climb'd the tree,
　　And thought himself unknown ;
　　But how surprised was he
　　When Jesus call'd him down !
　The Lord beheld him, though conceal'd.
　And by a word his power reveal'd.

2　Wonder and joy at once
　　Were painted in his face ;
　　" Does he my name pronounce,
　　And does he know my case ?
　Will Jesus deign with me to dine ?
　Lord, I, with all I have, are thine."

3　Thus, where the gospel's preach'd,
　　And sinners come to hear,
　　The hearts of some are reach'd
　　Before they are aware :
　The word directly speaks to them,
　And seems to point them out by name.

4　'Tis curiosity
　　Oft brings them in the way,
　　Only the man to see
　　And hear what he can say ;
　But how the sinner starts to find
　The preacher knows his inmost mind !

5    His long-forgotten faults
Are brought again in view,
And all his secrets thoughts
Reveal'd in public too.
Though compass'd with a crowd about,
The searching word has found him out.

6    While thus distressing pain
And sorrow fill his heart,
He hears a voice again,
That bids his fears depart,
Then like Zaccheus he is blest,
And Jesus deigns to be his guest.

## 108.

*The Believer's Danger, Safety, and Duty.—*
Luke, xxii, 31, 32.

1   " Simon beware," the Saviour said,—
Satan, your subtle foe,
Already has his measures laid
Your soul to overthrow.

2   " He wants to sift you all as wheat,
And thinks his vict'ry sure;
But I his malice will defeat,—
My pray'r shall faith secure."

3   Believers, tremble and rejoice,
Your help and danger view;
This warning has to you a voice,
This promise speaks to you.

4   Satan beholds with jealous eye
Your privilege and joy;
He's always watchful, always nigh,
To tear and to destroy.

5   But Jesus lives to intercede,
That faith may still prevail;
· He will support in time of need,
And Satan's art shall fail.

6   Yet let us not the warning slight,
But watchful still be found;

Though faith cannot be slain in fight,
It may receive a wound.

7 While Satan watches dare we sleep?
  We must our guard maintain;
But, Lord, do thou the city keep,
  Or else we watch in vain.

## 109.

*Father, forgive them.*—Luke, xxiii, 34.

1 " FATHER, forgive," the Saviour said,
  " They know not what they do:"
His heart was moved when thus he pray'd
  For me, my friends, and you.

2 He saw that as the Jews abused
  And crucified his flesh,
So he by us would be refused,
  And crucified afresh.

3 Through love of sin we long were prone
  To act as Satan bid;
But now with grief and shame we own
  We knew not what we did.

4 We knew not the desert of sin,
  Nor whom we thus defied;
Nor where our guilty souls had been
  If Jesus had not died.

5 We knew not what a law we broke,
  How holy, just, and pure!
Nor what a God we durst provoke,
  But thought ourselves secure.

6 But Jesus all our guilt foresaw,
  And shed his precious blood,
To satisfy the holy law,
  And make our peace with God.

7 My sin, dear Saviour, made thee bleed,
  Yet didst thou pray for me!
I knew not what I did, indeed,
  When ignorant of thee.

## 110.

*The two Malefactors.*—Luke, xxiii, 39—43.

1 SOVEREIGN grace has power alone
  To subdue a heart of stone;
  And the moment grace is felt,
  Then the hardest heart will melt.

2 When our Lord was crucified
  Two transgressors with him died!
  One, with vile blaspheming tongue,
  Scoff'd at Jesus as he hung.

3 Thus he spent his wicked breath
  In the very jaws of death;
  Perish'd, as too many do,
  With the Saviour in his view.

4 But the other, touch'd with grace,
  Saw the danger of his case,—
  Faith received to own the Lord,
  Whom the scribes and priests abhorr'd.

5 " Lord," he pray'd, " remember me
  When in glory thou shalt be!"
  " Soon with me," the Lord replies,
  " Thou shalt rest in paradise."

6 This was wondrous grace indeed,
  Grace vouchsafed in time of need!
  Sinners, trust in Jesus' name,
  You shall find him still the same.

7 But beware of unbelief,
  Think upon the harden'd thief;
  If the gospel you disdain,
  Christ to you will die in vain.

## 111.

*The Woman of Samaria.*—John, iv, 28.

1 JESUS, to what didst thou submit,
  To save thy dear-bought flock from hell!
  Like a poor trav'ler see him sit
  Athirst and weary by the well.

2 The woman who for water came
  (What great events on small depend!)
  Then learn'd the glory of his name,
  The well of life, the sinner's Friend!

3 Taught from her birth to hate the Jews,
  And fill'd with party pride, at first
  Her zeal induced her to refuse
  Water, to quench the Saviour's thirst.

4 But soon she knew the gift of God,
  And Jesus, whom she scorn'd before,
  Unask'd, that drink on her bestow'd
  Which whoso tastes shall thirst no more.

5 His words her prejudice removed,
  Her sin she felt, relief she found;
  She saw and heard, believed and loved,
  And ran to tell her neighbours round.

6 O come, this wondrous man behold,
  The promised Saviour! this is he
  Whom ancient prophecies foretold,
  Born from our guilt to set us free.

7 Like her, in ignorance content,
  I worshipp'd long I knew not what;
  Like her, on other things intent,
  I found him when I sought him not.

8 He told me all that e'er I did,
  And told me all was pardon'd too;
  And now, like her, as he has bid,
  I live to point him out to you.

## 112.

*The Pool of Bethesda.**—John, v, 2—4.

1 BESIDE the gospel pool,
    Appointed for the poor,
  From year to year my helpless soul
    Has waited for a cure.

* Book iii, Hymn 7.

2　How often have I seen
　　The healing waters move,
　And others, round me, stepping in,
　　Their efficacy prove!

3　But my complaints remain:
　　I feel the very same;
　As full of guilt and fear and pain
　　As when at first I came.

4　O would the Lord appear
　　My malady to heal;
　He knows how long I've languish'd here,
　　And what distress I feel.

5　How often have I thought,
　　Why should I longer lie?
　Surely the mercy I have sought
　　Is not for such as I?

6　But whether can I go?
　　There is no other pool
　Where streams of sovereign virtue flow
　　To make a sinner whole.

7　Here, then, from day to day,
　　I'll wait and hope and try;
　Can Jesus hear a sinner pray,
　　Yet suffer him to die!

8　No: he is full of grace;
　　He never will permit
　A soul that fain would see his face
　　To perish at his feet.

## 113.

### Another.

1　HERE at Bethesda's pool, the poor,
　　The wither'd, halt, and blind,
　With waiting hearts expect a cure,
　　And free admittance find.

2　Here streams of wondrous virtue flow,
　　To heal the sin-sick soul,—

To wash the filthy white as snow,
And make the wounded whole.

3 The dumb break forth in songs of praise,
The blind their sight receive,
The cripple runs in wisdom's ways,
The dead revive and live.

4 Restrain'd to no one case or time,
These waters always move;
Sinners in every age and clime
Their vital influence prove.

5 Yet numbers daily near them lie,
Who meet with no relief;
With life in view they pine and die
In hopeless unbelief.

6 'Tis strange they should refuse to bathe,
And yet frequent the pool;
But none can even wish for faith,
While love of sin bears rule.

7 Satan their consciences has seal'd
And stupifies their thought;
For were they willing to be heal'd,
The cure would soon be wrought.

8 Do thou, dear Saviour, interpose,
Their stubborn wills constrain;
Or else to them the water flows
And grace is preached in vain.

## 114.

*The Disciples at Sea.*—John, vi, 16—21.

1 CONSTRAIN'D by their Lord to embark,
And venture without him to sea,
The season tempestuous and dark,
How grieved the disciples must be!
But though he remain'd on the shore,
He spent the night for them in pray'r;
They still were as safe as before,
And equally under his care.

Book ii, Hymn 87.

2 They strove, though in vain, for awhile,
The force of the waves to withstand,
But when they were wearied with toil
They saw their dear Saviour at hand:
They gladly received him on board,
His presence their spirits revived,
The sea became calm at his word,
And soon at their port they arrived.

3 We, like the disciples, are toss'd,
By storms on a perilous deep;
But cannot be possibly lost,
For Jesus has charge of the ship:
Though billows and winds are enraged,
And threaten to make us their sport;
This pilot his word has engaged
To bring us in safety to port.

4 If sometimes we struggle alone,
And he is withdrawn from our view,
It makes us more willing to own
We nothing without him can do:
Then Satan our hopes would assail,
But Jesus is still within call,
And when our poor efforts quite fail
He comes in good time and does all.

5 Yet, Lord, we are ready to shrink
Unless we thy presence perceive;
O save us, (we cry,) or we sink;
We would, but we cannot believe!
The night has been long and severe,
The winds and the seas are still high,
Dear Saviour, this moment appear,
And say to our souls, "It is I!"*

## 115.

*Will ye also go away?*—John, vi, 67—69.

1 WHEN any turn from Zion's way—
Alas! what numbers do!—

* Book iii, Hymn 18.

Methinks I hear my Saviour say,
    " Wilt thou forsake me too?"

2 Ah, Lord! with such a heart as mine,
    Unless thou hold me fast,
I feel I must, I shall decline,
    And prove like them at last.

3 Yet thou alone hast power, I know,
    To save a wretch like me;
To whom, or whither, could I go,
    If I should turn from thee?

4 Beyond a doubt I rest assured
    Thou art the Christ of God,
Who hast eternal life secured
    By promise and by blood.

5 The help of men and angels join'd
    Could never reach my case;
Nor can I hope relief to find
    But in thy boundless grace.

6 No voice but thine can give me rest,
    And bid my fears depart;
No love but thine can make me bless'd.
    And satisfy my heart.

7 What anguish has that question stirr'd.
    If I will also go?
Yet, Lord, relying on thy word.
    I humbly answer—No.

## 116.

*The Resurrection and the Life.*—John, xi, 25.

1 " I AM," saith Christ, " your glorious head,"
    (May we attention give,)
" The resurrection of the dead,
    The life of all that live.

2 " By faith in me the soul receives
    New life, though dead before;
And he that in my name believes,
    Shall live to die no more.

3 " The sinner, sleeping in his grave,
　　Shall at my voice awake;
And when I once begin to save,
　　My work I ne'er forsake."

4 Fulfill thy promise, gracious Lord,
　　On us assembled here;
Put forth thy Spirit with the word,
　　And cause the dead to hear.

5 Preserve the power of faith alive
　　In those who love thy name;
For sin and Satan daily strive
　　To quench the sacred flame.

6 Thy power and mercy first prevail'd
　　From death to set us free;
And often since our life had fail'd,
　　If not renew'd by thee.

7 To thee we look, to thee we bow,
　　To thee for help we call;
Our life and resurrection thou,
　　Our hope, our joy, our all.

## 117.

*Weeping Mary.*—John xx, 11—16.

1 MARY to her Saviour's tomb
Hasted at the early dawn;
Spice she brought, and sweet perfume;
But the Lord she loved was gone.
For awhile she weeping stood,
Struck with sorrow and surprise,
Shedding tears, a plenteous flood,
For her heart supplied her eyes.

2 Jesus, who is always near,
Though too often unperceived,
Came, his drooping child to cheer,
Kindly asking, " Why she grieved?"
Though at first she knew him not,
When he call'd her by her name
Then her griefs were all forgot,
For she found he was the same.

3 Grief and sighing quickly fled
When she heard his welcome voice:
Just before she thought him dead,
Now he bids her heart rejoice.
What a change his word can make,
Turning darkness into day!
You who weep for Jesu's sake,
He will wipe your tears away.

4 He who came to comfort her,
When she thought her all was lost,
Will for your relief appear,
Though you now are tempest-toss'd:
On his word your burden cast,
On his love your thoughts employ;
Weeping for awhile may last,
But the morning brings the joy.

## 118.

*Lovest thou me?*—John, xxi, 16. C.

1 HARK, my soul! it is the Lord;
'Tis thy Saviour, hear his word:
Jesus speaks, and speaks to thee:
" Say, poor sinner, lov'st thou me?

2 " I deliver'd thee when bound,
And, when bleeding, heal'd thy wound,
Sought thee wand'ring, set thee right,
Turn'd thy darkness into light.

3 " Can a woman's tender care
Cease towards the child she bare?
Yes, she may forgetful be,
Yet will I remember thee.

4 " Mine is an unchanging love,
Higher than the heights above,
Deeper than the depths beneath,
Free and faithful, strong as death.

5 " Thou shalt see my glory soon,
When the work of grace is done,—

Partner of my throne shalt be,
Say, poor sinner, lov'st thou me?"

6 Lord, it is my chief complaint,
That my love is weak and faint;
Yet I love thee and adore,
Oh for grace to love thee more?

## 119.

### *Another.*

1 'Tis a point I long to know,
Oft it causes anxious thought—
Do I love the Lord, or no?
Am I his, or am I not?

2 If I love, why am I thus?
Why this dull, this lifeless frame?
Hardly sure can they be worse
Who have never heard his name!

3 Could my heart so hard remain,
Pray'r a task and burden prove,
Every trifle give me pain,
If I knew a Saviour's love?

4 When I turn my eyes within,
All is dark and vain and wild:
Fill'd with unbelief and sin,
Can I deem myself a child?

5 If I pray or hear or read,
Sin is mix'd with all I do;
You that love the Lord indeed,
Tell me, is it thus with you?

6 Yet I mourn my stubborn will,
Find my sin a grief and thrall:
Should I grieve for what I feel,
If I did not love at all?

7 Could I joy his saints to meet,
Choose the ways I once abhorr'd,
Find, at times, the promise sweet,
If I did not love the Lord?

8 Lord, decide the doubtful case!
Thou who art thy people's sun,
Shine upon thy work of grace,
If it be indeed begun.

9 Let me love thee more and more,
If I love at all, I pray;
If I have not loved before,
Help me to begin to-day.

## 120.

*The Death of Stephen.*—Acts, vii, 54—60.

1 As some tall rock amidst the waves
The fury of the tempest braves,
While the fierce billows, tossing high,
Break at its foot, and murm'ring, die:

2 Thus they who in the Lord confide,
Though foes assault on every side,
Cannot be moved or overthrown,
For Jesus makes their cause his own.

3 So faithful Stephen, undismay'd,
The malice of the Jews survey'd;
The holy joy which fill'd his breast,
A lustre on his face impress'd.

4 " Behold," he said, " the world of light
Is open'd to my strengthen'd sight;
My glorious Lord appears in view,
That Jesus whom ye lately slew."

5 With such a friend and witness near,
No form of death could make him fear;
Calm, amidst showers of stones, he kneels,
And only for his murderers feels.

6 May we by faith perceive thee thus,
Dear Saviour, ever near to us!
This sight our peace through life shall keep,
And death be fear'd no more than sleep.

## 121.

*The Rebel's surrender to Grace.—Lord, what wilt thou*
*have me to do?—Acts, ix, 6.*

1 LORD, thou hast won,—at length I yield,—
My heart, by mighty grace compell'd,
    Surrenders all to thee;
Against thy terrors long I strove,
But who can stand against thy love?
    Love conquers even me.

2 All that a wretch could do I tried,—
Thy patience scorn'd, thy power defied,
    And trampled on thy laws:
Scarcely thy martyrs at the stake
Could stand more steadfast for thy sake
    Than I in Satan's cause.

3 But since thou hast thy love reveal'd,
And shown my soul a pardon seal'd,
    I can resist no more:
Couldst thou for such a sinner bleed?
Canst thou for such a rebel plead?
    I wonder and adore!

4 If thou hadst bid thy thunders roll,
And lightnings flash, to blast my soul,
    I still had stubborn been;
But mercy has my heart subdued,—
A bleeding Saviour I have view'd,
    And now I hate my sin.

5 Now, Lord, I would be thine alone;
Come, take possession of thine own,
    For thou hast set me free:
Released from Satan's hard command,
See all my powers waiting stand
    To be employ'd by thee.

6 My will conform'd to thine would move;
On thee, my hope, desire, and love,
    In fix'd attention join;
My hands, my eyes, my ears, my tongue,
Have Satan's servants been too long,
    But now they shall be thine.

H          46

7 And can I be the very same
    Who lately durst blaspheme thy name,
        And on thy gospel tread?
    Surely each one who hears my case
    Will praise thee and confess thy grace
        Invincible indeed!


## 122.

*Peter released from Prison.*—Acts, xii, 5—8.

1 FERVENT persevering prayers
    Are faith's assured resource;
Brazen gates and iron bars
    In vain withstand their force:
Peter, when in prison cast,
    Though by soldiers kept with care,
Though the doors were bolted fast,
    Was soon released by prayer.

2 While he slept, an angel came,
    And spread a light around,
Touch'd and call'd him by his name,
    And raised him from the ground:
All his chains and fetters burst,
    Every door wide open flew;
Peter thought he dream'd at first,
    But found the vision true.

3 Thus the Lord can make a way
    To bring his saints relief;
'Tis their part to wait and pray
    In spite of unbelief:
He can break through walls of stone,
    Sink the mountain to a plain:
They to whom his name is known
    Can never pray in vain.

4 Thus in chains of guilt and sin,
    Poor sinners sleeping lie;
No alarm is felt within,
    Although condemn'd to die,

Till, descending from above,
(Mercy smiling in his eyes,)
Jesus, with a voice of love,
   Awakes, and bids them rise.

5 Glad the summons they obey,
  And liberty desire:
Straight their fetters melt away
   Like wax before the fire:
By the word of Him who died,
Guilty pris'ners to release,
Every door flies open wide,
   And they depart in peace.


## 123.

*The trembling Gaoler.*—Acts, xvi, 29—31.

1 A BELIEVER, free from care,
  May in chains or dungeons sing,
If the Lord be with him there,
  And be happier than a king:
Paul and Silas thus confined,
Though their backs were torn by whips,
Yet, possessing peace of mind,
  Sung his praise with joyful lips.

2 Suddenly the prison shook,
  Open flew the iron doors;
And the gaoler, terror-struck,
  Now his captives' help implores:
Trembling at their feet he fell,
" Tell me, sirs, what must I do
To be saved from guilt and hell?
  None can tell me this but you."

3 " Look to Jesus," they replied,
  " If on him thou canst believe,
By the death which he has died,
  Thou salvation shalt receive."
While the living word he heard,
Faith sprung up within his heart,
And released from all he fear'd,
  In their joy his soul had part.

4 Sinners, Christ is still the same;
  O that you could likewise fear!
  Then the mention of his name
  Would be music to your ear:
  Jesus rescues Satan's slaves,
  His dear wounds still plead, " Forgive!"
  Jesus to the utmost saves;
  Sinners, look to him and live.

## 124.

### The Exorcists.—Acts, xix, 13—16.

1 WHEN the apostle wonders wrought,
  And heal'd the sick in Jesu's name,
  The sons of Sceva vainly thought
  That they had power to do the same.

2 On one possess'd they tried their art,
  And naming Jesus preach'd by Paul,
  They charged the spirit to depart,
  Expecting he'd obey their call.

3 The spirit answer'd with a mock,
  " Jesus I know, and Paul I know;
  I must have gone if Paul had spoke:
  But who are ye that bid me go?"

4 With fury then the man he fill'd,
  Who on the poor pretenders flew;
  Naked and wounded, almost kill'd,
  They fled in all the people's view.

5 Jesus! that name pronounced by faith,
  Is full of wonder-working power:
  It conquers Satan, sin, and death,
  And cheers in trouble's darkest hour.

6 But they who are not born again
  Know nothing of it but the sound;
  They do but take his name in vain
  When most their zeal and pains abound.

7 Satan their vain attempts derides,
  Whether they talk or pray or preach:

Long as the love of sin abides,
His power is safe beyond their reach.

8 But you, believers, may rejoice,
Satan well knows your mighty Friend;
He trembles at your Saviour's voice,
And owns he cannot gain his end.

## 125.

*Paul's Voyage.*—Acts, xxvii.

1 If Paul in Cesar's court must stand,
He need not fear the sea,
Secured from harm on every hand
By the divine decree.

2 Although the ship in which he sail'd
By dreadful storms was toss'd,
The promise over all prevail'd,
And not a life was lost.

3 Jesus! the God whom Paul adored,
Who saves in time of need;
Was then confess'd by all on board,
A present help indeed!

4 Though neither sun nor stars were seen,
Paul knew the Lord was near;
And faith preserved his soul serene,
When others shook for fear.

5 Believers thus are toss'd about,
On life's tempestuous main;
But grace assures beyond a doubt,
They shall their port attain.

6 They must, they shall appear one day
Before their Saviour's throne;
The storms they meet with by the way
But make his power known.

7 Their passage lies across the brink
Of many a threat'ning wave;
The world expects to see them sink,
But Jesus lives to save.

8 Lord, though we are but feeble worms,
  Yet since thy word is past,
We'll venture through a thousand storms,
  To see thy face at last.

## 126.

*The Good that I would do, I do not.*—Rom. vii, 19.

1 I WOULD, but cannot sing,—
  Guilt has untuned my voice,
The serpent sin's envenom'd sting
  Has poison'd all my joys.

2 I know the Lord is nigh,
  And would, but cannot pray;
For Satan meets me when I try,
  And frights my soul away.

3 I would, but can't repent,
  Though I endeavour oft;
This stony heart can ne'er relent
  Till Jesus make it soft.

4 I would, but cannot love,
  Though woo'd by love divine :
No arguments have power to move
  A soul so base as mine.

5 I would, but cannot rest
  In God's most holy will;
I know what he appoints is best,
  Yet murmur at it still.

6 O could I but believe!
  Then all would easy be;
I would, but cannot—Lord, relieve ;
  My help must come from thee!

7 But if indeed I would,
  Though I can nothing do;
Yet the desire is something good,
  For which my praise is due.

8   By nature prone to ill,
      Till thine appointed hour,
  I was as destitute of will,
      As now I am of power.

9   Wilt thou not crown at length
      The work thou hast begun,
  And with a will afford me strength
      In all thy ways to run?

## 127.

*Salvation drawing nearer.*—Rom. xiii, 11, 12.

1   DARKNESS overspreads us here,
      But the night wears fast away;
    Jacob's Star will soon appear,
      Leading on eternal day!
    Now 'tis time to rouse from sleep,
      Trim our lamps, and stand prepared,
    For our Lord strict watch to keep,
      Lest he find us off our guard.

2   Let his people courage take,
      Bear with a submissive mind
    All they suffer for his sake,—
      Rich amends they soon will find:
    He will wipe away their tears,
      Near himself appoint their lot;
    All their sorrows, pains, and fears,
      Quickly then will be forgot.

3   Though already saved by grace,
      From the hour we first believed;
    Yet while sin and war have place,
      We have but a part received:
    Still we for salvation wait,
      Every hour it nearer comes!
    Death will break the prison gate
      And admit us to our homes.

4   Sinners, what can you expect,
      You who now the Saviour dare,
    Break his laws, his grace reject?
      You must stand before his bar!

Tremble, lest he say, depart!
Oh! the horrors of that sound!
Lord, make every careless heart
Seek thee while thou may'st be found.

## 128.

*That Rock was Christ.*—1 Cor. x, 4.

1 WHEN Isr'el's tribes were parch'd with thirst,
Forth from the rock the waters burst,
And all their future journey through
Yielded them drink and gospel too?

2 In Moses' rod a type they saw
Of His severe and fiery law;
The smitten rock prefigured Him
From whose pierced side all blessings stream.

3 But ah! the types were all too faint
His sorrows or His worth to paint;
Slight was the stroke of Moses' rod,
But He endured the wrath of God.

4 Their outward rock could feel no pain,
But ours was wounded, torn, and slain;
The rock gave but a wat'ry flood,
But Jesus pour'd forth streams of blood.

5 The earth is like their wilderness,
A land of drought and sore distress,
Without one stream from pole to pole
To satify a thirsty soul.

6 But let the Saviour's praise resound;
In him refreshing streams are found,
Which pardon, strength, and comfort give,
And thirsty sinners drink and live.

## 129.

*My Grace is sufficient for thee.*—2 Cor. xii, 9.

1 OPPRESS'D with unbelief and sin,
Fightings without, and fears within,
While earth and hell, with force combined,
Assault and terrify my mind;

2 What strength have I against such foes,
Such hosts and legions to oppose?
Alas! I tremble, faint, and fall;
Lord, save me, or I give up all.

3 Thus sorely press'd, I sought the Lord,
To give me some sweet cheering word;
Again I sought, and yet again;
I waited long, but not in vain.

4 Oh! 'twas a cheering word indeed!
Exactly suited to my need;
"Sufficient for thee is my grace,
Thy weakness my great power displays."

5 Now I despond and mourn no more,
I welcome all I fear'd before:
Though weak, I'm strong, though troubled, blest,
For Christ's own power shall on me rest.

6 My grace would soon exhausted be,
But his is boundless as the sea;
Then let me boast with holy Paul,
That I am nothing, Christ is all.

## 130.

*The Inward Warfare.*—Gal. v, 17.

1 STRANGE and mysterious is my life,
What opposites I feel within!
A stable peace, a constant strife;
The rule of grace, the power of sin :
    Too often I am captive led,
    Yet daily triumph in my Head.

2 I prize the privilege of prayer,
But oh! what backwardness to pray!
Though on the Lord I cast my care,
I feel its burden every day;
    I seek *his* will in all I do,
    Yet find my own is working too.

3 I call the promises my own,
And prize them more than mines of gold;

H 2

Yet though their sweetness I have known,
They leave me unimpress'd and cold:
    One hour upon the truth I feed,
    The next I know not what to read.

4 I love the holy day of rest,
  When Jesus meets his gather'd saints:
Sweet day, of all the week the best!
For its return my spirit pants:
    Yet often through my unbelief,
    It proves a day of guilt and grief.

5 While on the Saviour I rely,
  I know my foes shall lose their aim:
And therefore dare their power defy,
Assured of conquest through his name:
    But soon my confidence is slain,
    And all my fears return again.

6 Thus diff'rent powers within me strive.
And grace and sin by turns prevail;
I grieve, rejoice, decline, revive,
And vict'ry hangs in doubtful scale:
    But Jesus has his promise past,
    That grace shall overcome at last.

## 131.

*Contentment.* \*—Phil. iv, 11.    C.

1 FIERCE passions discompose the mind.
  As tempests vex the sea;
But calm content and peace we find
  When, Lord, we turn to thee.

2 In vain by reason and by rule
  We try to bend the will;
For none but in the Saviour's school
  Can learn the heavenly skill.

3 Since at his feet my soul has sat.
  His gracious words to hear;
Contented with my present state,
  I cast on him my care.

       \* Book iii, Hymn 55.

4 " Art thou a sinner, soul?" he said,
    " Then how canst thou complain?
  How light thy troubles here, if weigh'd
    With everlasting pain?

5 If thou of murm'ring wouldst be cured,
    Compare thy griefs with mine;
  Think what my love for thee endured,
    And thou wilt not repine.

6 'Tis I appoint thy daily lot,
    And I do all things well:
  Thou soon shalt leave this wretched spot,
    And rise with me to dwell.

7 In life, my grace shall strength supply
    Proportion'd to thy day;
  At death, thou still shalt find me nigh,
    To wipe thy tears away."

8 Thus I, who once my wretched days
    In vain repinings spent,
  Taught in my Saviour's school of grace,
    Have learn'd to be content.

## 132.

*Old Testament Gospel.*—Heb. iv, 2.    C.

1 Isr'el, in ancient days,
    Not only had a view
    Of Sinai in a blaze,
    But learn'd the gospel too:
  The types and figures were a glass
  In which they saw a Saviour's face.

2 The paschal sacrifice,
    And blood be-sprinkled door,
    Seen with enlighten'd eyes,
    And once applied with power,
  Would teach the need of other blood
  To reconcile an angry God.

3 The Lamb, the Dove, set forth
    His perfect innocence,
    Whose blood of matchless worth
    Should be the soul's defence:

For He who can for sin atone
Must have no failings of his own.

4 The scape-goat on his head
  The people's trespass bore,
  And to the desert led,
  Was to be seen no more:
In him our Surety seem'd to say,
"Behold! I bear your sins away."

5 Dipt in his fellow's blood,
  The living bird went free;
  The type, well understood,
  Express'd the sinner's plea;
Described a guilty soul enlarged,
And by a Saviour's death discharged

6 Jesus, I love to trace
  Throughout the sacred page
  The footsteps of thy grace,
  The same in every age!
O grant that I may faithful be
To clearer light vouchsafed to me!

## 133.

*The word quick and powerful.*—Heb. iv, 12. 13.

1 THE word of Christ our Lord,
  With whom we have to do,
  Is sharper than a two-edged sword
  To pierce the sinner through!

2 Swift as the lightning's blaze
  When awful thunders roll,
  It fills the conscience with amaze,
  And penetrates the soul.

3 No heart can be conceal'd
  From his all-piercing eyes:
  Each thought and purpose stands reveal'd,
  Naked without disguise.

4 He sees his people's fears,
  He notes their mournful cry;

He counts their sighs and falling tears,
And helps them from on high.

5   Though feeble is their good,
It has its kind regard;
Yea, all they would do, if they could,
Shall find a sure reward.

6   He sees the wicked too,
And will repay them soon,
For all the evil deeds they do,
And all they would have done.

7   Since all our secret ways
Are mark'd and known by thee,
Afford us, Lord, thy light of grace,
That we ourselves may see.

## 134.

*Looking unto Jesus.*—Heb. xii, 2.

1 By various maxims, forms, and rules,
That pass for wisdom in the schools,
I strove my passion to restrain;
But all my efforts proved in vain.

2 But since the Saviour I have known,
My rules are all reduced to one,
To keep my Lord by faith in view;
This strength supplies and motives too.

3 I see him lead a suff'ring life,
Patient amidst reproach and strife;
And from his pattern courage take
To bear and suffer for his sake.

4 Upon the cross I see him bleed,
And by the sight from guilt am freed;
This sight destroys the life of sin,
And quickens heav'nly life within.

5 To look to Jesus as he rose,
Confirms my faith, disarms my foes;
Satan I shame and overcome,
By pointing to my Saviour's tomb.

6 Exalted on his glorious throne,
   I see him make my cause his own;
   Then all my anxious cares subside,
   For Jesus lives, and will provide.

7 I see him look with pity down,
   And hold in view the conq'ror's crown.
   If press'd with griefs and cares before,
   My soul revives, nor asks for more.

8 By faith I see the hour at hand,
   When in his presence I shall stand;
   Then it will be my endless bliss
   To see him where and as he is.

## 135.

*Love Tokens.*—Heb. xii, 5—11.

1 AFFLICTIONS do not come alone,
   A voice attends the rod;
   By both he to his saints is known,
   A Father and a God.

2 " Let not my children slight the stroke
   I for chastisement send,
   Nor faint beneath my kind rebuke,
   For still I am their Friend.

3 " The wicked I perhaps may leave
   Awhile, and not reprove;
   But all the children I receive,
   I scourge, because I love.

4 " If therefore you were left without
   This needful discipline,
   You might with cause admit a doubt
   If you indeed were mine.

5 " Shall earthly parents then expect
   Their children to submit?
   And will not you, when I correct,
   Be humbled at my feet?

6 " To please themselves they oft chastise,
   And put their sons to pain;

But you are precious in my eyes,
  And shall not smart in vain.

7 " I see your hearts at present fill'd
  With grief and deep distress;
But soon these bitter seeds shall yield
  The fruits of righteousness."

8 Break through the clouds, dear Lord,
    and shine!
Let us perceive thee nigh!
And to each mourning child of thine
  These gracious words apply.

## 136.

*Ephesus.*—Rev. ii, 1—7.

1 Thus saith the Lord to Ephesus,
  And thus he speaks to some of us,—
"Amidst my churches, lo, I stand,
  And hold the pastors in my hand.

2 " Thy works to me are fully known,
  Thy patience and thy toil I own;
Thy views of gospel truth are clear,
  Nor canst thou other doctrine bear.

3 " Yet I must blame while I approve;
  Where is thy first, thy fervent love?
Dost thou forget my love to thee,
  That thine is grown so faint to me?

4 " Recall to mind the happy days
  When thou wast fill'd with joy and praise ;
Repent—thy former works renew—
  Then I'll restore thy comforts too.

5 " Return at once, when I reprove,
  Lest I thy candlestick remove;
And thou too late thy loss lament:
  I warn before I strike—Repent."

6 Hearken to what the Spirit saith,
  " To him that overcomes by faith,
The fruit of life's unfading tree
  In paradise his food shall be."

## 137.

*Smyrna.*—Rev. ii. 11.

1 THE message first to Smyrna sent,
   A message full of grace,
   To all the Saviour's flock is meant
   In every age and place.

2 Thus to his church, his chosen bride,
   Saith the great First and Last,
   Who ever lives, though once he died,
   " Hold thy profession fast.

3 " Thy works and sorrow well I know,
   Perform'd and borne for me ;
   Poor though thou art, despised and low,
   Yet who is rich like thee ?

4 " I know thy foes, and what they say,
   How long they have blasphemed ;
   The synagogue of Satan they,
   Though they would Jews be deem'd.

5 " Though Satan for a season rage,
   And prisons be your lot,
   I am your Friend, and I engage
   You shall not be forgot.

6 " Be faithful unto death, nor fear
   A few short days of strife ;
   Behold ! the prize you soon shall wear,
   A crown of endless life !"

7 Hear what the Holy Spirit saith,
   Of all who overcome ;
   " They shall escape the second death,
   The sinner's awful doom !"

## 138.

*Sardis.*—Rev. iii, 1—6.    C.

1 " WRITE to Sardis," (saith the Lord.)
   And write what he declares.
   He whose Spirit and whose word
   Upholds the seven stars :

"All thy works and ways I search,
Find thy zeal and love decay'd ;
Thou art call'd a living church,
    But thou art cold and dead.

2 " Watch, remember, seek, and strive,
    Exert thy former pains :
Let thy timely care revive,
    And strengthen what remains :
Cleanse thine heart, thy works amend,
Former times to mind recall,
Lest my sudden stroke descend,
    And smite thee once for all.

3 " Yet I number now in thee
    A few that are upright ;
These my Father's face shall see,
    And walk with me in white :
When in judgment I appear,
They for mine shall be confess'd,
Let my faithful servants hear,
    And woe be to the rest !"

## 139.

*Philadelphia.*—Rev. iii, 7—13.

1 Thus saith the Holy One and true,
To his beloved faithful few,
    " Of heaven and hell I hold the keys,
To shut or open as I please.

2 " I know thy works, and I approve,
Though small thy strength, sincere
            thy love ;
Go on, my word and name to own,
For none shall rob thee of thy crown.

3 " Before thee see my mercy's door
Stands open wide to shut no more ;
Fear not temptation's fiery day,
For I will be thy strength and stay.

4 " Thou hast my promise, hold it fast,
The trying hour will soon be past ;

Rejoice, for lo! I quickly come
To take thee to my heav'nly home.

5 "A pillar there no more to move,
Inscribed with all my names of love,
A monument of mighty grace,
Thou shalt for ever have a place."

6 Such is the conqueror's reward,
Prepared and promised by the Lord!
Let him that hath the ear of faith,
Attend to what the Spirit saith.

## 140.

*Laodicea.*—Rev. iii, 14—20.

1 HEAR what the Lord, the great Amen,
The true and faithful Witness, says;
He form'd the vast creation's plan,
And searches all our hearts and ways.

2 To some he speaks as once of old,
"I know thee, thy profession's vain;
Since thou art neither hot nor cold,
I'll spit thee from me with disdain.

3 "Thou boasted, ' I am wise and rich,
Increased in goods and nothing need;'
And dost not know thou art a wretch,
Naked and poor and blind and dead.

4 "Yet while I thus rebuke I love,
My message is in mercy sent;
That thou may'st my compassion prove,
I can forgive if thou repent.

5 "Wouldst thou be truly rich and wise!
Come, buy my gold in fire well tried,
My ointment to anoint thine eyes,
My robe thy nakedness to hide.

6 "See, at thy door I stand and knock!
Poor sinner, shall I wait in vain?
Quickly thy stubborn heart unlock,
That I may enter with my train.

7  " Thou canst not entertain a king,
      Unworthy thou of such a guest!
      But I my own provisions bring,
      To make thy soul a heavenly feast."

## 141.

### The Little Book.*—Rev. x.

1  WHEN the beloved disciple took
      The angel's little open book,
      Which by the Lord's command he eat,
      It tasted bitter after sweet.

2  Thus when the gospel is embraced,
      At first 'tis sweeter to the taste
      Than honey or the honey-comb,
      But there's a bitterness to come.

3  What sweetness does the promise yield,
      When by the Spirit's power seal'd!
      The longing soul is fill'd with good,
      Nor feels a wish for other food.

4  By these inviting tastes allured,
      We pass to what must be endured;
      For soon we find it is decreed,
      That bitter must to sweet succeed.

5  When sin revives and shows its power,
      When Satan threatens to devour,
      When God afflicts, and men revile,
      We draw our steps with pain and toil.

6  When thus deserted, tempest-toss'd,
      The sense of former sweetness lost,
      We tremble lest we were deceived
      In thinking that we once believed.

7  The Lord first makes the sweetness known,
      To win and fix us for his own;
      And though we now some bitter meet,
      We hope for everlasting sweet.

                * Book iii, Hymn 27.

# OLNEY HYMNS.

## BOOK II.

### ON OCCASIONAL SUBJECTS.

### I. SEASONS.

#### NEW-YEAR'S HYMNS.

### 1.

*Time how Swift.*

1 WHILE with ceaseless course the sun
  Hasted through the former year,
  Many souls their race have run,
  Never more to meet us here:
  Fix'd in an eternal state,
  They have done with all below;
  We a little longer wait,
  But how little—none can know.

2 As the winged arrow flies,
  Speedily the mark to find;
  As the lightning from the skies
  Darts, and leaves no trace behind;
  Swiftly thus our fleeting days
  Bear us down life's rapid stream;
  Upwards, Lord, our spirits raise,
  All below is but a dream.

3 Thanks for mercies past receive,
  Pardon of our sins renew;
Teach us, henceforth, how to live
  With eternity in view;
Bless thy word to young and old,
  Fill us with a Saviour's love;
And when life's short tale is told,
  May we dwell with thee above!

## 2.

### *Time how Short.*

TIME, with an unwearied hand,
  Pushes round the seasons past;
And in life's frail glass the sand
  Sinks apace, not long to last:
Many who, as you or I,
  The last year assembled thus,
In their silent graves now lie:
  Graves will open soon for us.

2 Daily sin and care and strife,
  While the Lord prolongs our breath,
Make it but a dying life,
  Or a kind of living death:
Wretched they and most forlorn,
  Who no better portion know;
Better ne'er to have been born,
  Than to have our all below.

3 When constrain'd to go alone,
  Leaving all your love behind,
Ent'ring on a world unknown,
  What will then support your mind?
When the Lord his summons sends,
  Earthly comforts lose their power:
Honour, riches, kindred, friends,
  Cannot cheer a dying hour.

4 Happy souls who fear the Lord!
  Time is not too swift for you;
When your Saviour gives the word,
  Glad you'll bid the world adieu:

Then he'll wipe away your tears,
Near himself appoint your place;
Swifter fly, ye rolling years,
Lord, we long to see thy face!

### 3.

#### *Uncertainty of Life.*

1 SEE! another year is gone!
Quickly have the seasons pass'd!
This we enter now upon
Will to many prove their last:
Mercy hitherto has spared,
But have mercies been improved?
Let us ask, Am I prepared,
Should I be this year removed?

2 Some we now no longer see,
Who their mortal race have run;
Seem'd as fair for life as we,
When the former year begun:
Some, but who God only knows,
Who are here assembled now,
Ere the present year shall close,
To the stroke of death must bow.

3 Life a field of battle is,
Thousands fall within our view:
And the next death-bolt that flies:
May be sent to me or you:
While we preach and while we hear,
Help us, Lord, each one to think
Vast eternity is near,
I am standing on the brink.

4 If from guilt and sin set free
By the knowledge of thy grace,
Welcome then the call will be
To depart and see thy face:
To thy saints while here below
With new years new mercies come;
But the happiest year they know
Is the last, which leads them home.

### 4.

*A New-Year's Thought and Prayer.*

1 TIME by moments steals away,
First the hour, and then the day;
Small the daily loss appears,
Yet it soon amounts to years:
Thus another year is flown,
Now it is no more our own,
If it brought or promised good,
Than the years before the flood.

2 But (may none of us forget)
It has left us much in debt:
Favours from the Lord received,
Sins that have his Spirit grieved,
Mark'd by an unerring hand,
In his book recorded stand;
Who can tell the vast amount
Placed to each of our account?

3 Happy the believing soul!
Christ for you has paid the whole:
While you own the debt is large.
You may plead a full discharge:
But, poor careless sinner, say,
What can you to justice pay?
Tremble, lest, when life is past,
Into prison you be cast!

4 Will you still increase the score?
Still be careless as before?
Oh, forbid it, gracious Lord,
Touch their spirits by thy word!
Now, in mercy to them show
What a mighty debt they owe!
All their unbelief subdue:
Let *them* find forgiveness too.

5 Spared to see another year,
Let thy blessing meet us here;
Come, thy dying work revive,
Bid thy drooping garden thrive:

Sun of righteousness, arise!
Warm our hearts, and bless our eyes;
Let our pray'r thy bowels move,
Make this year a time of love.

## 5.

### *Death and War.* 1778.

1 HARK! how Time's wide-sounding bell
Strikes on each attentive ear!
Tolling loud the solemn knell
Of the late departed year:
Years, like mortals, wear away,
Have their birth and dying day,
Youthful spring and wintry age,
Then to others quit the stage.

2 Sad experience may relate
What a year the last has been:
Crops of sorrow have been great
From the fruitful seeds of sin:
Oh! what numbers, gay and blithe,
Fell by Death's unsparing scythe,
While they thought the world their own,
Suddenly he mow'd them down!

3 See how War, with dreadful stride,
Marches at the Lord's command,
Spreading desolation wide
Through a once much-favour'd land:
War, with heart and arms of steel,
Preys on thousands at a meal;
Daily drinking human gore,
Still he thirsts and calls for more.

4 If the God whom we provoke
Hither should his way direct;
What a sin-avenging stroke
May a land like this expect!
They who now securely sleep,
Quickly then would wake and weep;
And too late would learn to fear,
When they saw the danger near.

I

5 You are safe who know his love;
  He will all his truth perform;
  To your souls a refuge prove
  From the rage of every storm:
  But we tremble for the youth!
  Teach them, Lord, thy saving truth;
  Join them to thy faithful few,
  Be to them a refuge too.


## 6.

### Earthly Prospects Deceitful.

1 Oft in vain the voice of truth
  Solemnly and loudly warns;
  Thoughtless, inexperienced youth,
  Though it hears, the warning scorns:
  Youth in fancy's glass surveys
  Life prolong'd to distant years,
  While the vast imagined space
  Fill'd with sweets and joys appears.

2 Awful disappointment soon
  Overclouds the prospect gay;
  Some their sun goes down at noon,
  Torn by death's strong hand away:
  Where are then their pleasing schemes?
  Where the joys they hoped to find?
  Gone for ever, like their dreams,
  Leaving not a trace behind.

3 Others, who are spared awhile,
  Live to weep o'er fancy's cheat;
  Find distress and pain and toil,
  Bitter things instead of sweet:
  Sin has spread a curse around,
  Poison'd all things here below;
  On this base polluted ground
  Peace and joy can never grow.

4 Grace alone can cure our ills,
  Sweeten life with all its cares,
  Regulate our stubborn wills,
  Save us from surrounding snares:

Though you oft have heard in vain,
Former years in folly spent,
Grace invites you yet again,
Once more calls you to repent.

5 Call'd again, at length beware,
Hear the Saviour's voice and live;
Lest he in his wrath should swear,
He no more will warning give;
Pray that you may hear and feel,
Ere the day of grace be past;
Lest your hearts grow hard as steel,
Or this year should prove your last.


HYMNS

Before Annual Sermons to Young People on New-Year's
Evenings.

## 7.

*Prayer for a Blessing.*

1 Now, gracious Lord, thine arm reveal,
And make thy glory known;
Now let us all thy presence feel,
And soften hearts of stone!

2 Help us to venture near thy throne,
And plead a Saviour's name;
For all that we can call our own
Is vanity and shame.

3 From all the guilt of former sin
May mercy set us free;
And let the year we now begin
Begin and end with thee.

4 Send down thy Spirit from above,
That saints may love thee more;
And sinners now may learn to love
Who never loved before.

5 And when before thee we appear,
    In our eternal home,
May growing numbers worship here,
    And praise thee in our room.

### 8.

*Another.    C.*

1 Bestow, dear Lord, upon our youth
    The gift of saving grace;
And let the seed of sacred truth
    Fall in a fruitful place.

2 Grace is a plant, where'er it grows,
    Of pure and heav'nly root;
But fairest in the youngest shows,
    And yields the sweetest fruit.

3 Ye careless ones, O hear betimes
    The voice of sovereign love!
Your youth is stain'd with many crimes,
    But mercy reigns above.

4 True, you are young, but there's a stone
    Within the youngest breast;
Or half the crimes which you have done
    Would rob you of your rest.

5 For you the public prayer is made,
    Oh! join the public prayer;
For you the sacred tear is shed,
    Oh! shed yourselves a tear.

6 We pray that you may early prove
    The Spirit's power to teach:
You cannot be too young to love
    That Jesus whom we preach.

### 9.

*Another.*

1 Now may fervent prayer arise,
Wing'd with faith, and pierce the skies;
Fervent prayer shall bring us down
Gracious answers from the throne.

2 Bless, O Lord, the opening year
  To each soul assembled here;
  Clothe thy word with power divine,
  Make us willing to be thine.

3 Shepherd of thy blood-bought sheep!
  Teach the stony heart to weep;
  Let the blind have eyes to see,
  See themselves and look on thee!

4 Let the minds of all our youth
  Feel the force of sacred truth;
  While the gospel call we hear,
  May they learn to love and fear.

5 Show them what their ways have been,
  Show them the desert of sin;
  Then thy dying love reveal,
  This shall melt a heart of steel.

6 Where thou hast thy work begun,
  Give new strength the race to run;
  Scatter darkness, doubts, and fears,
  Wipe away the mourner's tears.

7 Bless us all, both old and young;
  Call forth praise from every tongue;
  Let the whole assembly prove
  All thy power and all thy love.

## 10.

### *Casting the Gospel Net.*

1 When Peter, through the tedious night,
  Had often cast his net in vain,
  Soon as the Lord appear'd in sight
  He gladly let it down again.

2 Once more the gospel net we cast;
  Do thou, O Lord, the effort own!
  We learn from disappointments past
  To rest our hope on thee alone.

3 Upheld by thy supporting hand,
  We enter on another year;

And now we meet at thy command,
To seek thy gracious presence here.

4 May this be a much-favour'd hour
To souls in Satan's bondage led;
O clothe thy word with sovereign power
To break the rocks and raise the dead!

5 Have mercy on our num'rous youth,
Who, young in years, are old in sin:
And by thy Spirit, and thy truth,
Show them the state their souls are in.

6 Then by a Saviour's dying love,
To every wounded heart reveal'd,
Temptations, fears, and guilt remove,
And be their sun and strength and shield

7 To mourners speak a cheering word,
On seeking souls vouchsafe to shine;
Let poor backsliders be restored,
And all thy saints in praises join.

8 O hear our prayer, and give us hope,
That when thy voice shall call us home,
Thou still wilt raise a people up
To love and praise thee in our room.

## 11.

*Pleading for and with Youth.* C.

1 SIN has undone our wretched race,
But Jesus has restored
And brought the sinner face to face
With his forgiving Lord.

2 This we repeat, from year to year,
And press upon our youth;
Lord, give them an attentive ear;
Lord, save them by thy truth.

3 Blessings upon the rising race!
Make this a happy hour,
According to thy richest grace
And thine almighty power.

4 We feel for your unhappy state,
    (May you regard it too!)
  And would awhile ourselves forget,
    To pour out prayer for you.

5 We see, though you perceive it not,
    Th' approaching awful doom;
  O tremble at the solemn thought,
    And flee the wrath to come!

6 Dear Saviour, let this new-born year
    Spread an alarm abroad;
  And cry in every careless ear
    " Prepare to meet thy God!"

## 12.

### *Prayer for Children.*   C.

1 Gracious Lord, our children see!
  By thy mercy we are free,
  But shall these, alas! remain
  Subjects still of Satan's reign?
  Isr'el's young ones, when of old
  Pharaoh threaten'd to withhold,
  Then thy messenger said, " No—
  Let the children also go."

2 When the angel of the Lord,
  Drawing forth his dreadful sword,
  Slew, with an avenging hand,
  All the first-born of the land.
  Then thy people's door he pass'd,
  Where the bloody sign was placed.
  Hear us now upon our knees,
  Plead the blood of Christ for these!

3 Lord, we tremble, for we know
  How the fierce malicious foe,
  Wheeling round his watchful flight,
  Keeps them ever in his sight.
  Spread thy pinions, King of kings!
  Hide them safe beneath thy wings,
  Lest the ravenous bird of prey
  Stoop, and bear the brood away.

## 13.

*The Shunammite.*—2 Kings, iv, 31.

1 THE Shunammite, oppress'd with grief,
　When she had lost the son she loved,
　Went to Elisha for relief,
　Nor vain her application proved.

2 He sent his servant on before,
　To lay a staff upon his head;
　This *he* could do, but do no more,—
　He left him as he found him, dead.

3 But when the Lord's almighty power
　Wrought with the prophet's prayer and faith,
　The mother saw a joyful hour,—
　She saw her child restored from death.

4 Thus, like the weeping Shunammite,
　For many dead in sin we grieve.
　Now, Lord, display thine arm of might,
　Cause them to hear thy voice and live.

5 Thy preachers bear the staff in vain,
　Though at thine own command we go.
　Lord, we have tried and tried again,
　We find them dead, and leave them so.

6 Come then thyself—to every heart
　The glory of thy name make known.
　The means are our appointed part,
　The power and grace are thine alone.

## 14.

*Elijah's Prayer.*—1 Kings, xviii.

1 DOES it not grief and wonder move,
　To think of Israel's shameful fall,
　Who needed miracles to prove
　Whether the Lord was God or Baal?

2 Methinks I see Elijah stand,
　His features glow with love and zeal.
　In faith and prayer he lifts his hand,
　And makes to Heaven his great appeal.

3 " O God! if I thy servant am,
    If 'tis thy message fills my heart,
    Now glorify thy holy name,
    And show this people who thou art."

4 He spake, and lo a sudden flame
    Consumed the wood, the dust, the stone.
    The people struck, at once proclaim—
    " The Lord is God, the Lord alone."

5 Like him we mourn an awful day,
    When more for Baal than God appear.
    Like him, believers, let us pray,
    And may the God of Israel hear.

6 Lord, if thy servant speak thy truth,
    If he indeed is sent by thee,
    Confirm the word to all our youth,
    And let them thy salvation see.

7 Now may the Spirit's holy fire
    Pierce every heart that hears thy word,
    Consume each hurtful vain desire,
    And make them know thou art the Lord!

## 15.

*Preaching to the Dry Bones.*—Ezek. xxxvii.

1 PREACHERS may from Ezekiel's case
    Draw hope in this declining day.
    A proof like this of sovereign grace
    Should chase our unbelief away.

2 When sent to preach to mould'ring bones,
    Who could have thought he would succeed?
    But well he knew the Lord from stones
    Could raise up Abr'am's chosen seed.

3 Can these be made a num'rous host,
    And such dry bones new life receive?
    The prophet answer'd—" Lord, thou know'st
    They shall, if thou commandment give."

4 Like him around I cast my eye,
    And oh! what heaps of bones appear;

I 2

Like him, by Jesus sent I'll try,
For he can cause the dead to hear.

5 Hear, ye dry bones, the Saviour's word.
He who when dying gasp'd—" Forgive,—
That gracious sinner-loving Lord
Says—" Look to me, dry bones, and live."

6 Thou heav'nly wind, awake and blow,
In answer to the prayer of faith.
Now thine almighty infl'ence show,
And fill dry bones with living breath.

7 O make them hear and feel and shake,
And at thy call obedient move.
The bonds of death and Satan break,
And bone to bone unite in love.

## 16.

### The Rod of Moses.

1 WHEN Moses waved his mystic rod,
What wonders follow'd while he spoke
Firm as a wall the waters stood,
Or gush'd in rivers from the rock.

2 At his command the thunders roll'd;
Lightning and hail his voice obey'd;
And Pharaoh trembled to behold
His land in desolation laid.

3 But what could Moses' rod have done
Had he not been divinely sent?
The power was from the Lord alone.
And Moses but the instrument.

4 O Lord, regard thy people's pray'rs!
Assist a worm to preach aright;
And since thy gospel-rod he bears,
Display thy wonders in our sight.

5 Proclaim the thunders of thy law,
Like lightning let thine arrows fly,
That careless sinners, struck with awe.
For refuge may to Jesus fly.

6 Make streams of godly sorrow flow
From rocky hearts, unused to feel;
And let the poor in spirit know
That thou art near their griefs to heal.

7 But chiefly we would now look up
To ask a blessing for our youth,
The rising generation's hope,
That they may know and love thy truth.

8 Arise, O Lord, afford a sign,
Now shall our pray'rs success obtain;
Since both the means and power are thine,
How can the rod be raised in vain?

## 17.

*God speaking from Mount Zion.*

1 THE God who once to Isr'el spoke
From Sinai's top in fire and smoke,
In gentler strains of gospel grace
Invites us now to seek his face.

2 He wears no terrors on his brow;
He speaks in love from Zion now;
It is the voice of Jesus' blood,
Calling poor wand'rers home to God.

3 The holy Moses quaked and fear'd
When Sinai's thund'ring *law* he heard:
But reigning grace, with accents mild,
Speaks to the sinner as a child.

4 Hark! how from Calvary it sounds,
From the Redeemer's bleeding wounds!
" Pardon and grace I freely give;
Poor sinner, look to me and live."

5 What other arguments can move
The heart that slights a Saviour's love!
Yet till almighty power constrain,
This matchless love is preach'd in vain.

6 O Saviour, let that power be felt,
And cause each stony heart to melt!

Deeply impress upon our youth
The light and force of gospel truth.

7 With this new year may they begin
To live to thee, and die to sin;
To enter by the narrow way
Which leads to everlasting day.

8 How will they else thy presence bear
When as a Judge thou shalt appear!
When slighted love to wrath shall turn,
And the whole earth like Sinai burn!

## 18.

### A Prayer for Power on the Means of Grace.

1 O Thou at whose almighty word
The glorious light from darkness sprung!
Thy quick'ning influence afford,
And clothe with power the preacher's tongue.

2 Though 'tis thy truth he hopes to speak,
He cannot give the hearing ear;
'Tis thine, the stubborn heart to break,
And make the careless sinner fear.

3 As when, of old, the water flow'd
Forth from the rock at thy command:
Moses in vain had waved his rod
Without thy wonder-working hand.

4 As when the walls of Jericho
Down to the earth at once were cast;
It was thy power that brought them low,
And not the trumpet's feeble blast.

5 Thus we would in the means be found,
And thus on thee alone depend;
To make the gospel's joyful sound
Effectual to the promised end.

6 Now, while we hear thy word of grace,
Let self and pride before it fall;
And rocky hearts dissolve apace,
In streams of sorrow at thy call.

7  On all our youth assembled here
The unction of thy Spirit pour;
Nor let them lose another year,
Lest thou shouldst strive and call no more.

## 19.

*Elijah's Mantle.*—2 Kings, ii, 11—14.

1  ELISHA, struck with grief and awe,
Cried, Ah! where now is Isr'el's stay?"
When he his honour'd master saw
Borne by a fiery car away.

2  But while he look'd a last adieu,
His mantle, as it fell, he caught;
The Spirit rested on him too,
And equal miracles he wrought.

3  "Where is Elijah's God?" he cried,
And with the mantle smote the flood;
His word control'd the swelling tide,
Th' obedient waters upright stood.

4  The wonder-working gospel thus
From hand to hand has been convey'd;
We have the mantle still with us,
But where, O where's the Spirit's aid?

5  When Peter first his mantle waved,
How soon it melted hearts of steel!
Sinners, by thousands, then were saved,
But now how few its virtues feel!

6  Where is Elijah's God, the Lord,
Thine Isr'el's hope and joy and boast?
Reveal thine arm, confirm thy word,
Give us another Pentecost!

7  Assist thy messenger to speak,
And while he aims to lisp thy truth,
The bonds of sin and Satan break,
And pour thy blessing on our youth.

8  For them we now approach thy throne:
Teach them to know and love thy name,
Then shall thy thankful people own,
Elijah's God is still the same.

## HYMNS

After Sermons to Young People on New-Year's Evenings,
suited to the Subjects.

### 20.

*David's Charge to Solomon.*—1 Chron. xxviii. 9.

1 O DAVID's Son and David's Lord!
   From age to age thou art the same,
   Thy gracious presence now afford,
   And teach our youth to know thy name.

2 Thy people, Lord, though oft distress'd,
   Upheld by thee, thus far are come;
   And now we long to see thy rest,
   And wait thy word to call us home.

3 Like David, when this life shall end,
   We trust in thee sure peace to find;
   Like him, to thee we now commend
   The children we must leave behind.

4 Ere long, we hope to be where care
   And sin and sorrow never come;
   But oh! accept our humble prayer,
   That these may praise thee in our room.

5 Show them how vile they are by sin,
   And wash them in thy cleansing blood;
   Oh, make them willing to be thine,
   And be to them a cov'nant God.

6 Long may thy light and truth remain
   To bless this place when we are gone,
   And numbers here be born again,
   To dwell for ever near thy throne.

### 21.

*The Lord's Call to his Children.*—2 Cor. vi, 17, 18.

1 LET us adore the grace that seeks
      To draw our hearts above!
   Attend, 'tis God the Saviour speaks,
      And every word is love.

2 Though fill'd with awe, before his throne
    Each angel veils his face;
  He claims a people for his own
    Amongst our sinful race.

3 Careless, awhile, they live in sin,
    Enslaved to Satan's power;
  But they obey the call divine
    In his appointed hour.

4 "Come forth," He says, "no more pursue
    The paths that lead to death;
  Look up, a bleeding Saviour view;
    Look, and be saved by faith.

5 "My sons and daughters you shall be
    Through the atoning blood;
  And you shall claim and find in me
    A Father and a God."

6 Lord, speak these words to every heart,
    By thine all-powerful voice;
  That we may now from sin depart,
    And make thy love our choice.

7 If now we learn to seek thy face
    By Christ the living way,
  We'll praise thee for this hour of grace,
    Through an eternal day.

### 22.

*The Prayer of Jabez.*—1 Chron. iv, 9, 10.

1 JESUS, who bought us with his blood,
    And makes our souls his care,
  Was known of old as Isr'el's God,
    And answer'd Jabez' prayer.

2 Jabez, a child of grief! the name
    Befits poor sinners well;
  For Jesus bore the cross and shame,
    To save our souls from hell.

3 Teach us, O Lord, like him to plea
    For mercies from above;

O come, and bless our souls indeed,
  With light and joy and love.

4 The gospel's promised land is wide,
  We fain would enter in:
But we are press'd on every side
  With unbelief and sin.

5 Arise, O Lord, enlarge our coast,
  Let us possess the whole,
That Satan may no longer boast
  He can thy work control.

6 Oh! may thy hand be with us still,
  Our guide and guardian be,
To keep us safe from every ill,
  Till death shall set us free.

7 Help us on thee to cast our care.
  And on thy word to rest;
That Isr'el's God, who heareth pray'r,
  Will grant us our request.

### 23.

*Waiting at Wisdom's Gates.*—Prov. viii, 34, 35.

1 ENSNARED too long my heart has been
  In folly's hurtful ways;
O may I now at length begin
  To hear what Wisdom says!

2 'Tis Jesus, from the mercy-seat,
  Invites me to his rest;
He calls poor sinners to his feet,
  To make them truly blest.

3 Approach, my soul, to Wisdom's gates
  While it is call'd to-day;
No one who watches there and waits
  Shall e'er be turn'd away.

4 He will not let me seek in vain,
  For all who trust his word
Shall everlasting life obtain,
  And favour from the Lord.

5 Lord! I have hated thee too long,
   And dared thee to thy face;
I've done my soul exceeding wrong
   In slighting all thy grace.

6 Now I would break my league with death,
   And live to thee alone;
Oh! let thy Spirit's seal of faith
   Secure me for thine own.

7 Let all the saints assembled here,
   Yea, let all heaven rejoice,
That I begin with this new year
   To make the Lord my choice.

## 24.

*Asking the Way to Zion.*—Jer. 1, 5.

1 Zion, the city of our God,
   How glorious is the place!
The Saviour there has his abode,
   And sinners see his face!

2 Firm against every adverse shock
   Its mighty bulwarks prove;
'Tis built upon the living Rock,
   And wall'd around with love.

3 There all the fruits of glory grow,
   And joys that never die;
And streams of grace and knowledge flow,
   The soul to satisfy.

4 Come, set your faces Zion-ward,
   The sacred road enquire;
And let a union to the Lord
   Be henceforth your desire.

5 The gospel shines to give you light;
   No longer, then, delay;
The Spirit waits to guide you right,
   And Jesus is the way.

6 O Lord, regard thy people's prayer,
   Thy promise now fulfill;
And young and old by grace prepare
   To dwell on Zion's hill.

## 25.

*We were Pharaoh's Bondmen.*—Deut. vi, 20—23.

1 BENEATH the tyrant Satan's yoke
   Our souls were long opprest,
Till grace our galling fetters broke,
   And gave the weary rest.

2 Jesus, in that important hour,
   His mighty arm made known;
He ransom'd us by price and power,
   And claim'd us for his own.

3 Now, freed from bondage, sin, and death,
   We walk in wisdom's ways:
And wish to spend our every breath
   In wonder, love, and praise.

4 Ere long, we hope with Him to dwell
   In yonder world above;
And now we only live to tell
   The riches of his love.

5 O might we, ere we hence remove,
   Prevail upon our youth
To seek, that they may likewise prove
   His mercy and his truth!

6 Like Simeon, we shall gladly go,
   When Jesus calls us home:
If they are left a seed below,
   To serve him in our room.

7 Lord, hear our prayer, indulge our hope,
   On these thy Spirit pour,
That they may take our story up,
   When we can speak no more.

## 26.

*Travailing in Birth for Souls,*—Gal. iv, 19.

1 WHAT contradictions meet
   In ministers' employ!
It is a bitter sweet,
   A sorrow full of joy:

No other post affords a place
For equal honour or disgrace!

2　Who can describe the pain
　Which faithful preachers feel,
　Constrain'd to speak in vain
　To hearts as hard as steel?
Or who can tell the pleasures felt
When stubborn hearts begin to melt!

3　The Saviour's dying love,
　The soul's amazing worth,
　Their utmost efforts move,
　And draw their bowels forth:
They pray and strive, their rest departs,
Till Christ be form'd in sinners' hearts.

4　If some small hope appear,
　They still are not content;
　But, with a jealous fear,
　They watch for the event:
Too oft they find their hopes deceived,
Then how their inmost souls are grieved!

5　But when their pains succeed,
　And from the tender blade
　The ripening ears proceed,
　Their toils are overpaid:
No harvest joy can equal theirs,
To find the fruit of all their cares.

6　On what has now been sown,
　Thy blessing, Lord, bestow;
　The power is thine alone,
　To make it spring and grow:
Do thou the gracious harvest raise,
And thou alone shalt have the praise.

## 27.

*We are Ambassadors for Christ.*—2 Cor. v, 20.

1　Thy message by the preacher seal,
　And let thy power be known,
That every sinner here may feel
　The word is not his own.

2 Amongst the foremost of the throng
   Who dare thee to thy face,
He in rebellion stood too long,
   And fought against thy grace.

3 But grace prevail'd, he mercy found,
   And now by thee is sent,
To tell his fellow-rebels round,
   And call them to repent.

4 In Jesus God is reconciled,
   The worst may be forgiven;
Come, and he'll own you as a child,
   And make you heir of heaven.

5 O may the word of gospel truth
   Your chief desires engage!
And Jesus be your guide in youth,
   Your joy in hoary age.

6 Perhaps the year that's now begun
   May prove to some their last;
The sands of life may soon be run,
   The day of grace be past.

7 Think, if you slight this embassy,
   And will not warning take,
When Jesus in the clouds you see,
   What answer will you make?

## 28.

*Paul's Farewell Charge.*—Acts, xx, 26, 27.

1 WHEN Paul was parted from his friends
   It was a weeping day;
But Jesus made them all amends,
   And wiped their tears away.

2 Ere long they met again with joy
   (Secure, no more to part,)
Where praises every tongue employ,
   And pleasure fills each heart.

3 Thus all the preachers of His grace
   Their children soon shall meet,

Together see their Saviour's face,
  And worship at his feet.

4 But they who heard the word in vain,
  Though oft and plainly warn'd,
Will tremble when they meet again
  The ministers they scorn'd.

5 On your own heads your blood will fall
  If any perish here;
The preachers who have told you *all*
  Shall stand approved and clear.

6 Yet, Lord, to save themselves alone
  Is not their utmost view;
Oh! hear their prayer, thy message own,
  And save their hearers too.

## 29.

*How shall I put thee among the Children?—*
Jer. iii, 19.

1 ALAS! by nature how depraved,
  How prone to every ill!
Our lives to Satan how enslaved,
  How obstinate our will!

2 And can such sinners be restored,
  Such rebels reconciled?
Can grace itself the means afford
  To make a foe a child?

  Yes, grace has found the wondrous means
    Which shall effectual prove,
  To cleanse us from our countless sins,
    And teach our hearts to love.

4 Jesus for sinners undertakes,
  And died that we may live;
His blood a full atonement makes,
  And cries aloud, "Forgive!"

5 Yet one thing more must grace provide,
  To bring us home to God,
Or we shall slight the Lord who died,
  And trample on his blood.

6 The Holy Spirit must reveal
　The Saviour's work and worth;
Then the hard heart begins to feel
　A new and heav'nly birth.

7 Thus bought with blood and born again,
　Redeem'd and saved by grace,
Rebels in God's own house obtain
　A son's and daughter's place.

### 30.

*Winter.*\*

1 SEE, how rude Winter's icy hand
　Has stripp'd the trees and seal'd the ground!
But Spring shall soon his rage withstand,
　And spread new beauties all around.

2 My soul a sharper winter mourns,
　Barren and fruitless I remain;
When will the gentle spring return,
　And bid my graces grow again?

3 Jesus, my glorious sun, arise!
　'Tis thine the frozen heart to move;
Oh! hush these storms and clear my skies,
　And let me feel thy vital love!

4 Dear Lord, regard my feeble cry,
　I faint and droop till thou appear;
Wilt thou permit thy plant to die?
　Must it be winter all the year.

5 Be still, my soul, and wait his hour
　With humble pray'r and patient faith;
Till he reveals his gracious power,
　Repose on what his promise saith.

6 He, by whose all-commanding word
　Seasons their changing course maintain,
In every change a pledge affords,
　That none shall seek his face in vain.

\* Book iii, Hymn 31.

## 31.

### *Waiting for Spring.*

1 Though cloudy skies and northern blasts
  Retard the gentle spring awhile,
  The sun will conq'ror prove at last,
  And nature wear a vernal smile.

2 The promise which from age to age
  Has brought the changing seasons round,
  Again shall calm the winter's rage,
  Perfume the air and paint the ground.

3 The virtue of that first command,
  I know still does and will prevail,
  That while the earth itself shall stand,
  The spring and summer shall not fail.

4 Such changes are for us decreed;
  Believers have their winters too;
  But spring shall certainly succeed,
  And all their former life renew.

5 Winter and spring have each their use,
  And each in turn his people know;
  One kills the weeds their hearts produce,
  The other makes their graces grow.

6 Though like dead trees awhile they seem,
  Yet, having life within their root,
  The welcome spring's reviving beam
  Draws forth their blossoms, leaves, and fruit.

7 But if the tree indeed be dead,
  It feels no change though spring return;
  Its leafless, naked, barren head,
  Proclaims it only fit to burn.

8 Dear Lord, afford our souls a spring,
  Thou know'st our winter has been long:
  Shine forth, and warm our hearts to sing,
  And thy rich grace shall be our song.

## 32.

### *Spring.*

1 BLEAK winter is subdued at length,
   And forced to yield the day;
The sun has wasted all his strength,
   And driven him away.

2 And now long-wish'd-for spring is come,
   How alter'd is the scene!
The trees and shrubs are dress'd in bloom,
   The earth array'd in green.

3 Where'er we tread, beneath our feet
   The clust'ring flowers spring;
The artless birds in concerts sweet,
   Invite our hearts to sing.

4 But ah! in vain I strive to join,
   Oppress'd with sin and doubt;
I feel 'tis winter still within,
   Though all is spring without.

5 Oh! would my Saviour from on high
   Break through these clouds and shine!
No creature then more bless'd than I,
   No song more loud than mine.

6 Till then no softly warbling thrush,
   Nor cowslip's sweet perfume,
Nor beauties of each painted bush,
   Can dissipate my gloom.

7 To Adam, soon as he transgress'd,
   Thus Eden bloom'd in vain:
Not Paradise could give him rest,
   Or sooth his heart-felt pain.

8 Yet here an emblem I perceive
   Of what the Lord can do:
Dear Saviour, help me to believe,
   That I may flourish too.

9 Thy word can soon my hopes revive,
  Can overcome my foes,
And make my languid graces thrive
And blossom like the rose.

## 33.

### *Another.*

1 PLEASING spring again is here;
  Trees and fields in bloom appear:
  Hark! the birds with artless lays,
  Warble their Creator's praise!
  Where, in winter, all was snow,
  Now the flow'rs in clusters grow,
  And the corn, in green array,
  Promises a harvest-day.

2 What a change has taken place!
  Emblem of the spring of grace;
  How the soul in winter mourns
  Till the Lord, the Sun, returns,—
  Till the Spirit's gentle rain
  Bids the heart revive again;
  Then the stone is turn'd to flesh,
  And each grace springs forth afresh.

3 Lord, afford a spring to me!
  Let me feel like what I see;
  Ah! my winter has been long,
  Chill'd my hopes and stopp'd my song!
  Winter threaten'd to destroy
  Faith and love and every joy;
  If thy life was in the root,
  Still I could not yield the fruit.

4 Speak, and by thy gracious voice
  Make my drooping soul rejoice;
  O beloved Saviour haste,
  Tell me all the storms are past!
  On thy garden deign to smile,
  Raise the plants, enrich the soil;
  Soon thy presence will restore
  Life to what seem'd dead before.

K                                46

5 Lord, I long to be at home,
  Where these changes never come,
  Where the saints no winter fear,
  Where 'tis spring throughout the year:
  How unlike this state below!
  There the flow'rs unwith'ring blow;
  There no chilling blasts annoy;
  All is love and bloom and joy.


## 34.

*Summer Storms.**

1 THOUGH the morn may be serene—
  Not a threat'ning cloud be seen,
  Who can undertake to say
  'Twill be pleasant all the day?
  Tempests suddenly may rise,
  Darkness overspread the skies,
  Lightnings flash and thunders roar,
  Ere a short-lived day be o'er.

2 Often thus the child of grace
  Enters on his Christian race;
  Guilt and fear are overborne,
  'Tis with him a summer's morn:
  While his new-felt joys abound,
  All things seem to smile around;
  And he hopes it will be fair
  All the day and all the year.

3 Should we warn him of a change
  He would think the caution strange;
  He no change or trouble fears
  Till the gath'ring storm appears; †
  Till dark clouds his sun conceal,
  Till temptation's power he feel;
  Then he trembles and looks pale,
  All his hopes and courage fail.

* Book iii, Hymn 68.          † Book i, Hymn 44.

4 But the wonder-working Lord
  Soothes the tempest by his word;
  Stills the thunder, stops the rain,
  And his sun breaks forth again:
  Soon the cloud again returns,
  Now he joys, and now he mourns;
  Oft his sky is overcast
  Ere the day of life be past.

5 Tried believers too can say,
  In the course of one short day,
  Though the morning has been fair,
  Proved a golden hour of pray'r,
  Sin and Satan, long ere night,
  Have their comforts put to flight;
  Ah! what heart-felt peace and joy
  Unexpected storms destroy!

6 Dearest Saviour, call us soon
  To thy high eternal noon;
  Never there shall tempest rise,
  To conceal thee from our eyes:
  Satan shall no more deceive,
  We no more thy Spirit grieve;
  But, through cloudless, endless days,
  Sound to golden harps thy praise.

## 35.

### *Hay-time.*

1 THE grass and flow'rs which clothe the field,
  And look so green and gay,
Touch'd by the scythe, defenceless yield,
  And fall and fade away.

2 Fit emblem of our mortal state!
  Thus, in the Scripture glass,
The young, the strong, the wise, the great,
  May see themselves but grass.

3 Ah! trust not to your fleeting breath,
  Nor call your time your own;
Around you see the scythe of death
  Is mowing thousands down.

4 And you, who hitherto are spared,
    Must shortly yield your lives;
  Your wisdom is to be prepared
    Before the stroke arrives.

5 The grass, when dead, revives no more:
    You die to live again;
  But oh! if death should prove the door
    To everlasting pain!

6 Lord, help us to obey thy call,
    That from our sins set free,
  When, like the grass, our bodies fall,
    Our souls may spring to thee.

### 36.

*Harvest.*

1 SEE the corn again in ear!
  How the fields and valleys smile!
  Harvest now is drawing near,
  To repay the farmer's toil.
  Gracious Lord, secure the crop,
  Satisfy the poor with food:
  In thy mercy is our hope;
  We have sinn'd, but thou art good.

2 While I view the plenteous grain,
  As it ripens on the stalk,
  May I not instruction gain
  Helpful to my daily walk?
  All this plenty of the field
  Was produced from foreign seeds:
  For the earth itself would yield
  Only crops of useless weeds.

3 Though when newly sown it lay
  Hid awhile beneath the ground,
  (Some might think it thrown away,)
  Now a large increase is found;
  Though conceal'd, it was not lost;
  Though it died, it lives again;
  Eastern storms and nipping frosts
  Have opposed its growth in vain.

4 Let the praise be all the Lord's,
  As the benefit is ours.
  He in season still affords
  Kindly heat and gentle showers.
  By his care the produce thrives,
  Waving o'er the furrow'd lands;
  And when harvest-time arrives,
  Ready for the reaper stands.

5 Thus in barren hearts he sows
  Precious seeds of heav'nly joy;
  Sin and hell in vain oppose,
  None can grace's crop destroy:
  Threaten'd oft, yet still it blooms,
  After many changes past;
  Death the reaper, when he comes,
  Finds it fully ripe at last.

CHRISTMAS.

## 37.

*Praise for the Incarnation.*

1 SWEETER sounds than music knows
    Charm me in Emmanuel's name;
  All her hopes my spirit owes
    To his birth and cross and shame.

2 When he came the angels sung—
    " Glory be to God on high!"
  Lord, unloose my stamm'ring tongue,
    Who should louder sing than I?

3 Did the Lord a man become,
    That he might the law fulfill,
  Bleed and suffer in my room,
    And canst thou, my tongue, be still?

4 No, I must my praises bring,
    Though they worthless are and weak;
  For should I refuse to sing,
    Sure the very stones would speak.

5 O my Saviour, Shield, and Sun,
    Shepherd, Brother, Husband, Friend,
  Every precious name in one,
    I will love thee without end.

## 38.

*Jehovah-Jesus.*  C.

1 My song shall bless the Lord of all,
  My praise shall climb to his abode.
  Thee, Saviour, by that name I call—
  The great supreme, the mighty God.

2 Without beginning or decline,
  Object of faith and not of sense—
  Eternal ages saw him shine,
  He shines eternal ages hence.

3 As much, when in the manger laid,
  Almighty Ruler of the sky,
  As when the six days' work he made
  Fill'd all the morning-stars with joy.

4 Of all the crowns Jehovah bears,
  Salvation is his dearest claim :
  That gracious sound well pleased he hears,
  And owns Emmanuel for his name.

5 A cheerful confidence I feel,
  My well-placed hopes with joy I see ;
  My bosom glows with heav'nly zeal
  To worship Him who died for me.

6 As man he pities my complaint,
  His power and truth are all divine—
  He will not fail, he cannot faint,
  Salvation's sure, and must be mine.

## 39.

*Man honoured above Angels.*

1 Now let us join with hearts and tongues,
  And emulate the angels' songs;
  Yea, sinners may address their King
  In songs that angels cannot sing.

2 They praise the Lamb who once was slain ;
But we can add a higher strain,—
Not only say " He suffer'd thus,
But that " He suffer'd all for us."

3 When angels by transgression fell,
Justice consign'd them all to hell;
But mercy form'd a wondrous plan.
To save and honour fallen man.

4 Jesus, who pass'd the angels by,
Assumed our flesh to bleed and die ;
And still he makes it his abode——
As man he fills the throne of God.

5 Our next of kin, our Brother now,
Is he to whom the angels bow;
They join with us to praise his name,
But *we* the nearest int'rest claim.

6 But ah! how faint our praises rise !
Sure, 'tis the wonder of the skies,
That we, who share his richest love,
So cold and unconcern'd should prove.

7 Oh glorious hour ! it comes with speed,
When we from sin and darkness freed,
Shall see the God who died for man,
And praise him more than angels can.

## 40.

### *Saturday Evening.*

1 Safely through another week
God has brought us on our way;
Let us now a blessing seek
On th' approaching Sabbath-day :
Day of all the week the best,
Emblem of eternal rest.

2 Mercies multiplied each hour
Through the week our praise demand ;
Guarded by Almighty power,
Fed and guided by his hand.
Though ungrateful we have been,—
Only made returns of sin.

3 While we pray for pard'ning grace,
  Through the dear Redeemer's name,
  Show thy reconciled face,
  Shine away our sin and shame.
  From our worldly care set free,
  May we rest this night with thee.

4 When the morn shall bid us rise
  May we feel thy presence near!
  May thy glory meet our eyes
  When we in thy house appear!
  There afford us, Lord, a taste
  Of our everlasting feast.

5 May thy gospel's joyful sound
  Conquer sinners—comfort saints;
  Make the fruits of grace abound,
  Bring relief for all complaints.
  Thus may all our Sabbaths prove
  Till we join the church above!

### THE CLOSE OF THE YEAR.

## 41.

*Ebenezer.*—1 Sam. vii, 12.

1 THE Lord, our salvation and light,
  The guide and the strength of our days,
  Has brought us together to-night,
  A new Ebenezer to raise.
  The year we have now passed through
  His goodness with blessings has crown'd;
  Each morning his mercies were new;
  Then let our thanksgivings abound.

2 Encompass'd with dangers and snares,
  Temptations and fears and complaints,
  His ear he inclined to our prayers,
  His hand open'd wide to our wants,
  We never besought him in vain;
  When burden'd with sorrow or sin,

He help'd us again and again,
Or where before now had we been?

3 His gospel throughout the long year,
From Sabbath to Sabbath he gave.
How oft has he met with us here,
And shown himself mighty to save!
His candlestick has been removed
From churches once privileged thus;
But though we unworthy have proved,
It still is continued to us.

4 For so many mercies received,
Alas! what returns have we made?
His Spirit we often have grieved,
And evil for good have repaid.
How well it becomes us to cry—
" Oh! who is a God like to thee?
Who passest iniquities by,
And plungest them deep in the sea!"

5 To Jesus, who sits on the throne,
Our best hallelujahs we bring.
To thee it is owing alone
That we are permitted to sing.
Assist us, we pray, to lament
The sins of the year that is past;
And grant that the next may be spent
Far more to thy praise than the last.

## 42.

*Another.*

1 LET hearts and tongues unite,
And loud thanksgivings raise:
'Tis duty, mingled with delight,
To sing the Saviour's praise.

2 To him we owe our breath,
He took us from the womb,
Which else had shut us up in death,
And proved an early tomb.

K 2

3   When on the breast we hung
    Our help was in the Lord.
  'Twas he first taught our infant tongue
    To form the lisping word.

4   When in our blood we lay,
    He would not let us die,
  Because his love had fix'd a day
    To bring salvation nigh.

5   In childhood and in youth
    His eye was on us still,
  Though strangers to his love and truth,
    And prone to cross his will.

6   And since his name we knew,
    How gracious has he been,
  What dangers has he led us through,
    What mercies have we seen!

7   Now through another year,
    Supported by his care,
  We raise our Ebenezer here,
    " The Lord has help'd thus far."

8   Our lot in future years
    Unable to foresee,
  He kindly, to prevent our fears,
    Says, " Leave it all to me."

9   Yea, Lord, we wish to cast
    Our cares upon thy breast.
  Help us to praise thee for the past,
    And trust thee for the rest.


ORDINANCES.

43.

*On Opening a Place for Social Prayer.*

1 O Lord, our languid souls inspire,
    For here we trust thou art;
  Send down a coal of heav'nly fire
    To warm each waiting heart.

2 Dear Shepherd of thy people, hear ;
    Thy presence now display :
  As thou hast given a place for pray'r,
    So give us hearts to pray.

3 Show us some token of thy love,
    Our fainting hope to raise ;
  And pour thy blessings from above,
    That we may render praise.

4 Within these walls let holy peace
    And love and concord dwell ;
  Here give the troubled conscience ease,
    The wounded spirit heal.

5 The feeling heart, the melting eye,
    The humbled mind bestow ;
  And shine upon us from on high,
    To make our graces grow !
6 May we in faith receive thy word,
    In faith present our pray'rs ;
  And in the presence of our Lord
    Unbosom all our cares !

7 And may the gospel's joyful sound,
    Enforced by mighty grace,
  Awaken many sinners round
    To come and fill the place !

## 44.

*Another.*  C.

1 JESUS, where'er thy people meet,
  There they behold thy mercy-seat ;
  Where'er they seek thee, thou art found,
  And every place is hallow'd ground.

2 For thou, within no walls confined,
  Inhabitest the humble mind ;
  Such ever bring thee where they come,
  And going, take thee to their home.

3 Dear Shepherd of thy chosen few,
  Thy former mercies here renew ;

Here to our waiting hearts proclaim
The sweetness of thy saving name.

4 Here may we prove the power of pray'r
To strengthen faith and sweeten care—
To teach our faint desires to rise,
And bring all heaven before our eyes.

5 Behold, at thy commanding word,
We stretch the curtain and the cord;
Come thou, and fill this wider space,
And bless us with a large increase.

6 Lord, we are few, but thou art near:
Nor short thine arm, nor deaf thine ear;
O rend the heavens, come quickly down,
And make a thousand hearts thine own!

## 45.

### The Lord's Day.

1 How welcome to the saints, when press'd
With six days' noise and care and toil,
Is the returning day of rest,
Which hides them from the world awhile!

2 Now from the throng withdrawn away,
They seem to breathe a diff'rent air;
Composed and soften'd by the day,
All things another aspect wear.

3 How happy if their lot is cast
Where statedly the gospel sounds!
The word is honey to their taste,
Renews their strength, and heals their wounds!

4 Though pinch'd with poverty at home,
With sharp afflictions daily fed,
It makes amends, if they can come
To God's own house for heav'nly bread!

5 With joy they hasten to the place
Where they their Saviour oft have met:
And while they feast upon his grace,
Their burdens and their griefs forget.

6 This favour'd lot, my friends, is ours ;
 May we the privilege improve,
 And find these consecrated hours
 Sweet earnest of the joys above.

7 We thank thee for thy day, O Lord !
 Here we thy promised presence seek ;
 Open thine hand, with blessings stored,
 And give us manna for the week.

### 46.

*Gospel Privileges.*

1 O HAPPY they who know the Lord,
 With whom he deigns to dwell !
 He feels and cheers them by his word,
 His arm supports them well.

2 To them, in each distressing hour,
 His throne of grace is near ;
 And when they plead his love and power,
 He stands engaged to hear.

3 He help'd his saints in ancient days,
 Who trusted in his name ;
 And we can witness, to his praise,
 His love is still the same.

4 Wand'ring in sin, our souls he found,
 And bade us seek his face ;
 Gave us to hear the gospel sound,
 And taste the gospel grace.

5 Oft in his house his glory shines
 Before our wond'ring eyes ;
 We wish not then for golden mines,
 Or aught beneath the skies.

6 His presence sweetens all our cares,
 And makes our burdens light ;
 A word from him dispels our fears,
 And gilds the gloom of night.

7 Lord, we expect to suffer here,
 Nor would we dare repine ;

But give us still to find thee near,
And own us still for thine.

8 Let us enjoy and highly prize
These tokens of thy love
Till thou shalt bid our spirits rise
To worship thee above.

## 47.

### *Another.*

1 HAPPY are they to whom the Lord
His gracious name makes known,
And by his Spirit and his word
Adopts them for his own!

2 He calls them to his mercy-seat,
And hears their humble pray'r;
And when within his house they meet,
They find his presence near.

3 The force of their united cries
No power can long withstand;
For Jesus helps them from the skies
By his almighty hand.

4 Then mountains sink at once to plains,
And light from darkness springs,
Each seeming loss improves their gains,
Each trouble comfort brings.

5 Though men despise them, or revile,
They count the trial small;
Whoever frowns, if Jesus smile,
It makes amends for all.

6 Though meanly clad, and coarsely fed,
And, like their Saviour, poor,
They would not change their gospel-bread
For all the worldling's store.

7 When cheer'd with faith's sublimer joys,
They mount on eagles' wings;
They can disdain, as children's toys,
The pride and pomp of kings.

8 Dear Lord, assist our souls to pay
 The debt of praise we owe,
That we enjoy a gospel-day
 And heaven begun below.


### 48.

*Prayer for the Continuance of the Gospel.**

1 ONCE, while we aim'd at Zion's songs,
 A sudden mourning check'd our tongues!
Then we were called to sow in tears
 The seeds of joy for future years.

2 Oft as that memorable hour
 The changing year brings round again,
We meet to praise the love and power
 Which heard our cries and eased our pain.

3 Come, ye who trembled for the ark,
 Unite in praise for answer'd prayer;
Did not the Lord our sorrows mark?
 Did not our sighing reach his ear?

4 Then smaller griefs were laid aside,
 And all our cares summ'd up in one;
" Let us but have thy word," we cried,
 " In other things thy will be done."

5 Since he has granted our request,
 And we still hear the gospel voice;
Although by many trials press'd,
 In this we can and will rejoice.

6 Though to our lot temptations fall,
 Though pain and want and cares annoy;
The precious gospel sweetens all,
 And yields us med'cine, food, and joy.

---

* Wherever a separation is threatened between a minister
and people who dearly love each other, this hymn may be as
seasonable as it was once at Olney.

### 49.

*A Famine of the Word.*

1 GLADNESS was spread through Isr'el's host
    When first they manna view'd:
They labour'd who should gather most,
    And thought it pleasant food.

2 But when they had it long enjoy'd,
    From day to day the same,
Their hearts were by the plenty cloy'd,
    Although from heav'n it came.

3 Thus gospel-bread at first is prized,
    And makes a people glad;
But afterwards too much despised
    When easy to be had.

4 But should the Lord, displeased, withhold
    The bread his mercy sends,
To have our houses fill'd with gold
    Would make but poor amends.

5 How tedious would the week appear,
    How dull the Sabbath prove,
Could we no longer meet to hear
    The precious truths we love!

6 How would believing parents bear
    To leave their heedless youth
Exposed to every fatal snare,
    Without the light of truth?

7 The gospel, and a praying few,
    Our bulwark long have proved;
But Olney sure the day will rue
    When these shall be removed.

8 Then sin, in this once favour'd town,
    Will triumph unrestrain'd;
And wrath and vengeance hasten down,
    No more by pray'r detain'd.

9 Preserve us from this judgment, Lord,
    For Jesus' sake, we plead;
A famine of the gospel-word
    Would be a stroke indeed!

## 50.

### *Prayer for Ministers.*

1 CHIEF Shepherd of thy chosen sheep,
   From death and sin set free ;
May every under shepherd keep
   His eye intent on thee !

2 With plenteous grace their hearts prepare
   To execute thy will,—
Compassion, patience, love, and care,
   And faithfulness and skill.

3 Inflame their minds with holy zeal
   Their flocks to feed and teach ;
And let them live, and let them feel
   The sacred truths they preach.

4 Oh, never let the sheep complain,
   That toys, which fools amuse,
Ambition, pleasure, praise, or gain,
   Debase the shepherd's views.

5 He that for these forbears to feed
   The souls whom Jesus loves,
Whate'er he may profess, or plead,
   An idle shepherd proves.

6 The sword of God shall break his arm,
   A blast shall blind his eye ;
His word shall have no power to warm,
   His gifts shall all grow dry.

7 O Lord, avert this heavy woe !
   Let all thy shepherds say ;
And grace and strength on each bestow,
   To labour while 'tis day.

## 51.

### *Prayer for a Revival.*

1 SAVIOUR, visit thy plantation,
   Grant us, Lord, a gracious rain !
All will come to desolation
   Unless thou return again :

Keep no longer at a distance,
 Shine upon us from on high,
Lest, for want of thine assistance,
 Every plant should droop and die.

2 Surely once thy garden flourish'd,
 Every part look'd gay and green;
Then thy word our spirits nourish'd.
 Happy seasons we have seen!
But a drought has since succeeded,
 And a sad decline we see;
Lord, thy help is greatly needed,
 Help can only come from thee.

3 Where are those we counted leaders,
 Fill'd with zeal and love and truth?
Old professors, tall as cedars,
 Bright examples to our youth?
Some, in whom we once delighted,
 We shall meet no more below;
Some, alas! we fear are blighted,—
 Scarce a single leaf they show.

4 Younger plants—the sight how pleasant—
 Cover'd thick with blossoms stood;
But they cause us grief at present,—
 Frosts have nipp'd them in the bud!
Dearest Saviour, hasten hither,
 Thou canst make them bloom again:
Oh, permit them not to wither,
 Let not all our hopes be vain!

5 Let our mutual love be fervent,
 Make us prevalent in pray'rs:
Let each one esteem'd thy servant
 Shun the world's bewitching snares;
Break the tempter's fatal power,
 Turn the stony heart to flesh:
And begin, from this good hour,
 To revive thy work afresh.

## 52.

### *Hoping for a Revival.*

1 My harp untuned, and laid aside,
  (To cheerful hours the harp belongs,)
  My cruel foes insulting cried,
  " Come, sing us one of Zion's songs."

2 Alas! when sinners, blindly bold,
  At Zion scoff, and Zion's King;
  When zeal declines, and love grows cold,
  Is this a day for me to sing?

3 Time was, whene'er the saints I met,
  With joy and praise my bosom glow'd!
  But now, like Eli, sad I sit,
  And tremble for the ark of God.

4 While thus to grief my soul gave way
  To see the work of God decline,
  Methought I heard my Saviour say,
  " Dismiss thy fears,—the ark is mine.

5 " Though for a time I hide my face,
  Rely upon my love and power;
  Still wrestle at a throne of grace,
  And wait for a reviving hour.

6 " Take down thy long-neglected harp;
  I've seen thy tears, and heard thy pray'r;
  The winter season has been sharp,
  But spring shall all its wastes repair."

7 Lord, I obey; my hopes revive;
  Come join with me, ye saints, and sing;
  Our foes in vain against us strive,
  For God will help and healing bring.

SACRAMENTAL HYMNS.

## 53.

*Welcome to the Table.*   C.

1 This is the feast of heav'nly wine,
    And God invites to sup;
  The juices of the living vine
    Were press'd to fill the cup.

2 O bless the Saviour, ye that eat,
    With royal dainties fed;
  Not heaven affords a costlier treat,
    For Jesus is the bread.

3 The vile, the lost, he calls to them.
    Ye trembling souls, appear!
  The righteous in their own esteem
    Have no acceptance here.

4 Approach, ye poor, nor dare refuse
    The banquet spread for you:
  Dear Saviour, this is welcome news,
    Then I may venture too.

5 If guilt and sin afford a plea,
    And may obtain a place,
  Surely the Lord will welcome me,
    And I shall see his face.

## 54.

*Christ Crucified.*

1 When on the cross my Lord I see,
  Bleeding to death for wretched me,
  Satan and sin no more can move,
  For I am all transform'd to love.

2 His thorns and nails pierce through my heart,
  In every groan I bear a part;
  I view his wounds with streaming eyes:
  But see! he bows his head and dies!

3 Come, sinners, view the Lamb of God,
Wounded and dead and bathed in blood!
Behold his side, and venture near,
The well of endless life is here.

4 Here I forget my cares and pains,
I drink—yet still my thirst remains;
Only the fountain-head above
Can satisfy the thirst of love.

5 Oh that I thus could always feel!
Lord, more and more thy love reveal!
Then my glad tongue shall loud proclaim
The grace and glory of thy name.

6 Thy name dispels my guilt and fear,
Revives my heart, and charms my ear,
Affords a balm for every wound,
And Satan trembles at the sound.

## 55.

*Jesus hasting to suffer.*    C.

1 THE Saviour, what a noble flame
Was kindled in his breast,
When, hasting to Jerusalem,
He march'd before the rest!

2 Good-will to men, and zeal for God,
His every thought engross;
He longs to be baptized with blood,
He pants to reach the cross.

3 With all his suff'rings full in view,
And woes to us unknown,
Forth to the task his spirit flew;
'Twas love that urged him on.

4 Lord, we return thee what we can!
Our hearts shall sound abroad,
Salvation to the dying Man,
And to the rising God!

5 And while thy bleeding glories here
Engage our wond'ring eyes,

We learn our lighter cross to bear,
And hasten to the skies.

### 56.

*It is good to be here.*

1 Let me dwell on Golgotha,
Weep and love my life away,
While I see Him on the tree
Weep and bleed and die for me!

2 That dear blood for sinners spilt
Shows my sin in all its guilt;
Ah! my soul, He bore thy load,—
Thou hast slain the Lamb of God.

3 Hark! his dying word, "Forgive!
Father, let the sinner live:
Sinner, wipe thy tears away,
I thy ransom freely pay."

4 While I hear this grace reveal'd,
And obtain a pardon seal'd,
All my soft affections move,
Waken'd by the force of love.

5 Farewell, world, thy gold is dross.
Now I see the bleeding cross:
Jesus died to set me free
From the law and sin and thee!

6 He has dearly bought my soul;
Lord, accept and claim the whole!
To thy will I all resign,
Now, no more my own, but thine.

### 57.

*Looking at the Cross.*

1 In evil long I took delight,
Unawed by shame or fear,
Till a new object struck my sight,
And stopp'd my wild career.

2 I saw one hanging on a tree,
In agonies and blood,

Who fix'd his languid eyes on me
  As near his cross I stood.

3 Sure never till my latest breath
  Can I forget that look;
It seem'd to charge me with his death,
  Though not a word He spoke.

4 My conscience felt, and own'd the guilt,
  And plunged me in despair;
I saw my sins his blood had spilt,
  And help'd to nail Him there.]

5 Alas! I knew not what I did:
  But now my tears are vain;
Where shall my trembling soul be hid?
  For I the Lord have slain.

6 A second look He gave, which said,
  " I freely all forgive;
This blood is for thy ransom paid,
  I die, that may may st live."

7 Thus while his death my sin displays
  In all its blackest hue,
(Such is the mystery of grace,)
  It seals my pardon too.

8 With pleasing grief and mournful joy
  My spirit now is fill'd,
That I should such a life destroy,
  Yet live by Him I kill'd.

## 58.

### *Supplies in the Wilderness.*

1 WHEN Isr'el, by divine command,
  The pathless desert trod,
They found, though 'twas a barren land,
  A sure resource in God.

2 A cloudy pillar mark'd their road,
  And screen'd them from the heat;
From the hard rocks the water flow'd,
  And manna was their meat.

3 Like them, we have a rest in view,
　　Secure from adverse pow'rs;
　Like them, we pass a desert too,
　　But Isr'el's God is ours.

4 Yes, in this barren wilderness
　　He is to us the same,
　By his appointed means of grace,
　　As once he was to them.

5 His word a light before us spreads,
　　By which our path we see;
　His love, a banner o'er our heads,
　　From harm preserves us free.

6 Jesus, the bread of life, is giv'n
　　To be our daily food;
　We drink a wondrous stream from heav'n,
　　'Tis water, wine, and blood.

7 Lord, 'tis enough, I ask no more;
　　These blessings are divine;
　I envy not the worldling's store
　　If Christ and heav'n are mine.

## 59.

*Communion with the Saints in Glory.*

1 REFRESHED by the bread and wine,
　The pledges of our Saviour's love,
　Now let our hearts and voices join
　In songs of praise with those above.

2 Do they sing, "Worthy is the Lamb"?
　Although we cannot reach their strains,
　Yet we through grace can sing the same,—
　For us he died, for us he reigns.

3 If they behold him face to face,
　While we a glimpse can only see,
　Yet, equal debtors to his grace,
　As safe and as beloved are we.

4 They had, like us, a suff'ring time,
　Our cares and fears and griefs they knew:

But they have conquer'd all through Him,
And we ere long shall conquer too.

5 Though all the songs of saints in light
Are far beneath His matchless worth,
His grace is such, He will not slight
The poor attempts of worms on earth.

ON PRAYER.

## 60.

*Exhortation to Prayer.*  C.

1 WHAT various hind'rances we meet
In coming to a mercy-seat!
Yet who that knows the worth of pray'r
But wishes to be often there?

2 Pray'r makes the darken'd cloud withdraw,
Pray'r climbs the ladder Jacob saw,
Gives exercise to faith and love,
Brings every blessing from above.

3 Restraining pray'r, we cease to fight:
Pray'r makes the Christian's armour bright;
And Satan trembles when he sees
The weakest saint upon his knees.

4 While Moses stood with arms spread wide,
Success was found on Isr'el's side;
But when through weariness they fail'd,
That moment Amalek prevail'd.

5 Have you no words? Ah! think again:
Words flow apace when you complain,
And fill your fellow-creature's ear
With the sad tale of all your care.

6 Were half the breath thus vainly spent
To Heaven in supplication sent,
Your cheerful song would oftener be,
" Hear what the Lord has done for me.

L

## 61.

*Power of Prayer.*

1 In themselves as weak as worms,
  How can poor believers stand,
  When temptations, foes, and storms,
  Press them close on every hand?

2 Weak, indeed, they feel they are,
  But they know the throne of grace;
  And the God who answers pray'r
  Helps them when they seek his face.

3 Though the Lord awhile delay,
  Succour they at length obtain;
  He who taught their hearts to pray
  Will not let them cry in vain.

4 Wrestling pray'r can wonders do,
  Bring relief in deepest straits:
  Pray'r can force a passage through
  Iron bars and brazen gates.

5 Hezekiah on his knees
  Proud Assyria's host subdued;
  And, when smitten with disease,
  Had his life by pray'r renew'd.

6 Peter, though confined and chain'd,
  Pray'r prevail'd and brought him out
  When Elijah pray'd it rain'd,
  After three long years of drought.

7 We can likewise witness bear,
  That the Lord is still the same;
  Though we fear'd he would not hear,
  Suddenly deliv'rance came.

8 For the wonders he has wrought,
  Let us now our praises give;
  And, by sweet experience taught,
  Call upon him while we live.

ON THE SCRIPTURE.

## 62.

*The Light and Glory of the Word.*    C.

1 THE Spirit breathes upon the word,
     And brings the truth to sight;
Precepts and promises afford
     A sanctifying light.

2 A glory gilds the sacred page,
     Majestic, like the sun ;
It gives a light to every age,
     It gives, but borrows none.

3 The hand that gave it still supplies
     The gracious light and heat;
His truths upon the nations rise,
     They rise, but never set.

4 Let everlasting thanks be thine
     For such a bright display
As makes a world of darkness shine
     With beams of heav'nly day.

5 My soul rejoices to pursue
     The steps of Him I love,
Till glory breaks upon my view
     In brighter worlds above.

## 63.

*The Word more precious than Gold.*

1 PRECIOUS BIBLE! what a treasure
     Does the Word of God afford!
All I want for life or pleasure,
     Food and med'cine, shield and sword;
Let the world account me poor,
     Having this I need no more.

2 Food, to which the world's a stranger,
     Here my hungry soul enjoys;

Of excess there is no danger,
  Though it fills, it never cloys:
On a dying Christ I feed,——
  He is meat and drink indeed!

3 When my faith is faint and sickly,
  Or when Satan wounds my mind,
Cordials to revive me quickly,
  Healing med'cines, here I find:
    To the promises I flee,
    Each affords a remedy.

4 In the hour of dark temptation,
  Satan cannot make me yield ;
For the word of consolation
  Is to me a mighty shield :
    While the Scripture truths are sure,
    From his malice I'm secure.

5 Vain his threats to overcome me
  When I take the Spirit's sword ;
Then with ease I drive him from me,——
  Satan trembles at the word :
    'Tis a sword for conquest made,
    Keen the edge and strong the blade.

6 Shall I envy then the miser,
  Doating on his golden store ?
Sure I am, or should be, wiser ;
  I am rich, 'tis he is poor :
    Jesus gives me, in his word,
    Food and med'cine, shield and sword.


### III. PROVIDENCES.

### 64.

*On the Commencement of Hostilities in America.*

1 The gath'ring clouds, with aspect dark,
  A rising storm presage ;
Oh! to be hid within the ark,
  And shelter'd from its rage !

2 See the commission'd angel frown!
   That vial in his hand,
Fill'd with fierce wrath, is pouring down
   Upon our guilty land!

3 Ye saints, unite in wrestling pray'r,
   If yet there may be hope ;
Who knows but mercy yet may spare,
   And bid the angel stop ?

4 Already is the plague begun,
   And, fired with hostile rage,
Brethren, by blood and int'rest one,
   With brethren now engage.

5 Peace spreads her wings, prepared for flight;
   And war, with flaming sword
And hasty strides, draws nigh, to fight
   The battles of the Lord.

6 The first alarm, alas, how few,
   While distant, seem to hear!
But they will hear, and tremble too,
   When God shall send it near.

7 So thunder o'er the distant hills
   Gives but a murm'ring sound ;
But as the tempest spreads, it falls
   And shakes the welkin * round.

8 May we, at least, with one consent,
   Fall low before the throne :
With tears the nation's sins lament,
   The church's, and our own.

9 The humble souls who mourn and pray
   The Lord approves and knows ;
His mark secures them in the day
   When vengeance strikes his foes.

* Firmament, or atmosphere.

FAST-DAY HYMNS.

## 65.

*Confession and Prayer.*   Dec. 13, 1776.

1 Ou may the pow'r which melts the rock
  Be felt by all assembled here!
  Or else our service will but mock
  The God whom we profess to fear.

2 Lord, while thy judgments shake the land,
  Thy people's eyes are fix'd on thee!
  We own thy just uplifted hand,
  Which thousands cannot, will not see.

3 How long hast thou bestow'd thy care
  On this indulged ungrateful spot,
  While other nations far and near
  Have envied and admired our lot!

4 Here peace and liberty have dwelt,
  The glorious gospel brightly shone;
  And oft our enemies have felt
  That God has made our cause his own.

5 But ah! both heaven and earth have heard
  Our vile requital of his love!
  We, whom like children he has rear'd,
  Rebels against his goodness prove.

6 His grace despised, his power defied,
  And legions of the blackest crimes,
  Profaneness, riot, lust, and pride,
  Are signs that mark the present times.

7 The Lord displeased has raised his rod;
  Ah, where are now the faithful few
  Who tremble for the ark of God,
  And know what Isr'el ought to do?

8 Lord, hear thy people every-where,
  Who meet to mourn, confess, and pray:
  The nation and thy churches spare,
  And let thy wrath be turn'd away!

## 66.

*Moses and Amalek.*—Exod. xvii, 9.    Feb. 27, 1778.

1 WHILE Joshua led the armed bands
    Of Israel forth to war;
  Moses apart with lifted hands
    Engaged in humble pray'r.

2 The armed bands had quickly fail'd,
    And perish'd in the fight,
  If Moses' pray'r had not prevail'd
    To put the foes to flight.

3 When Moses' hands through weakness dropp'd
    The warriors fainted too;
  Isr'el's success at once was stopp'd,
    And Am'lek bolder grew.

4 A people, always prone to boast,
    Were taught by this suspense,
  That not a num'rous armed host,
    But God, was their defence.

5 We now of fleets and armies vaunt,
    And ships and men prepare;
  But men like Moses most we want,
    To save the state by pray'r.

6 Yet, Lord, we hope thou hast prepared
    A hidden few to-day,
  (The nation's secret strength and guard,)
    To weep and mourn and pray.

7 Oh hear their pray'rs, and grant us aid,
    Bid war and discord cease;
  Heal the sad breach which sin has made,
    And bless us all with peace.

## 67.

*The Hiding-place.*    Feb. 10, 1779.

1 SEE the gloomy gath'ring cloud.
  Hanging o'er a sinful land!

Sure the Lord proclaims aloud, ·
Times of trouble are at hand.
Happy they who love his name,
They shall always find him near ;
Though the earth were wrapp'd in flame,
They have no just cause for fear.

2 Hark ! his voice in accents mild,
(Oh, how comforting and sweet!)
Speaks to every humble child,
Pointing out a sure retreat!
Come and in my chambers hide,
To my saints of old well known ;
There you safely may abide
Till the storm be overblown.

3 You have only to repose
On my wisdom, love, and care ;
When my wrath consumes my foes,
Mercy shall my children spare :
While *they* perish in the flood,
You that bear my holy mark,
Sprinkled with atoning blood,
Shall be safe within the ark.

4 Sinners, see the ark prepared !
Haste to enter while there's room !
Though the Lord his arm has bared,
Mercy still retards your doom :
Seek him while there yet is hope,
Ere the day of grace be past,
Lest in wrath he give you up,
And this call should prove your last.

## 68.

*On the Earthquake.* Sept. 8, 1775.

1 ALTHOUGH on massy pillars built,
The earth has lately shook :
It trembles under Britain's guilt
Before its Maker's look.

2 Swift as the shock amazement spreads,
  And sinners tremble too ;
  What flight can screen their guilty heads,
  If earth itself pursue ?

3 But mercy spared us while it warn'd,——
  The shock is felt no more :
  And mercy, now, alas ! is scorn'd
  By sinners, as before.

4 But if these warnings prove in vain,
  Say, sinner, canst thou tell
  How soon the earth may quake again,
  And open wide to hell ?

5 Repent before the Judge draws nigh ;
  Or else, when he comes down,
  Thou wilt in vain for earthquakes cry,
  To hide thee from his frown.

6 But happy they who love the Lord,
  And his salvation know ;
  The hope that's founded on his word,
  No change can overthrow.

7 Should the deep-rooted hills be hurl'd,
  And plunged beneath the seas,
  And strong convulsions shake the world,
  Your hearts may rest in peace.

8 Jesus, your Shepherd, Lord, and Chief,
  Shall shelter you from ill,
  And not a worm or shaking leaf
  Can move but at his will.

## 69.

*On the Fire at Olney.*    Sept. 22, 1777.

1 WEARIED by day with toils and cares,
  How welcome is the peaceful night !
  Sweet sleep our wasted strength repairs,
  And fits us for returning light.

2 Yet when our eyes in sleep are closed,
  Our rest may break ere well begun ;

L 2

To dangers every hour exposed
We neither can foresee nor shun.

3 'Tis of the Lord that we can sleep
A single night without alarms;
His eye alone our lives can keep
Secure amidst a thousand harms.

4 For months and years of safety past
Ungrateful we, alas! have been;
Though patient long, he spoke at last.
And bid the fire rebuke our sin.

5 The shout of *fire!* a dreadful cry,
Impress'd each heart with deep dismay,
While the fierce blaze and redd'ning sky
Made midnight wear the face of day.

6 The throng and terror who can speak?
The various sounds that fill'd the air!
The infant's wail, the mother's shriek,
The voice of blasphemy and pray'r!

7 But pray'r prevail'd, and saved the town:
The few who loved the Saviour's name
Were heard, and mercy hasted down,
To change the wind and stop the flame.

8 Oh, may that night be ne'er forgot!
Lord, still increase thy praying few!
Were Olney left without a Lot,
Ruin like Sodom's would ensue.

## 70.

### *A Welcome to Christian Friends.*

1 KINDRED in Christ, for his dear sake,
A hearty welcome here receive;
May we together now partake
The joys which only he can give!

2 To you and us by grace 'tis given
To know the Saviour's precious name,
And shortly we shall meet in heaven,
Our hope, our way, our end, the same.

3 May he, by whose kind care we meet,
  Send his good Spirit from above,
  Make our communications sweet,
  And cause our hearts to burn with love!

4 Forgotten be each worldly theme,
  When Christians see each other thus:
  We only wish to speak of Him
  Who lived and died and reigns for us.

5 We'll talk of all He did and said,
  And suffer'd for us here below;
  The path He mark'd for us to tread,
  And what He's doing for us now.

6 Thus, as the moments pass away,
  We'll love and wonder and adore,
  And hasten on the glorious day
  When we shall meet to part no more.

## 71.

### At Parting.

1 As the sun's enliv'ning eye
  Shines on every place the same;
  So the Lord is always nigh
  To the souls that love his name.

2 When they move at duty's call,
  He is with them by the way;
  He is ever near them all,
  Those who go, and those who stay.

3 From his holy mercy-seat
  Nothing can their souls confine;
  Still in spirit they may meet,
  And in sweet communion join.

4 For a season call'd to part,
  Let us then ourselves commend
  To the gracious eye and heart
  Of our ever-present Friend.

5 Jesus, hear our humble pray'r!
  Tender Shepherd of thy sheep,

Let thy mercy and thy care
All our souls in safety keep.

6 In thy strength may we be strong,
Sweeten every cross and pain;
Give us, if we live, ere long,
Here to meet in peace again.

7 Then if thou thy help afford,
Ebenezers shall be rear'd;
And our souls shall praise the Lord,
Who our poor petitions heard.


FUNERAL HYMNS.


### 72.

*On the Death of a Believer.*

1 In vain our fancy strives to paint
The moment after death,
The glories that surround the saints
When yielding up their breath.

2 One gentle sigh their fetters breaks;
We scarce can say, "They're gone!"
Before the willing spirit takes
Her mansion near the throne.

3 Faith strives, but all its efforts fail
To trace her in her flight;
No eye can pierce within the veil
Which hides that world of light.

4 Thus much (and this is all) we know,
They are completely bless'd—
Have done with sin and care and woe,
And with their Saviour rest.

5 On harps of gold they praise his name,
His face they always view;
Then let us foll'wers be of them,
That we may praise him too.

6 Their faith and patience, love and zeal,
    Should make their mem'ry dear;
And, Lord, do thou the pray'rs fulfill
    They offer'd for us here.

7 While they have gain'd we losers are,
    We miss them day by day:
But thou canst every breach repair,
    And wipe our tears away.

8 We pray, as in Elisha's case,
    When great Elijah went—
May double portions of thy grace
    To us who stay be sent.

## 73.

*On the Death of a Minister.*  C.

1 HIS master taken from his head,
    Elisha saw him go;
And in desponding accents said—
    "Ah, what must Isr'el do?"

2 But he forgot the Lord who lifts
    The beggar to the throne;
Nor knew that all Elijah's gifts
    Will soon be made his own.

3 What, when a Paul has run his course,
    Or when Apollos dies,
Is Isr'el left without resource?
    And have we no supplies?

4 Yes, while the dear Redeemer lives,
    We have a boundless store,
And shall be fed with what he gives,
    Who lives for evermore.

## 74.

*The Tolling Bell.*

1 OFT as the bell, with solemn toll,
    Speaks the departure of a soul,
Let each one ask himself—"Am I
    Prepared, should I be call'd to die?"

2 Only this frail and fleeting breath
  Preserves me from the jaws of death;
  Soon as it fails at once I'm gone,
  And plunged into a world unknown.

3 Then leaving all I loved below,
  To God's tribunal I must go,—
  Must hear the Judge pronounce my fate,
  And fix my everlasting state.

4 But could I bear to hear him say,
  " Depart, accursed, far away ;
  With Satan in the lowest hell,
  Thou art for ever doom'd to dwell " ?

5 Lord Jesus ! help me now to flee,
  And seek my hope alone in thee ;
  Apply thy blood, thy Spirit give,
  Subdue my sin and let me live.

6 Then when the solemn bell I hear,
  If saved from guilt I need not fear;
  Nor would the thought distressing be—
  Perhaps it next may toll for me.

7 Rather my spirit would rejoice,
  And long and wish to hear thy voice ;
  Glad when it bids me earth resign,
  Secure of heaven if thou art mine.

## 75.

*Hope beyond the Grave.*

1 My soul, this curious house of clay,
    Thy present frail abode,
  Must quickly fall to worms a prey,
    And thou return to God.

2 Canst thou by faith survey with joy
    The change before it come ?
  And say—" Let death this house destroy,
    I have a heav'nly home ?"

3 The Saviour, whom I then shall see
    With new admiring eyes,

Already has prepared for me
A mansion in the skies.

4 I feel this mud-wall cottage shake,
And long to see it fall,
That I my willing flight may take
To Him who is my all.

5 Burden'd and groaning then no more,
My rescued soul shall sing,
As up the shining path I soar,
"Death, thou hast lost thy sting!"

6 Dear Saviour, help us now to seek,
And know thy grace's power,
That we may all this language speak
Before the dying hour.

## 76.

### *There the Weary are at Rest.*

1 COURAGE, my soul! behold the prize
The Saviour's love provides—
Eternal life beyond the skies
For all whom here he guides.

2 The wicked cease from troubling there,
The weary are at rest;
Sorrow and sin and pain and care
No more approach the blest.

3 A wicked world and wicked heart
With Satan now are join'd;
Each acts a too successful part
In harassing my mind.

4 In conflict with this threefold troop,
How weary, Lord, am I!
Did not thy promise bear me up
My soul must faint and die:

5 But fighting in my Saviour's strength,
Though mighty are my foes,
I shall a conq'ror be at length
O'er all that can oppose.

6 Then why, my soul, complain or fear?
    The crown of glory see!
The more I toil and suffer here,
    The sweeter rest will be.

## 77.

### The Day of Judgment.

1 DAY of judgment, day of wonders!
    Hark! the trumpet's awful sound,
Louder than a thousand thunders,
    Shakes the vast creation round!
How the summons will the sinner's heart confound!

2 See the Judge our nature wearing,
    Clothed in majesty divine!
You who long for his appearing
    Then shall say—" This God is mine!"
Gracious Saviour, own me in that day for thine.

3 At his call the dead awaken,
    Rise to life from earth and sea.
All the powers of nature, shaken
    By his looks, prepare to flee.
Careless sinner, what will then become of thee?

4 Horrors past imagination
    Will surprise your trembling heart,
When you hear your condemnation,
    " Hence, accursed wretch, depart!
Thou with Satan and his angels have thy part!"

5 Satan, who now tries to please you,
    Lest you timely warning take,
When that word is past, will seize you,
    Plunge you in the burning lake:
Think, poor sinner, thy eternal all's at stake.

6 But to those who have confessed,
    Loved and served the Lord below,
He will say—" Come near, ye blessed,
    See the kingdom I bestow:
You for ever shall my love and glory know."

7   Under sorrows and reproaches,
     May this thought your courage raise,
Swiftly God's great day approaches,
     Sighs shall then be changed to praise.
We shall triumph when the world is in a blaze.

## 78.

### *The Day of the Lord.* *

1   God with one piercing glance looks through
     Creation's wide-extended frame;
     The past and future in his view,
     And days and ages are the same.

2   Sinners who dare provoke his face,
     Who on his patience long presume,
     And trifle out his day of grace,
     Will find he has a day of doom,

3   As pangs the labouring woman feels,
     Or as the thief in midnight sleep,
     So comes that day for which the wheels
     Of time their ceaseless motion keep!

4   Hark! from the sky the trump proclaims
     Jesus the Judge approaching nigh!
     See the creation wrapt in flames,
     First kindled by his vengeful eye!

5   When thus the mountains melt like wax;
     When earth and air and sea shall burn;
     When all the frame of nature breaks;
     Poor sinner, whither wilt thou turn?

6   The puny works which feeble men
     Now boast or covet or admire;
     Their pomp and arts and treasures then
     Shall perish in one common fire.

7   Lord, fix our hearts and hopes above,
     Since all below to ruin tends;
     Here may we trust, obey, and love,
     And there be found amongst thy friends.

\* Book iii, Hymn 4.

## 79.

*The Great Tribunal.*—Rev. xx, 11, 12.

1 John in vision saw the day
  When the Judge will hasten down:
  Heaven and earth shall flee away
  From the terror of his frown.
  Dead and living, small and great,
  Raised from the earth and sea,
  At his bar shall hear their fate:
  What will then become of me ?

2 Can I bear his awful looks?
  Shall I stand in judgment then,
  When I see the open'd books,
  Written by th' Almighty's pen ?
  If he to remembrance bring,
  And expose to public view,
  Every work and secret thing,
  Ah, my soul, what canst thou do ?

3 When the list shall be produced
  Of the talents I enjoy'd,
  Means and mercies how abused,
  Time and strength how misemploy'd,
  Conscience, then compell'd to read,
  Must allow the charge is true ;
  Say, my soul, what canst thou plead—
  In that hour what wilt thou do ?

4 But the book of life I see ;
  May my name be written there :
  Then from guilt and danger free,
  Glad I'll meet him in the air.
  That's the book I hope to plead,—
  'Tis the gospel open'd wide.
  Lord, I am a wretch indeed,—
  I have sinn'd, but thou hast died.

5 Now my soul knows what to do;
  Thus I shall with boldness stand,
  Number'd with the faithful few,
  Own'd and saved at thy right hand.

If thou help a feeble worm
To believe thy promise now,
Justice will at last confirm
What thy mercy wrought below.

## IV. CREATION.

## 80.

### *The Old and New Creation.*

1 That was a wonder-working word
Which could the vast creation raise!
Angels, attendant on their Lord
Admired the plan, and sung his praise.

2 From what a dark and shapeless mass
All nature sprang at his command!
Let there be light! and light there was,
And sun and stars and sea and land.

3 With equal speed the earth and seas
Their mighty Maker's voice obey'd;
He spake, and straight the plants and trees
And birds and beasts and man were made.

4 But man, the lord and crown of all,
By sin his honour soon defaced,
His heart (how alter'd since the fall!)
Is dark, deform'd, and void and waste.

5 The new creation of the soul
Does now no less his power display,
Than when he form'd the mighty whole,
And kindled darkness into day.

6 Though self-destroy'd, O Lord, we are,
Yet let us feel what thou canst do;
Thy word the ruin can repair,
And all our hearts create anew.

## 81.

### *The Book of Creation.*

1 THE book of nature open lies,
    With much instruction stored:
But till the Lord anoints our eyes
    We cannot read a word.

2 Philosophers have pored in vain,
    And guess'd from age to age;
For reason's eye could ne'er attain
    To understand a page.

3 Though to each star they give a name,
    Its size and motions teach,
The truths which all the stars proclaim
    Their wisdom cannot reach.

4 With skill to measure earth and sea,
    And weigh the subtile air,
They cannot, Lord, discover thee
    Though present everywhere.

5 The knowledge of the saints excels
    The wisdom of the schools;
To them his secrets God reveals
    Though men account them fools.

6 To them the sun and stars on high,
    The flow'rs that paint the field,
And all the artless birds that fly,
    Divine instructions yield.

7 The creatures on their senses press,
    As witnesses to prove
Their Saviour's power and faithfulness.
    His providence and love.

8 Thus may we study nature's book,
    To make us wise indeed!
And pity those who only look
    At what they cannot read.

## 82.

### *The Rainbow.*

1 WHEN the sun with cheerful beams
Smiles upon a low'ring sky,
Soon its aspect soften'd seems,
And a rainbow meets the eye:
While the sky remains serene
This bright arch is never seen.

2 Thus the Lord's supporting pow'r
Brightest to his saints appears,
When affliction's threat'ning hour
Fills their sky with clouds and fears:
He can wonders then perform,
Paint a rainbow on the storm.

3 All their graces doubly shine
When their troubles press them sore;
And the promises divine
Give them joys unknown before:
As the colours of the bow
To the cloud their brightness owe.

4 Favour'd John a rainbow saw,
Circling round a throne above;
Hence the saints a pledge may draw
Of unchanging cov'nant love:
Clouds awhile may intervene,
But the bow will still be seen.

## 83.

### *Thunder.*

1 WHEN a black o'erspreading cloud
Has darken'd all the air,
And peals of thunder, roaring loud,
Proclaim the tempest near;

2 Then guilt and fear, the fruits of sin,
The sinner oft pursue;
A louder storm is heard within,
And conscience thunders too.

3 The law a fiery language speaks,
   His danger he perceives;
Like Satan, who his ruin seeks,
   He trembles and believes.

4 But when the sky serene appears,
   And thunders roll no more,
He soon forgets his vows and fears,
   Just as he did before.

5 But whither shall the sinner flee
   When nature's mighty frame,
The pond'rous earth and air and sea,
   Shall all dissolve in flame?

6 Amazing day! It comes apace!
   The Judge is hasting down!
Will sinners bear to see his face,
   Or stand before his frown?

7 Lord, let thy mercy find a way
   To touch each stubborn heart,
That they may never hear thee say,
   " Ye cursed ones, depart!"

8 Believers, you may well rejoice!
   The thunder's loudest strains
Should be to you a welcome voice,
   That tells you, " Jesus reigns!"

## 84.

### *Lightning in the Night.*

1 A GLANCE from heav'n with sweet effect,
Sometimes my pensive spirit cheers;
But, ere I can my thoughts collect,
As suddenly it disappears.

2 So lightning in the gloom of night
Affords a momentary day;
Disclosing objects full in sight,
Which, soon as seen, are snatch'd away.

3 Ah! what avail these pleasing scenes!
They do but aggravate my pain;

While darkness quickly intervenes,
And swallows up my joys again.

4 But shall I murmur at relief?
Though short, it was a precious view,
Sent to control my unbelief,
And prove that what I read was true,

5 The lightning's flash did not create
The opening prospect it reveal'd;
But only showed the real state
Of what the darkness had conceal'd.

6 Just so, we by a glimpse discern
The glorious things within the veil,—
That, when in darkness, we may learn
To live by faith till light prevail.

7 The Lord's great day will soon advance,
Dispersing all the shades of night;
Then we no more shall need a glance,
But see by an eternal light.

## 85.

*On the Eclipse of the Moon.*  July 30, 1776.

1 THE moon in silver glory shone,
    And not a cloud in sight,
When suddenly a shade begun
    To intercept her light.

2 How fast across her orb it spread!
    How fast her light withdrew!
A circle, tinged with languid red,
    Was all appear'd in view.

3 While many, with unmeaning eye,
    Gaze on thy works in vain,
Assist me, Lord, that I may try
    Instruction to obtain.

4 Fain would my thankful heart and lips
    Unite in praise of thee,
And meditate on thy eclipse
    In sad Gethsemane.

5 Thy people's guilt, a heavy load,
   (When standing in their room,)
Deprived thee of the light of God,
   And fill'd thy soul with gloom.

6 How punctu'lly eclipses move,
   Obedient to thy will!
Thus shall thy faithfulness and love
   Thy promises fulfill.

7 Dark, like the moon without the sun,
   I mourn thine absence, Lord!
For light or comfort I have none
   But what thy beams afford.

8 But, lo! the hour draws near apace,
   When changes shall be o'er;
Then I shall see thee face to face,
   And be eclipsed no more.

## 86.

### *Moonlight.*

1 THE moon has but a borrow'd light,
   A faint and feeble ray;
She owes her beauty to the night,
   And hides herself by day.

2 No cheering warmth her beam conveys,
   Though pleasing to behold;
We might upon her brightness gaze
   Till we were starved with cold.

3 Just such is all the light to man
   Which reason can impart;
It cannot show one object plain,
   Nor warm the frozen heart.

4 Thus moonlight views of truth divine
   To many fatal prove;
For what avail in gifts to shine,
   Without a spark of love?

5 The gospel, like the sun at noon,
   Affords a glorious light;

Then fallen reason's boasted moon
   Appears no longer bright.

6 And grace, not light alone, bestows,
   But adds a quick'ning power;
The desert blossoms like the rose,
   And sin prevails no more.

## 87.

*The Sea.**

1 If for a time the air be calm,
Serene and smooth the sea appears,
And shows no danger to alarm
Th' inexperienced landsman's fears;

2 But if the tempest once arise,
The faithless water swells and raves;
Its billows foaming to the skies,
Disclose a thousand threat'ning graves.

3 My untried heart thus seem'd to me
(So little of myself I knew,)
Smooth as the calm unruffled sea,
But ah! it proved as treach'rous too.

4 The peace of which I had a taste
When Jesus first his love reveal'd,
I fondly hoped would always last
Because my foes were then conceal'd.

5 But when I felt the tempter's power
Rouse my corruptions from their sleep,
I trembled at the stormy hour,
And saw the horrors of the deep.

6 Now on presumption's billows borne,
My spirit seem'd the Lord to dare;
Now, quick as thought, a sudden turn
Plunged me in gulfs of black despair.

7 Lord, save me, or I sink, I pray'd;
He heard, and bid the tempest cease;

Book i, Hymn 115.
M

46

The angry waves his word obey'd,
And all my fears were hush'd to peace.

8 The peace is his, and not my own ;
My heart (no better than before)
Is still to dreadful changes prone,
Then let me never trust it more.

## 88.

### The Flood.

1 Though small the drops of falling rain
If one be singly view'd,
Collected, they o'erspread the plain.
And form a mighty flood.

2 The house it meets with in its course
Should not be built on clay,
Lest, with a wild, resistless force,
It sweep the whole away.

3 Though for awhile it seem secure.
It will not bear the shock
Unless it has foundations sure,
And stands upon a rock.

4 Thus sinners think their evil deeds.
Like drops of rain, are small ;
But it the power of thought exceeds
To count the sum of all.

5 One sin can raise, though small it seem.
A flood to drown the soul :
What then, when countless million streams
Shall join to swell the whole!

6 Yet, while they think the weather fair,
If warn'd they smile or frown :
But they will tremble and despair,
When the fierce flood comes down.

7 Oh! then on Jesus ground your hope.
That Stone in Zion laid ;
Lest your poor building quickly drop,
With ruin on your head.

## 89.

### *The Thaw.*

1 THE ice and snow we lately saw,
  Which cover'd all the ground,
Are melted soon before the thaw,
  And can no more be found.

2 Could all the art of man suffice
  To move away the snow,
To clear the rivers from the ice,
  Or make the waters flow?

3 No, 'tis the work of God alone;
  An emblem of the power
By which he melts the heart of stone
  In his appointed hour.

4 All outward means, till he appears,
  Will ineffectual prove;
Though much the sinner sees and hears,
  He cannot learn to love.

5 But let the stoutest sinner feel
  The soft'ning warmth of grace,
Though hard as ice or rocks or steel,
  His heart dissolves apace.

6 Seeing the blood which Jesus spilt
  To save his soul from woe,
His hatred, unbelief, and guilt,
  All melt away like snow.

7 Jesus, we in thy name entreat,
  Reveal thy gracious arm;
And grant thy Spirit's kindly heat,
  Our frozen hearts to warm.

## 90.

### *The Loadstone.*

1 As needles point towards the pole
  When touch'd by the magnetic stone;
So faith in Jesus gives the soul
  A tendency before unknown.

2  Till then, by blinded passions led,
   In search of fancied good we range;
   The paths of disappointment tread,
   To nothing fix'd but love of change.

3  But when the Holy Ghost imparts
   A knowledge of the Saviour's love,
   Our wand'ring, weary, restless hearts
   Are fix'd at once, no more to move.

4  Now a new principle takes place,
   Which guides and animates the will;
   This love, another name for grace,
   Constrains to good, and bars from ill.

5  By love's pure light we soon perceive
   Our noblest bliss and proper end;
   And gladly every idol leave,
   To love and serve our Lord and Friend.

6  Thus, borne along by faith and hope,
   We feel the Saviour's words are true;
   "And I, if I be lifted up,
   Will draw the sinner upward too."

## 91.

### The Spider and Bee.

1  On the same flow'r we often see
   The loathsome spider and the bee:
   But what they get by working there
   Is diff'rent as their natures are.

2  The bee a sweet reward obtains,
   And honey well repays his pains;
   Home to the hive he bears the store,
   And then returns in quest of more.

3  But no sweet flow'rs that grace the field
   Can honey to the spider yield;
   A cobweb all that he can spin,
   And poison all the stores within.

4  Thus in that sacred field, the Word,
   With flow'rs of God's own planting stored,

Like bees his children feed and thrive,
And bring home honey to the hive.

5 There, spider-like, the wicked come,
And seem to taste the sweet perfume;
But the vile venom of their hearts
To poison all their food converts.

6 From the same truths believers prize
They weave vain refuges of lies;
And from the promise license draw
To trifle with the holy law.

7 Lord, shall thy word of life and love
The means of death to numbers prove?
Unless thy grace our hearts renew *
We sink to hell with heaven in view.

## 92.

### *The Bee saved from the Spider.*

1 THE subtle spider often weaves
 His unsuspected snares
Among the balmy flowers and leaves,
 To which the bee repairs.

2 When in his web he sees one hang,
 With a malicious joy
He darts upon it with his fang,
 To poison and destroy.

3 How welcome then some pitying friend,
 To save the threaten'd bee,
The spider's treach'rous web to rend,
 And set the captive free!

4 My soul has been in such a case:
 When first I knew the Lord,
I hasted to the means of grace,
 Where sweets I knew were stored.

5 Little I thought of danger near,
 That soon my joys would ebb;
But ah! I met a spider there,
 Who caught me in his web.

* Book iii, Hymn 71.

6 Then Satan raised his pois'nous sting,
    And aim'd his blows at me :
  While I, poor helpless trembling thing.
    Could neither fight nor flee.

7 But oh! the Saviour's pitying eye
    Relieved me from despair ;
  He saw me at the point to die,
    And broke the fatal snare.

8 My case his heedless saints should warn,
    Or cheer them if afraid ;
  May you from me your danger learn,
    And where to look for aid !

## 93.

### The tamed Lion.

1 A LION, though by nature wild,
    The art of man can tame ;
  He stands before his keeper mild
    And gentle as a lamb.

2 He watches, with submissive eye.
    The hand that gives him food,
  As if he meant to testify
    A sense of gratitude.

3 But man himself, who thus subdues
    The fiercest beasts of prey,
  A nature more unfeeling shows
    And far more fierce than they.

4 Though by the Lord preserved and fed.
    He proves rebellious still ;
  And while he eats his Maker's bread
    Resists his holy will.

5 Alike in vain, of grace that saves.
    Or threat'ning law. he hears ;
  The savage scorns, blasphemes, and raves,
    But neither loves nor fears.

6 O Saviour ! how thy wondrous power
    By angels is proclaim'd !

When in thine own appointed hour
   They see this lion tamed!

7 The love thy bleeding cross displays
   The hardest heart subdues!
Here furious lions, while they gaze,
   Their rage and fierceness lose.

8 Yet we are but renew'd in part,
   The lion still remains ;
Lord, drive him wholly from my heart,
   Or keep him fast in chains.

## 94.

### *Sheep.*

1 THE Saviour calls his people sheep,
   And bids them on his love rely;
For he alone their souls can keep,
   And he alone their wants supply.

2 The bull can fight, the hare can flee,
   The ant in summer food prepare ;
But helpless sheep, and such are we,
   Depend upon the shepherd's care.

3 Jehovah is our Shepherd's name,
   Then what have we, though weak, to fear?
Our sin and folly we proclaim
   If we despond while he is near.

4 When Satan threatens to devour,
   When troubles press on every side,
Think on our Shepherd's care and power,
   He can defend, He will provide.

5 See the rich pastures of his grace,
   Where in full streams salvation flows!
There he appoints our resting-place,
   And we may feel secure from foes.

6 There, 'midst the flock, the Shepherd dwells,
   The sheep around in safety lie ;
The wolf in vain with malice swells,
   For he protects them with his eye.

7 Dear Lord, if I am one of thine,
    From anxious thoughts I would be free :
    To trust and love and praise is mine,
    The care of all belongs to thee.

## 95.

### *The Garden.*

1 A GARDEN contemplation suits,
    And may instruction yield
Sweeter than all the flow'rs and fruits
    With which the spot is fill'd.

2 Eden was Adam's dwelling-place
    While blest with innocence ;
But sin o'erwhelm'd him with disgrace,
    And drove the rebel thence.

3 Oft as the garden-walk we tread
    We should bemoan his fall ;
The trespass of our legal head
    In ruin plunged us all.

4 The garden of Gethsemane
    The second Adam saw
Oppress'd with woe, to set us free
    From the avenging law.

5 How stupid we, who can forget,
    With gardens in our sight,
His agonies and bloody sweat
    In that tremendous night !

6 His church as a fair garden stands,
    Which walls of love enclose ;
Each tree is planted by his hands,
    And by his blessing grows.

7 Believing hearts are gardens too,
    For grace has sown its seeds
Where once, by nature, nothing grew
    But thorns and worthless weeds.

8 Such themes to those who Jesus love
    May constant joys afford,

And make a barren desert prove
The garden of the Lord.

## 96.

*For a Garden-seat or Summer-house.*

1 A SHELTER from the rain or wind,
  A shade from scorching heat,
A resting-place you here may find,
  To ease your weary feet,

2 Enter, but with a serious thought,
  Consider who is near!
This is a consecrated spot,—
  The Lord is present here!

3 A question of the utmost weight,
  While reading, meets your eye;
May conscience witness to your state,
  And give a true reply!

4 Is Jesus to your heart reveal'd
  As full of truth and grace?
And is his name your hope and shield,
  Your rest and hiding-place?

5 If so, for all events prepared,
  Whatever storms may rise,
He whom you love will safely guard,
  And guide you to the skies.

6 No burning sun or storm or rain
  Will there your peace annoy;
No sin, temptation, grief, or pain,
  Intrude to damp your joy.

7 But if his name you have not known,
  Oh, seek him while you may!
Lest you should meet his awful frown
  In that approaching day.

8 When the avenging Judge you see
  With terrors on his brow,
Where can you hide, or whither flee,
  If you reject him now?

## 97.

*The Creatures in the Lord's hands.*

1 THE water stood like walls of brass,
To let the sons of Isr'el pass,
And from the rock in rivers burst,
At Moses' pray'r, to quench their thirst.

2 The fire, restrain'd by God's commands,
Could only burn his people's bands:
Too faint, when he was with them there,
To singe their garments or their hair.

3 At Daniel's feet the lions lay
Like harmless lambs, nor touch'd their prey;
And ravens, which on carrion fed,
Procured Elijah flesh and bread.

4 Thus creatures only can fulfill
Their great Creator's holy will;
And when his servants need their aid,
His purposes must be obey'd.

5 So, if his blessing he refuse,
Their pow'r to help they quickly lose;
Sure as on creatures we depend,
Our hopes in disappointment end.

6 Then let us trust the Lord alone,
And creature-confidence disown:
Nor if they threaten need we fear,
They cannot hurt if he be near.

7 If instruments of pain they prove,
Still they are guided by his love:
As lancets by the surgeon's skill,
Which wound to cure, and not to kill.

## 98.

*On Dreaming.*

1 WHEN slumber seals our weary eyes,
The busy fancy wakeful keeps;
The scenes which then before us rise
Prove something in us never sleeps.

2 As in another world we seem,
  A new creation of our own;
  All appears real, though but a dream,
  And all familiar, though unknown.

3 Sometimes, the mind beholds again
  The past day's business in review——
  Resumes the pleasure or the pain,
  And sometimes all we meet is new.

4 What schemes we form, what pains we take!
  We fight, we run, we fly, we fall;
  But all is ended when we wake,
  We scarcely then a trace recall.

5 But though our dreams are often wild,
  Like clouds before the driving storm;
  Yet some important may be styled,
  Sent to admonish or inform.

6 What mighty agents have access,
  What friends from heaven, or foes from hell,
  Our minds to comfort or distress,
  When we are sleeping, who can tell?

7 One thing, at least, and 'tis enough,
  We learn from this surprising fact——
  Our dreams afford sufficient proof,
  The soul without the flesh can act.

8 This life, which mortals so esteem,
  That many choose it for their all,
  They will confess, was but a dream,
  When waken'd by death's awful call.

## 99.

### *The World.*

1 SEE, the world for youth prepares,
  Harlot-like, her gaudy snares!
  Pleasures round her seem to wait,
  But 'tis all a painted cheat.

2 Rash and unsuspecting youth
  Thinks to find thee always smooth,

Always kind, till better taught,
By experience dearly bought.

3 So the calm but faithless sea,
(Lively emblem, world, of thee,)
Tempts the shepherd from the shore,
Foreign regions to explore.

4 While no wrinkled wave is seen,
While the sky remains serene,
Fill'd with hopes and golden schemes,
Of a storm he little dreams.

5 By ere long the tempest raves,
Then he trembles at the waves,
Wishes then he had been wise,
But too late—he sinks and dies.

6 Hapless, thus, are they, vain world,
Soon on rocks of ruin hurl'd,
Who, admiring thee untried,
Court thy pleasure, wealth, or pride.

7 Such a shipwreck had been mine,
Had not Jesus (name divine!)
Saved me with a mighty hand,
And restored my soul to land.

8 Now, with gratitude I raise
Ebenezers to his praise;
Now my rash pursuits are o'er,
I can trust thee, world, no more.

## 100.

### The Enchantment Dissolved.

1 BLINDED in youth by Satan's arts,
The world to our unpractised hearts
A flatt'ring prospect shows;
Our fancy forms a thousand schemes
Of gay delights, and golden dreams,
And undisturb'd repose.

2 So in the desert's dreary waste,
By magic power produced in haste,
(As ancient fables say,)

Castles and groves and music sweet,
The senses of the trav'ler meet,
  And stop him in his way.

3 But while he listens with surprise,
The charm dissolves, the vision dies——
  'Twas but enchanted ground.
Thus if the Lord our spirit touch,
The world, which promised us so much,
  A wilderness is found.

4 At first we start and feel distress'd,
Convinced we never can have rest
  In such a wretched place;
But he whose mercy breaks the charm,
Reveals his own almighty arm,
  And bids us seek his face,

5 Then we begin to live indeed,
When from our sin and bondage freed
  By this beloved Friend:
We follow him from day to day,
Assured of grace through all the way,
  And glory at the end.

# OLNEY HYMNS.

## BOOK III.

### ON THE RISE, PROGRESS, CHANGES, AND COMFORTS OF THE SPIRITUAL LIFE.

I. SOLEMN ADDRESSES TO SINNERS.

II. SEEKING, PLEADING, AND HOPING.

III. CONFLICT.

V. COMFORT.

V. DEDICATION AND SURRENDER.

VI. CAUTIONS.

VII. PRAISE.

VIII. SHORT HYMNS.

## I. SOLEMN ADDRESSES TO SINNERS.

### 1.

#### *Expostulation.*

1 No words can declare,
No fancy can paint,
What rage and despair,
What hopeless complaint,
Fill Satan's dark dwelling,
The prison beneath,—
What weeping and yelling
And gnashing of teeth!

2 Yet sinners will choose
This dreadful abode!
Each madly pursues
The dangerous road;

Though God give them warning,
They onward will go,
They answer with scorning,
And rush upon woe,

3  How sad to behold
The rich and the poor,
The young and the old,
All blindly secure!
All posting to ruin,
Refusing to stop.
Ah! think what you're doing,
While yet there is hope!

4  How weak is your hand
To fight with the Lord!
How can you withstand
The edge of his sword?
What hope of escaping
For those who oppose,
When hell is wide gaping
To swallow his foes?

5  How oft have you dared
The Lord to his face!
Yet still you are spared
To hear of his grace.
O pray for repentance
And life-giving faith
Before the just sentence
Consign you to death.

6  It is not too late
To Jesus to flee;
His mercy is great,
His pardon is free!
His blood has such virtue
For all that believe
That nothing can hurt you
If him you receive.

## 2.

### *Alarm.*

1 STOP, poor sinner! stop and think,
  Before you farther go!
Will you sport upon the brink
  Of everlasting woe?
Once again I charge you, stop;
For unless you warning take,
Ere you are aware you drop
  Into the burning lake.

2 Say, have you an arm like God,
  That you his will oppose?
Fear you not that iron rod
  With which he breaks his foes?
Can you stand in that dread day
When he judgment shall proclaim,
And the earth shall melt away
  Like wax before the flame?

3 Pale-faced death will quickly come
  To drag you to his bar;
Then to hear your awful doom
  Will fill you with despair:
All your sins will round you crowd,
Sins of a blood-crimson dye;
Each for vengeance crying loud,
  And what can you reply?

4 Though your heart be made of steel,
  Your forehead lined with brass,
God at length will make you feel
  He will not let you pass:
Sinners then in vain will call,
(Though they now despise his grace)
Rocks and mountains, on us fall,
  And hide us from his face!

5 But as yet there is a hope
  You may his mercy know;
Though his arm is lifted up,
  He still forbears the blow:

'Twas for sinners Jesus died,
Sinners he invites to come;
None who come shall be denied,——
He says——" There still is room."

3.

*We were once as you are.*

1 SHALL men pretend to pleasure
  Who never knew the Lord?
Can all the worldling's treasure
  True peace of mind afford?
They shall obtain this jewel
  In what their hearts desire
When they by adding fuel
  Can quench the flame of fire.

2 Till you can bid the ocean,
  When furious tempests roar,
Forget its wonted motion,
  And rage and swell no more;
In vain your expectation
  To find content in sin;
Or freedom from vexation
  While passions reign within.

3 Come, turn your thoughts to Jesus,
  If you would good possess;
'Tis he alone that frees us
  From guilt and from distress:
When he by faith is present
  The sinner's troubles cease;
His ways are truly pleasant,
  And all his paths are peace.

4 Our time in sin we wasted,
  And fed upon the wind;
Untill his love we tasted
  No comfort could we find:
But now we stand to witness
  His power and grace to you;
May you perceive its fitness,
  And call upon him too!

5 Our pleasure and our duty,
   Though opposite before,
Since we have seen his beauty,
   Are join'd to part no more:
It is our highest pleasure,
   No less than duty's call,
To love him beyond measure,
   And serve him with our all.

4.

*Prepare to meet God.*

1 SINNER, art thou still secure?
   Wilt thou still refuse to pray?
Can thy heart or hands endure
   In the Lord's avenging day?
See his mighty arm is bared!
   Awful terrors clothe his brow!
For his judgment stand prepared,
   Thou must either break or bow.

2 At his presence nature shakes,
   Earth affrighted hastes to flee,
Solid mountains melt like wax,
   What will then become of thee?
Who his advent may abide?
   You that glory in your shame,
Will you find a place to hide
   When the world is wrapt in flame?

3 Then the rich, the great, the wise,
   Trembling, guilty, self-condemn'd,
Must behold the wrathful eyes
   Of the Judge they once blasphemed.
Where are now their haughty looks?
   Oh their horror and despair,
When they see the open'd books,
   And their dreadful sentence hear!

4 Lord, prepare us by thy grace!
   Soon we must resign our breath,
And our souls be call'd to pass
   Through the iron gate of death:

Let us now our day improve,
Listen to the gospel-voice,
Seek the things that are above,
Scorn the world's pretended joys.

5 Oh! when flesh and heart shall fail,
Let thy love our spirits cheer,
Strengthen'd thus we shall prevail
Over Satan, sin, and fear:
Trusting in thy precious name,
May we thus our journey end;
Then our foes shall lose their aim,
And the Judge will be our Friend.

### 5.

#### *Invitation.*

1 SINNERS, hear the Saviour's call,
   He now is passing by;
He has seen thy grievous thrall,
   And heard thy mournful cry.
He has pardons to impart,
   Grace to save thee from thy fears:
See the love that fills his heart,
   And wipe away thy tears.

2 Why art thou afraid to come
   And tell him all thy case?
He will not pronounce thy doom,
   Nor frown thee from his face:
Wilt thou fear Emmanuel?
Wilt thou dread the Lamb of God,
Who to save thy soul from hell,
   Has shed his precious blood?

3 Think how on the cross he hung,
   Pierced with a thousand wounds!
Hark from each, as with a tongue
   The voice of pardon sounds!
See from all his bursting veins,
Blood of wondrous virtue flow!
Shed to wash away thy stains,
   And ransom thee from woe.

4 Though his majesty be great,
      His mercy is no less;
   Though he thy transgressions hate,
      He feels for thy distress:
   By himself the Lord has sworn,
   He delights not in thy death;
   But invites thee to return,
      That thou may'st live by faith.

5 Raise thy downcast eyes, and see
      What throngs his throne surround!
   These, though sinners once like thee,
      Have full salvation found:
   Yield not then to unbelief,
   While he says, " There yet is room;
   Though of sinners, thou art chief,
      Since Jesus calls thee, come.

SIMILAR HYMNS.

Book   I.   Hymns 75, 91.
Book  II.   Hymns 1, 2, 3, 4, 6, 35, 77, 78, 83.


II. SEEKING, PLEADING, AND HOPING.

## 6.

### *The burdened Sinner.*

1 An! what can I do,
      Or where be secure?
   If justice pursue,
      What heart can endure ?
   The heart breaks asunder,
      Though hard as a stone,
   When God speaks in thunder,
      And makes himself known.

2 With terror I read
      My sins' heavy score,
   The number exceed
      The sands on the shore:

Guilt makes me unable
To stand or to flee;
So Cain murder'd Abel,
And trembled like me.

3 Each sin, like his blood,
With a terrible cry,
Calls loudly on God
To strike from on high;
Nor can my repentance,
Extorted by fear,
Reverse the just sentence :
'Tis just, though severe.

4 The case is too plain,
I had my own choice;
Again, and again,
I slighted his voice,——
His warnings neglected,
His patience abused,
His gospel rejected,
His mercy refused.

5 And must I then go
For ever to dwell
In torments and woe
With devils in hell?
Oh where is the Saviour
I scorn'd in times past?
His word in my favour
Would save me at last.

6 Lord Jesus, on thee
I venture to call,
Oh look upon me
The vilest of all!
For whom didst thou languish,
And bleed on the tree ?
Oh pity my anguish,
And say, "Twas for thee."

7 A case such as mine
Will honour thy power;
All hell will repine,
All heaven adore;

If in condemnation
Strict justice takes place,
It shines in salvation
More glorious through grace.

## 7.

*Behold, I am vile.*

1 O LORD, how vile am I,
  Unholy and unclean!
How can I dare to venture nigh
  With such a load of sin?

2 Is this polluted heart
  A dwelling fit for thee;
Swarming, alas! in every part,
  What evils do I see!

3 If I attempt to pray,
  And lisp thy holy name,
My thoughts are hurried soon away,
  I know not where I am.

4 If in thy word I look,
  Such darkness fills my mind,
I only read a sealed book,
  But no relief can find.

5 Thy gospel oft I hear,
  But hear it still in vain:
Without desire or love or fear,
  I like a stone remain.

6 Myself can hardly bear
  This wretched heart of mine;
How hateful then must it appear
  To those pure eyes of thine!

7 And must I then indeed
  Sink in despair and die?
Fain would I hope that thou didst bleed
  For such a wretch as I.

8 That blood which thou hast spilt,
  That grace which is thine own,

Can cleanse the vilest sinner's guilt,
   And soften hearts of stone.

9   Low at thy feet I bow,
   Oh pity and forgive;
Here will I lie, and wait till thou
   Shalt bid me raise and live.

### 8.

*The shining Light.*   C.

1  My former hopes are fled,
   My terror now begins:
   I feel, alas! that I am dead
   In trespasses and sins.

2  Ah, whither shall I fly?
   I hear the thunder roar:
   The law proclaims destruction nigh,
   And vengeance at the door.

3  When I review my ways,
   I dread impending doom;
   But sure a friendly whisper says,
   "Flee from the wrath to come."

4  I see, or think I see,
   A glimm'ring from afar;
   A beam of day that shines for me,
   To save me from despair.

5  Forerunner of the sun,
   It marks the pilgrim's way:
   I'll gaze upon it while I run,
   And watch the rising day.

### 9.

*Encouragement.*

1  My soul is beset
   With grief and dismay.
   I owe a vast debt,
   And nothing can pay:
   I must go to prison
   Unless that dear Lord

Who died and is risen
His pity afford.

2 The death that he died,
The blood that he spilt,
To sinners applied,
Discharge from all guilt:
This great Intercessor
Can give, if he please,
The vilest transgressor
Immediate release.

3 When nail'd to the tree,
He answer'd the pray'r
Of one who, like me,
Was nigh to despair;
He did not upbraid him
With all he had done,
But instantly made him
A saint and a son.

4 The jailor, I read,
A pardon received:
And how was he freed?
He only believed:
His case mine resembled,—
Like me he was foul,
Like me too he trembled,
But faith made him whole.

5 Though Saul in his youth,
To madness enraged,
Against the Lord's truth
And people engaged;
Yet Jesus, the Saviour,
Whom long he reviled,
Received him to favour,
And made him a child.

6 A foe to all good,
In wickedness skill'd,
Manasseh with blood
Jerusalem fill'd;

N                              16

In evil long harden'd,
The Lord he defied;
Yet he too was pardon'd,
When mercy he cried.

7 Of sinners the chief,
And viler than all,
The jailor or thief,
Manasseh or Saul:
Since they were forgiven,
Why should I despair
While Christ is in heaven
And still answers prayer?

## 10.

### *The waiting Soul.*

1 BREATHE from the gentle south, O Lord,
And cheer me from the north;
Blow on the treasures of thy word,
And call the spices forth!

2 I wish, thou know'st, to be resign'd,
And wait with patient hope;
But hope delay'd fatigues the mind
And drinks the spirits up.

3 Help me to reach the distant goal,
Confirm my feeble knee,
Pity the sickness of a soul
That faints for love of thee.

4 Cold as I feel this heart of mine,
Yet since I *feel* it so,
It yields some hope of life divine
Within, however low.

5 I seem forsaken and alone,
I hear the lion roar;
And every door is shut but one,
And that is mercy's door.

6 There, till the dear Deliv'rer come,
I'll wait with humble pray'r;

And when he calls his exile home,
The Lord shall find him there.

## 11.

### *The Effort.*

1 CHEER up, my soul, there is a mercy-seat,
Sprinkled with blood, where Jesus answers pray'r ;
There humbly cast thyself beneath his feet,
For never needy sinner perish'd there.

2 Lord, I am come! thy promise is my plea.
Without thy word I durst not venture nigh!
But thou hast call'd the burden'd soul to thee,
A weary burden'd soul, O Lord, am I!

3 Bow'd down beneath a heavy load of sin,
By Satan's fierce temptations sorely press'd,
Beset without, and full of fears within,
Trembling and faint, I come to thee for rest.

4 Be thou my refuge, Lord, my hiding-place !
I know no force can tear me from thy side ;
Unmoved I then may all accusers face,
And answer every charge with " Jesus died."

5 Yes, thou didst weep and bleed and groan and die—
Well hast thou known what fierce temptations mean—
Such was thy love, and now, enthroned on high,
The same compassions in thy bosom reign.

6 Lord, give me faith—he hears—what grace is this!
Dry up thy tears, my soul, and cease to grieve :
He shows me what he did, and who he is,
I must, I will, I can, I do believe.

## 12.

### *The Effort—in another Measure.*

1 APPROACH, my soul, the mercy-seat
Where Jesus answers pray'r ;
There humbly fall before his feet,
For none can perish there.

2 Thy promise is my only plea,
   With this I venture nigh :
Thou callest burden'd souls to thee,
   And such, O Lord, am I.

3 Bow'd down beneath a load of sin,
   By Satan sorely press'd;
By war without and fears within,
   I come to thee for rest.

4 Be thou my shield and hiding-place!
   That, shelter'd near thy side,
I may my fierce accuser face,
   And tell him, ' Thou hast died.'

5 Oh wond'rous love, to bleed and die,
   To bear the cross and shame,
That guilty sinners, such as I,
   Might plead thy gracious name.

6 " Poor tempest-tossed soul, be still.
   My promised grace receive :"
'Tis Jesus speaks—I must, I will,
   I can, I do believe.

## 13.

*Seeking the Beloved.*   C.

1 To those who know the Lord I speak,
   Is my Beloved near ?
The Bridegroom of my soul I seek,
   Oh ! when will he appear ?

2 Though once a man of grief and shame,
   Yet now he fills a throne,
And bears the greatest, sweetest name,
   That earth or heaven have known.

3 Grace flies before, and love attends
   His steps where'er he goes ;
Though none can see him but his friends,
   And they were once his foes.

4 He speaks—obedient to his call
   Our warm affections move :

Did he but shine alike on all,
Then all alike would love.

5 Then love in every heart would reign,
And war would cease to roar;
And cruel and blood-thirsty men
Would thirst for blood no more.

6 Such Jesus is, and such his grace,
Oh may it shine on you!
And tell him, when you see his face,
I long to see him too.

## 14.

*Rest for weary Souls.*

1 DOES the gospel-word proclaim
Rest for those who weary be?
Then my soul put in thy claim,
Sure that promise speaks to thee:
Marks of grace I cannot show,
All polluted is my best;
Yet I weary am, I know,
And the weary long for rest.

2 Burden'd with a load of sin,
Harass'd with tormenting doubt,
Hourly conflicts from within,
Hourly crosses from without:
All my little strength is gone,
Sink I must without supply;
Sure upon the earth is none
Can more weary be than I.

3 In the ark the weary dove
Found a welcome resting-place;
Thus my spirit longs to prove
Rest in Christ, the ark of grace:
Tempest-toss'd I long have been,
And the flood increases fast,
Open, Lord, and take me in
Till the storm be overpast.

4 Safely lodged within thy breast,
What a wondrous change I find!

Now I know thy promised rest
Can compose a troubled mind.
You that weary are like me:
Hearken to the gospel call,
To the ark for refuge flee,
Jesus will receive you all!

SIMILAR HYMNS.

Book I.   Hymns 45, 69, 82, 83, 84, 96.
Book II.  Hymn 29.

III   CONFLICT.

15.

*Light shining out of Darkness.*   C.

1 God moves in a mysterious way
    His wonders to perform;
  He plants his footsteps in the sea,
    And rides upon the storm.

2 Deep in unfathomable mines
    Of never-failing skill,
  He treasures up his bright designs,
    And works his sovereign will.

3 Ye fearful saints, fresh courage take,—
    The clouds ye so much dread,
  Are big with mercy, and shall break
    In blessings on your head.

4 Judge not the Lord by feeble sense,
    But trust him for his grace;
  Behind a frowning providence
    He hides a smiling face.

5 His purposes will ripen fast,
    Unfolding every hour;
  The bud may have a bitter taste,
    But sweet will be the flower.

6 Blind unbelief is sure to err,
   And scan his work in vain;
God is his own interpreter,
   And he will make it plain.

## 16.

### *Welcome Cross.*   C.

1 'Tis my happiness below
  Not to live without the cross,
But the Saviour's pow'r to know,
  Sanctifying every loss.
Trials must and will befall;
  But with humble faith to see
Love inscribed upon them all,
  This is happiness to me.

2 God in Isr'el sows the seeds
  Of affliction, pain, and toil:
These spring up and choak the weeds
  Which would else o'erspread the soil.
Trials make the promise sweet;
  Trials give new life to pray'r;
Trials bring me to his feet,
  Lay me low and keep me there.

3 Did I meet no trials here,
  No chastisement by the way,
Might I not with reason fear,
  I should prove a cast-away?
Bastards may escape the rod,
  Sunk in earthly vain delight;
But the true-born child of God
  Must not, would not, if he might.

## 17.

### *Afflictions sanctified by the Word.*   C.

1 O now I love thy holy word,
  Thy gracious covenant, O Lord!
It guides me in the peaceful way,
  I think upon it all the day.

2 What are the mines of shining wealth,
 The strength of youth, the bloom of health;
 What are all joys compared with those
 Thine everlasting word bestows?

3 Long unafflicted, undismay'd,
 In pleasure's path secure I stray'd;
 Thou madest me feel thy chast'ning rod,
 And straight I turn'd unto my God.

4 What though it pierced my fainting heart,
 I bless'd thine hand that caused the smart!
 It taught my tears awhile to flow,
 But saved me from eternal woe.

5 Oh! hadst thou left me unchastised,
 Thy precept I had still despised;
 And *still* the snare in secret laid
 Had my unwary feet betray'd.

6 I love thee, therefore, O my God,
 And breathe towards thy dear abode,
 Where in thy presence fully bless'd,
 Thy chosen saints for ever rest.

## 18.

*Temptation.* C.

1 The billows swell, the winds are high,
 Clouds overcast my wintry sky:
 Out of the depths to thee I call,
 My fears are great, my strength is small.

2 O Lord, the pilot's part perform,
 And guide and guard me through the storm:
 Defend me from each threat'ning ill,
 Control the waves, say—" Peace, be still!"

3 Amidst the roaring of the sea,
 My soul still hangs her hopes on thee;
 Thy constant love, thy faithful care,
 Is all that saves me from despair.

4 Dangers of every shape and name
 Attend the foll'wers of the Lamb.

Who leave the world's deceitful shore,
And leave it to return no more.

5 Though tempest-toss'd and half a wreck,
My Saviour through the floods I seek;
Let neither winds nor stormy main
Force back my shatter'd bark again.

## 19.

*Looking upwards in a Storm.* C.

1 God of my life, to thee I call,
Afflicted at thy feet I fall;
When the great water-floods prevail,
Leave not my trembling heart to fail!

2 Friend of the friendless and the faint,
Where should I lodge my deep complaint?
Where but with thee, whose open door
Invites the helpless and the poor?

3 Did ever mourner plead with thee,
And thou refuse that mourner's plea?
Does not the word still fix'd remain
That none shall seek thy face in vain?

4 That were a grief I could not bear,
Didst thou not hear and answer pray'r;
But a pray'r-hearing, answ'ring God,
Supports me under every load.

5 Fair is the lot that's cast for me,
I have an Advocate with thee:
They whom the world caresses most
Have no such privilege to boast.

6 Poor though I am, despised, forgot,
Yet God, my God, forgets me not;
And he is safe and must succeed,
For whom the Lord vouchsafes to plead.

N 2

## 20.

### The Valley of the Shadow of Death.   C.

1 My soul is sad and much dismay'd;
   See, Lord, what legions of my foes,
   With fierce Apollyon at their head,
   My heavenly pilgrimage oppose!

2 See from the ever-burning lake,
   How like a smoky cloud they rise!
   With horrid blasts my soul they shake,—
   With storms of blasphemies and lies.

3 Their fiery arrows reach the mark,
   My throbbing heart with anguish tear:
   Each lights upon a kindred spark,
   And finds abundant fuel there.

4 I hate the thought that wrongs the Lord:
   Ah! I would drive it from my breast,
   With thy own sharp two-edged sword,
   Far as the east is from the west.

5 Come then and chase the cruel host,
   Heal the deep wounds I have received!
   Nor let the pow'rs of darkness boast
   That I am foil'd and thou art grieved!

## 21.

### The Storm is hushed.

1 'Tis past—the dreadful stormy night
   Is gone, with all its fears!
   And now I see returning light,—
   The Lord, my Sun, appears.

2 The tempter, who but lately said
   I soon should be his prey,
   Has heard my Saviour's voice, and fled
   With shame and grief away.

3 Ah! Lord, since thou didst hide thy face
   What has my soul endured?
   But now 'tis past, I feel thy grace,
   And all my wounds are cured!

4 O wondrous change! but just before
　　Despair beset me round;
　I heard the lion's horrid roar,
　　And trembled at the sound:

5 Before corruption, guilt, and fear,
　　My comforts blasted fell;
　And unbelief discover'd near
　　The dreadful depths of hell:

6 But Jesus pitied my distress,
　　He heard my feeble cry,
　Reveal'd his blood and righteousness,
　　And brought salvation nigh.

7 Beneath the banner of his love
　　I now secure remain;
　The tempter frets, but dares not move
　　To break my peace again.

8 Lord, since thou thus hast broke my bands,
　　And set the captive free,
　I would devote my tongue, my hands,
　　My heart, my all to thee.

## 22.

### *Help in the Time of Need.*

1 UNLESS the Lord had been my stay,
　　(With trembling joy my soul may say,)
　My cruel foe had gain'd his end:
　But he appear'd for my relief,
　And Satan sees, with shame and grief,
　That I have an almighty Friend.

2 Oh! 'twas a dark and trying hour,
　When harass'd by the tempter's power,
　I felt my strongest hopes decline!
　You only who have known his arts,
　You only who have felt his darts,
　Can pity such a case as mine.

3 Loud in my ears a charge he read,
　(My conscience witness'd all he said,)
　My long black list of outward sin:

Then bringing forth my heart to view,
Too well what's hidden there he knew,
He show'd me ten times worse within.

4  'Tis all too true, my soul replied,
But I remember Jesus died,
And now he fills a throne of grace :
I'll go, as I have done before,
His mercy I may still implore;
I have his promise—" Seek my face."

5  But as when sudden fogs arise
The trees and hills, the sun and skies
Are all at once conceal'd from view :
So clouds of horror, black as night,
By Satan raised, hid from my sight
The throne of grace and promise too.

6  Then, while beset with guilt and fear,
He tried to urge me to despair,
He tried and he almost prevail'd :
But Jesus by a heavenly ray
Drove clouds and guilt and fear away,
And all the tempter's malice fail'd.

## 23.

### *Peace after a Storm.*   C.

1  WHEN darkness long has veil'd my mind,
And smiling day once more appears,
Then, my Redeemer, then I find
The folly of my doubts and fears.

2  Straight I upbraid my wand'ring heart,
And blush that I should ever be
Thus prone to act so base a part,
Or harbour one hard thought of thee.

3  Oh! let me then at length be taught
What I am still so slow to learn:
That God is love and changes not,
Nor knows the shadow of a turn.

4  Sweet truth, and easy to repeat!
But when my faith is sharply tried,

I find myself a learner yet,
Unskilful, weak, and apt to slide.

5 But, O my Lord, one look from thee
Subdues the disobedient will;
Drives doubt and discontent away,
And thy rebellious worm is still.

6 Thou art as ready to forgive,
As I am ready to repine;
Thou, therefore, all the praise receive;
Be shame and self-abhorrence mine.

### 24.

*Mourning and Longing.* C.

1 THE Saviour hides his face!
My spirit thirsts to prove
Renew'd supplies of pard'ning grace,
And never-fading love.

2 The favour'd souls who know
What glories shine in him
Pant for his presence, as the roe
Pants for the living stream.

3 What trifles tease me now!
They swarm like summer flies,
They cleave to every thing I do,
And swim before my eyes.

4 How dull the Sabbath-day,
Without the Sabbath's Lord!
How toilsome then to sing and pray
And wait upon the word?

5 Of all the truths I hear,
How few delight my taste!
I glean a berry here and there,
But mourn the vintage past.

6 Yet let me (as I ought)
Still hope to be supplied;
No pleasure else is worth a thought,
Nor shall I be denied.

7    Though I am but a worm,
       Unworthy of his care,
The Lord will my desire perform,
       And grant me all my pray'r.

25.

*Rejoice the Soul of thy Servant.*

1  WHEN my pray'rs are a burden and task,
    No wonder I little receive;
    O Lord, make me willing to ask,
    Since thou art so ready to give:
    Although I am bought with thy blood,
    And all thy salvation is mine,
    At a distance from thee, my chief good,
    I wander and languish and pine.

2  Of thy goodness of old, when I read,
    To those who were sinners like me,
    Why may I not wrestle and plead,
    With them a partaker to be?
    Thine arm is not shorten'd since then,
    And those who believe in thy name
    Ever find thou art Yea and Amen,
    Through all generations the same.

3  While my spirit within me is press'd
    With sorrow, temptation, and fear,
    Like John I would flee to thy breast,
    And pour my complaints in thine ear:
    How happy and favour'd was he
    Who could on thy bosom repose!
    Might this favour be granted to me,
    I'd smile at the rage of my foes.

4  I have heard of thy wonderful name,
    How great and exalted thou art;
    But ah! I confess to my shame,
    It faintly impresses my heart:
    The beams of thy glory display,
    As Peter once saw thee appear;
    That, transported like him, I might say,
    " It is good for my soul to be here."

5 What a sorrow and weight didst thou feel,
  When nail'd, for my sake, to the tree!
  My heart sure is harder than steel,
  To feel no more sorrow for thee:
  Oh! let me with Thomas descry
  The wounds in thy hands and thy side,
  And have feelings like his when I cry,
  "My God and my Saviour has died!"

6 But if thou hast appointed me still
  To wrestle and suffer and fight;
  O make me resign'd to thy will,
  For all thy appointments are right:
  This mercy, at least I entreat,
  That, knowing how vile I have been,
  I, with Mary, may wait at thy feet,
  And weep o'er the pardon of sin.

## 26.

### *Self-Acquaintance.*   C.

1 DEAR Lord! accept a sinful heart,
  Which of itself complains,
And mourns, with much and frequent smart,
  The evil it contains.

2 There fiery seeds of anger lurk,
  Which often hurt my frame;
And wait but for the tempter's work,
  To fan them to a flame.

3 Legality holds out a bribe
  To purchase life from thee;
And discontent would fain prescribe
  How thou shalt deal with me.

4 While unbelief withstands thy grace,
  And puts the mercy by,
Presumption, with a brow of brass,
  Says, " Give me, or I die."

5 How eager are my thoughts to roam
  In quest of what they love!

But ah! when duty calls them home,
  How heavily they move!

6 Oh, cleanse me in a Saviour's blood,
  Transform me by thy power,
And make me thy beloved abode,
  And let me rove no more!

## 27.

### Bitter and Sweet.

1 KINDLE, Saviour, in my heart
  A flame of love divine;
Hear, for mine I trust thou art,
  And sure I would be thine:
If my soul has felt thy grace,
If to me thy name is known;
Why should trifles fill the place
  Due to thyself alone?

2 'Tis a strange mysterious life
  I live from day to day;
Light and darkness, peace and strife,
  Bear an alternate sway:
When I think the battle won,
I have to fight it o'er again;
When I say I'm overthrown,
  Relief I soon obtain.

3 Often at the mercy-seat,
  While calling on thy name,
Swarms of evil thoughts I meet,
  Which fill my soul with shame.
Agitated in my mind,
Like a feather in the air,
Can I thus a blessing find?
  My soul, can this be pray'r?

4 But when Christ, my Lord and Friend,
  Is pleased to show his power,
All at once my troubles end,
  And I've a golden hour:

Then I see his smiling face,
Feel the pledge of joys to come,
Often, Lord, repeat this grace
    Till thou shalt call me home.

## 28.

### *Prayer for Patience.*   C.

1 LORD, who hast suffer'd all for me,
My peace and pardon to procure,
The lighter cross I bear for thee
Help me with patience to endure.

2 The storm of loud repining hush,
I would in humble silence mourn;
Why should th' unburnt though burning bush
Be angry as the crackling thorn?

3 Man should not faint at thy rebuke,
Like Joshua falling on his face,
When the cursed thing that Achan took
Brought Isr'el into just disgrace.

4 Perhaps some golden wedge suppress'd,
Some secret sin, offends my God;
Perhaps that Babylonish vest,
Self-righteousness, provokes the rod.

5 Ah! were I buffeted all day,
Mock'd, crown'd with thorns, and spit upon,
I yet should have no right to say,
My great distress is mine alone.

6 Let me not angrily declare
No pain was ever sharp like mine;
Nor murmur at the cross I bear,
But rather weep, rememb'ring thine.

## 29.

### *Submission.*   C.

1 O LORD, my best desire fulfill,
    And help me to resign
Life, health, and comfort to thy will,
    And make thy pleasure mine.

2 Why should I shrink at thy command,
    Whose love forbids my fear s
Or tremble at the gracious hand
    That wipes away my tears?

3 No, rather let me freely yield
    What most I prize to thee,
Who never hast a good withheld,
    Nor wilt withhold from me.

4 Thy favour all my journey through,
    Thou art engaged to grant;
What else I want, or think I do,
    'Tis better still to want.

5 Wisdom and mercy guide my way,
    Shall I resist them both?
A poor blind creature of a day,
    And crush'd before the moth!

6 But ah! my inward spirit cries,
    Still bind me to thy sway;
Else the next cloud that veils the skies,
    Drives all these thoughts away.

## 30.

### *Why should I complain?*

1 WHEN my Saviour, my Shepherd, is near,
How quickly my sorrows depart?
New beauties around me appear,
New spirits enliven my heart:
His presence gives peace to my soul,
And Satan assaults me in vain;
While my Shepherd his power controls
I think I no more shall complain.

2 But, alas! what a change do I find,
When my Shepherd withdraws from my sight!
My fears all return to my mind,
My day is soon changed into night;
Then Satan his efforts renews
To vex and ensnare me again;
All my pleasing enjoyments I lose,
And can only lament and complain.

3  By these changes I often pass through
  I am taught my own weakness to know;
  I am taught what my Shepherd can do,
  And how much to his mercy I owe:
  It is he that supports me through all;
  When I faint he revives me again;
  He attends to my pray'r when I call,
  And bids me no longer complain.

4  Wherefore then should I murmur and grieve,
  Since my Shepherd is always the same,
  And has promised he never will leave
  The soul that confides in his name?
  To relieve me from all that I fear,
  He was buffeted, tempted, and slain;
  And at length he will surely appear,
  Though he leaves me awhile to complain.

5  While I dwell in an enemy's land,
  Can I hope to be always in peace?
  'Tis enough that my Shepherd's at hand,
  And that shortly this warfare will cease:
  For ere long he will bid me remove
  From this region of sorrow and pain,
  To abide in his presence above,
  And then I no more shall complain,

## 31.

*Return, O Lord, how long?*

1  RETURN to bless my waiting eyes,
  And cheer my mourning heart, O Lord!
  Without thee all beneath the skies
  No real pleasure can afford.

2  When thy loved presence meets my sight
  It softens care and sweetens toil,
  The sun shines forth with double light,
  The whole creation wears a smile.

3  Upon thine arm of love I rest,
  Thy gracious voice forbids my fear;
  No storms disturb my peaceful breast,
  No foes assault when thou art near.

4 But, ah! since thou hast been away,
  Nothing but trouble have I known;
  And Satan marks me for his prey.
  Because he sees me left alone.

5 My sun is hid, my comforts lost,
  My graces droop, my sins revive;
  Distress'd, dismay'd, and tempest-toss'd,
  My soul is only just alive!

6 Lord, hear my cry, and come again!
  But all mine enemies to shame;
  And let them see 'tis not in vain
  That I have trusted in thy name.

## 32.

*Cast down, but not destroyed.*

1 THOUGH sore beset with guilt and fear,
  I cannot, dare not, quite despair;
  If I must perish, would the Lord
  Have taught my heart to love his word?
  Would he have given me eyes to see
  My danger and my remedy;
  Reveal'd his name, and bid me pray.
  Had he resolved to say me nay?

2 No——though cast down, I am not slain!
  I fall, but I shall rise again;
  The present, Satan, is thy hour,
  But Jesus shall control thy pow'r:
  His love will plead for my relief,
  He hears my groans, he sees my grief:
  Nor will he suffer thee to boast
  A soul that sought his help was lost.

3 'Tis true, I have unfaithful been,
  And grieved his Spirit by my sin:
  Yet still his mercy he'll reveal,
  And all my wounds and follies heal:
  Abounding sin I must confess,
  But more abounding is his grace:
  He once vouchsafed for me to bleed,
  And now he lives my cause to plead.

4 I'll cast myself before his feet,
I see him on his mercy-seat,
('Tis sprinkled with atoning blood);
There sinners find access to God:
Ye burden'd souls, approach with me,
And make the Saviour's name your plea:
Jesus will pardon all who come,
And strike your fierce accuser dumb.

## 33.

### The benighted Traveler.

1 FOREST beasts that live by prey,
Seldom show themselves by day;
But when day-light is withdrawn,
Then they rove and roar till dawn.

2 Who can tell the trav'ler's fears
When their horrid yells he hears?
Terror almost stops his breath,
While each step he looks for death.

3 Thus, when Jesus is in view,
Cheerful I my way pursue;
Walking by my Saviour's light
Nothing can my soul affright.

4 But when he forbears to shine,
Soon the trav'ler's case is mine;
Lost, benighted, struck with dread,
What a painful path I tread!

5 Then my soul with terror hears,
Worse than lions, wolves, or bears,
Roaring loud in every part,
Through the forest of my heart.

6 Wrath, impatience, envy, pride,
Satan and his host beside,
Press around me to devour;
How can I escape their power?

7 Gracious Lord, afford me light,
Put these beasts of prey to flight;
Let thy pow'r of love be shown;
Save me, for I am *thine* own!

## 34.

### *The Prisoner.*

1  WHEN the poor pris'ner, through a grate,
    Sees others walk at large,
How does he mourn his lonely state,
    And long for a discharge!

2  Thus I, confined in unbelief,
    My loss of freedom mourn;
And spend my hours in fruitless grief
    Untill my Lord return.

3  The beam of day, which pierces through
    The gloom in which I dwell,
Only discloses to my view
    The horrors of my cell.

4  Ah! how my pensive spirit faints
    To think of former days!
When I could triumph with the saints,
    And join their songs of praise!

5  But now my joys are all cut off,
    In prison I am cast;
And Satan, with a cruel scoff,
    Says, "Where's your God at last?"

6  Dear Saviour, for thy mercy's sake,
    My strong, my only plea,
These gates and bars in pieces break,
    And set the pris'ner free!

7  Surely my soul shall sing to thee,
    For liberty restored;
And all thy saints admire to see
    The mercies of the Lord.

## 35.

### *Perplexity Relieved.*

1  UNCERTAIN how the way to find
    Which to salvation led,
I listen'd long, with anxious mind,
    To hear what others said.

2 When some of joys and comforts told,
  I fear'd that I was wrong;
  For I was stupid, dead, and cold—
  Had neither joy nor song.

3 The Lord my lab'ring heart relieved,
  And made my burden light;
  Then for a moment I believed,
  Supposing all was right.

4 Of fierce temptations others talk'd,
  Of anguish, and dismay—
  Through what distresses they had walk'd
  Before they found the way.

5 Ah! then I thought my hopes were vain,
  For I had lived at ease;
  I wish'd for all my fears again,
  To make me more like these.

6 I had my wish: the Lord disclosed
  The evils of my heart,
  And left my naked soul exposed
  To Satan's fiery dart.

7 Alas! "I now must give it up,"
  I cried in deep despair;
  How could I dream of drawing hope
  From what I cannot bear?

8 Again my Saviour brought me aid,
  And when he set me free,
  "Trust simply on my word," he said,
  "And leave the rest to me."

## 36.

*Prayer answered by Crosses.*

1 I ASK'D the Lord, that I might grow
  In faith and love and every grace,
  Might more of his salvation know,
  And seek more earnestly his face.

2 'Twas he who taught me thus to pray,
  And he, I trust, has answer'd pray'r;

But it has been in such a way
As almost drove me to despair.

3 I hoped that in some favour'd hour
At once he'd answer my request;
And by his love's constraining power
Subdue my sins and give me rest.

4 Instead of this, he made me feel
The hidden evils of my heart;
And let the angry pow'rs of hell
Assault my soul in every part.

5 Yea more, with his own hand he seem'd
Intent to aggravate my woe;
Cross'd all the fair designs I schemed,
Blasted my gourds, and laid me low.

6 Lord, why is this, I trembling cried,
Wilt thou pursue thy worm to death?
" 'Tis in this way," the Lord replied,
" I answer pray'r for grace and faith.

7 " These inward trials I employ,
From self and pride to set thee free:
And break thy schemes of earthly joy,
That thou may'st seek thy all in me."

## 37.

*I will trust and not be afraid.*

1 BEGONE, unbelief,
My Saviour is near,
And for my relief
Will surely appear:
By pray'r let me wrestle,
And he will perform;
With Christ in the vessel,
I smile at the storm.

2 Though dark be my way,
Since he is my guide,
'Tis mine to obey,
'Tis his to provide;

Though cisterns be broken,
And creatures all fail,
The word he has spoken
Will surely prevail.

3 His love in time past
Forbids me to think
He'll leave me at last
In trouble to sink;
Each sweet Ebenezer
I have in review
Confirms his good pleasure
To help me quite through.

4 Determined to save,
He watch'd o'er my path,
When, Satan's blind slave,
I sported with death;
And can he have taught me
To trust in his name,
And thus far have brought me,
To put me to shame?

5 Why should I complain
Of want or distress,
Temptation or pain?
He told me no less:
The heirs of salvation,
I know from his word,
Through much tribulation
Must follow their Lord.

6 How bitter that cup,
No heart can conceive,
Which he drank quite up,
That sinners might live!
His way was much rougher
And darker than mine;
Did Jesus thus suffer,
And shall I repine?

7 Since all that I meet
Shall work for my good,

O                              46

The bitter is sweet,
The med'cine is food;
Though painful at present,
'Twill cease before long,
And then, O! how pleasant
The conqueror's song!

## 38.

### Questions to Unbelief.

1 IF to Jesus for relief
    My soul has fled by pray'r,
Why should I give way to grief,
    Or heart-consuming care?
Are not all things in his hand?
    Has he not his promise pass'd?
Will he then regardless stand,
    And let me sink at last?

2 While I know his providence
    Disposes each event,
Shall I judge by feeble sense,
    And yield to discontent?
If he worms and sparrows feed,
    Clothe the grass in rich array,
Can he see a child in need,
    And turn his eye away?

3 When his name was quite unknown,
    And sin my life employ'd,
Then he watch'd me as his own,
    Or I had been destroy'd!
Now his mercy-seat I know,
    Now by grace am reconciled;
Would he spare me while a foe,
    To leave me when a child?

4 If he all my wants supplied
    When I disdain'd to pray;
Now his Spirit is my guide,
    How can he say me nay?
If he would not give me up
    When my soul against him fought,

.    Will he disappoint the hope
       Which he himself has wrought?

5 If he shed his precious blood
       To bring me to his fold,
   Can I think that meaner good
       He ever will withhold?
   Satan, vain is thy device!
       Here my hope rests assured,
   In that great redemption price
       I see the whole secured.

## 39.

### Good Effects by weak Means.

1 UNBELIEF the soul dismays,
   What objections will it raise!
   But true faith securely leans
   On the promise, in the means.

2 If to faith it once be known,
   God has said, " It shall be done,
   And in this appointed way,"
   Faith has then no more to say.

3 Moses' road, by faith uprear'd,
   Through the sea a path prepared;
   Jericho's devoted wall
   At the trumpet's sound must fall.

4 With a pitcher and a lamp
   Gideon overthrew a camp:
   And a stone, well aim'd by faith,
   Proved the arm'd Philistine's death.

5 Thus the Lord is pleased to try
   Those who on his help rely;
   By the means he makes it known
   That the power is all his own.

6 Yet the means are not in vain,
   If the end we would obtain;
   Though the breath of pray'r be weak,
   None shall find but they who seek.

7 God alone the heart can reach,
  Yet the ministers must preach:
  'Tis their part the seed to sow,
  And 'tis his to make it grow.

## 40.

### *Why art thou cast down?*

1 Be still, my heart! these anxious cares
  To thee are burdens, thorns, and snares;
  They cast dishonour on thy Lord,
  And contradict his gracious word.

2 Brought safely by his hand thus far,
  Why wilt thou now give place to fear?
  How canst thou want if he provide,
  Or lose thy way with such a guide?

3 When first before his mercy-seat
  Thou didst to him thy all commit,
  He gave the warrant from that hour,
  To trust his wisdom, love, and power.

4 Did ever trouble yet befall,
  And he refuse to hear thy call?
  And has he not his promise pass'd,
  That thou shalt overcome at last?

5 Like David thou may'st comfort draw,
  Saved from the bear's and lion's paw;
  Goliath's rage I may defy,
  For God, my Saviour, still is nigh.

6 He who has help'd me hitherto,
  Will help me all my journey through,
  And give me daily cause to raise
  New Ebenezers to his praise.

7 Though rough and thorny be the road,
  It leads thee home apace to God;
  Then count thy present trials small,
  For heav'n will make amends for all.

## 41.

### The Way of Access.

1 ONE glance of thine, eternal Lord,
  Pierces all nature through;
Nor heaven nor earth nor hell afford
  A shelter from thy view!

2 The mighty whole, each smaller part,
  At once before thee lies;
And every thought of every heart
  Is open to thine eyes.

3 Though greatly from myself conceal'd,
  Thou seest my inward frame;
To thee I always stand reveal'd
  Exactly as I am.

4 Since, therefore, I can hardly bear
  What in myself I see,
How vile and black must I appear
  Most holy God, to thee!

5 But since my Saviour stands between,
  In garments dyed in blood,
'Tis he, instead of me, is seen,
  When I approach to God.

6 Thus, though a sinner, I am safe;
  He pleads before the throne
'Tis life and death in my behalf,
  And calls my sins his own.

7 What wondrous love, what mysteries,
  In this appointment shine!
My breaches of the law are his,
  And his obedience mine.

## 42.

### The Pilgrim's Song.

1 FROM Egypt lately freed
  By the Redeemer's grace,
A rough and thorny path we tread,
  In hopes to see his face.

2    The flesh dislikes the way,
      But faith approves it well!
   This only leads to endless day,
      All others lead to hell.

3    The promised land of peace
      Faith keeps in constant view:
   How diff'rent from the wilderness
      We are now passing through!

4    Here often from our eyes
      Clouds hide the light divine:
   There we shall have unclouded skies,
      Our sun will always shine.

5    Here griefs and cares and pains
      And fears distress us sore!
   But there eternal pleasure reigns,
      And we shall weep no more.

6    Lord, pardon our complaints,
      We follow at thy call;
   The joy prepared for suff'ring saints
      Will make amends for all.

SIMILAR HYMNS.

Book I. Hymns 10, 13, 21, 22, 24, 27, 40, 43, 44, 51, 56,
   63, 76, 88, 107, 115, 126, 130, 131, 136, 142.
Book II. Hymns 30, 31, 84, 87, 91.


IV. COMFORT.


43.

*Faith a new and comprehensive Sense.*

1 SIGHT, hearing, feeling, taste, and smell,
      Are gifts we highly prize;
   But faith does singly each excel,
      And all the five comprise.

2 More piercing than the eagle's sight,
      It views the world unknown,

Surveys the glorious realms of light,
    And Jesus on the throne.

3 It hears the mighty voice of God,
    And ponders what he saith.
His word and works, his gifts and rod,
    Have each a voice to faith.

4 It feels the touch of heav'nly power,
    And from that boundless source
Derives fresh vigour every hour
    To run its daily course.

5 The truth and goodness of the Lord
    Are suited to its taste;
Mean is the worldling's pamper'd board,
    To faith's perpetual feast.

6 It smells the dear Redeemer's name
    Like ointment poured forth;
Faith only knows, or can proclaim,
    Its savour or its worth.

7 Till saving faith possess the mind,
    In vain of sense we boast;
We are but senseless, tasteless, blind,
    And deaf and dead and lost.

## 44.

*The happy Change.*  C.

1 How blest thy creature is, O God,
    When, with a single eye,
He views the lustre of thy word—
    The day-spring from on high!

2 Through all the storms that veil the skies,
    And frown on earthly things,
The Sun of Righteousness he eyes,
    With healing on his wings.

3 Struck by that light, the human heart,
    A barren soil no more,
Sends the sweet smell of grace abroad,
    Where serpents lurk'd before.

4 The soul, a dreary province once
    Of Satan's dark domain,
  Feels a new empire form'd within,
    And owns a heav'nly reign.

5 The glorious orb, whose golden beams
    The fruitful year control,
  Since first, obedient to thy word,
    He started from the goal,

6 Has cheer'd the nations with the joys
    His orient rays impart:
  But, Jesus, 'tis thy light alone
    Can shine upon the heart.


## 45.

### *Retirement.*    C.

1 Far from the world, O Lord, I flee,
    From strife and tumult far!
  From scenes where Satan wages still
    His most successful war.

2 The calm retreat, the silent shade,
    With pray'r and praise agree;
  And seem by thy sweet bounty made
    For those who follow thee.

3 There, if thy Spirit touch the soul,
    And grace her mean abode,
  Oh with what peace and joy and love
    She communes with her God!

4 There like the nightingale she pours
    Her solitary lays;
  Nor asks a witness of her song,
    Nor thirsts for human praise.

5 Author and Guardian of my life,
    Sweet source of light divine,
  And (all harmonious names in one)
    My Saviour, thou art mine!

6 What thanks I owe thee, and what love,
    A boundless, endless store,

Shall echo through the realms above
When time shall be no more.

## 46.

*Jesus my All.*

1 WHY should I fear the darkest hour,
　Or tremble at the tempter's power!
　Jesus vouchsafes to be my tower.

2 Though hot the fight, why quit the field,
　Why must I either flee or yield,
　Since Jesus is my mighty shield?

3 When creature-comforts fade and die,
　Worldlings may weep, but why should I,—
　Jesus still lives, and still is nigh?

4 Though all the flocks and herds were dead,
　My soul a famine need not dread,
　For Jesus is my living bread.

5 I know not what may soon betide,
　Or how my wants shall be supplied;
　But Jesus knows, and will provide.

6 Though sin would fill me with distress,
　The throne of grace I dare address,
　For Jesus is my righteousness.

7 Though faint my pray'rs, and cold my love,
　My steadfast hope shall not remove
　While Jesus intercedes above.

8 Against me earth and hell combine,
　But on my side is power divine;
　Jesus is all, and he is mine.

## 47.

*The hidden Life.*   C.

1 To tell the Saviour all my wants,
　How pleasing is the task!
　Nor less to praise him when he grants
　Beyond what I can ask.

O 2

2  My lab'ring spirit vainly seeks
      To tell but half the joy ;
   With how much tenderness he speaks,
      And helps me to reply.

3  Nor were it wise, nor should I choose,
      Such secrets to declare ;
   Like precious wines, their taste they lose
      Exposed to open air.

4  But this with boldness I proclaim,
      Nor care if thousands hear,
   Sweet is the ointment of his name,
      Not life is half so dear.

5  And can you frown, my former friends,
      Who knew what once I was ;
   And blame the song that thus commends
      The Man who bore the cross?

6  Trust me, I draw the likeness true,
      And not as fancy paints ;
   Such honour may he give to you,
      For such have all his saints.

### 48.

*Joy and Peace in Believing.*   C.

1  SOMETIMES a light surprises
      The Christian while he sings ;
   It is the Lord who rises
      With healing in his wings.
   When comforts are declining,
      He grants the soul again
   A season of clear shining,
      To cheer it after rain.

2  In holy contemplation,
      We sweetly then pursue
   The theme of God's salvation,
      And find it ever new :
   Set free from present sorrow,
      We cheerfully can say,
   E'en let th' unknown to-morrow
      Bring with it what it may.

3 It can bring with it nothing
    But he will bear us through;
Who gives the lilies clothing
    Will clothe his people too:
Beneath the spreading heavens
    No creature but is fed;
And He who feeds the ravens
    Will give his children bread.

4 Though vine nor fig-tree neither
    Their wonted fruit shall bear,
Though all the field should wither,
    Nor flocks nor herds be there:
Yet God the same abiding,
    His praise shall tune my voice;
For, while in him confiding,
    I cannot but rejoice.

## 49.

### *True Pleasure.*   C.

1 LORD, my soul with pleasure springs
    When Jesus' name I hear,
And when God the Spirit brings
    The word of promise near:
Beauties too, in holiness,
Still delighted I perceive;
Nor have words that can express
    The joys thy precepts give.

2 Clothed in sanctity and grace,
    How sweet it is to see
Those who love thee, as they pass,
    Or when they wait on thee!
Pleasant too, to sit and tell
What we owe to love divine;
Till our bosoms grateful swell
    And eyes begin to shine.

3 Those the comforts I possess,
    Which God shall still increase:
All his ways are pleasantness,
    And all his paths are peace.

Nothing Jesus did or spoke,
Henceforth let me ever slight:
For I love his easy yoke,
  And find his burden light.

## 50.

### The Christian.   C.

1 Honour and happiness unite
  To make the Christian's name a praise;
  How fair the scene, how clear the light,
  That fill the remnant of his days!

2 A kingly character he bears,
  No change his priestly office knows;
  Unfading is the crown he wears,
  His joys can never reach a close.

3 Adorn'd with glory from on high,
  Salvation shines upon his face;
  His robe is of th' ethereal dye,
  His steps are dignity and grace.

4 Inferior honours he disdains,
  Nor stoops to take applause from earth:
  The King of kings himself maintains
  Th' expenses of his heavenly birth.

4 The noblest creature seen below,
  Ordain'd to fill a throne above;
  God gives him all he can bestow—
  His kingdom of eternal love!

6 My soul is ravish'd at the thought!
  Methinks from earth I see him rise!
  Angels congratulate his lot,
  And shout him welcome to the skies!

## 51.

### Lively Hope and gracious Fear.   C.

1 I was a grov'ling creature once,
  And basely cleaved to earth;
  I wanted spirit to renounce
    The clod that gave me birth.

2 But God has breathed upon a worm,
    And sent me from above
Wings, such as clothe an angel's form,
    The wings of joy and love.

3 With these to Pisgah's top I fly,
    And there delighted stand,
To view, beneath a shining sky,
    The spacious promised land.

4 The Lord of all the vast domain
    Has promised it to me;
The length and breadth of all the plain,
    As far as faith can see.

5 How glorious is my privilege!
    To thee for help I call;
I stand upon a mountain's edge,
    Oh, save me, lest I fall!

6 Though much exalted in the Lord,
    My strength is not my own;
Then let me tremble at his word,
    And none shall cast me down.

## 52.

### *Confidence.*

1 YES! since God himself has said it,
    On the promise I rely;
His good word demands my credit,
    What can unbelief reply;
    He is strong, and *can* fulfill;
    He is truth, and therefore *will.*

2 As to all the doubts and questions
    Which my spirit often grieve,
These are Satan's sly suggestions,
    And I need no answer give.
    He would fain destroy my hope,
    But the promise bears it up.

3 Sure the Lord thus far has brought me
    By his watchful tender care;

Sure 'tis he himself has taught me
How to seek his face by pray'r:
After so much mercy past,
Will he give me up at last?

4 True, I've been a foolish creature,
And have sinn'd against his grace!
But forgiveness is his nature,
Though he justly hides his face;
Ere he call'd me, well he knew
What a heart like mine would do.

5 In my Saviour's intercession
Therefore I will still confide;
Lord, accept my free confession,
I have sinn'd but thou hast died:
This is all I have to plead,
This is all the plea I need.

## 53.

### *Peace restored.*

1 Oh! speak that gracious word again,
  And cheer my drooping heart;
No voice but thine can soothe my pain,
  Or bid my fears depart.

2 And canst thou still vouchsafe to own
  A wretch so vile as I?
And may I still approach thy throne,
  And Abba, Father, cry?

3 Oh then let saints and angels join,
  And help me to proclaim
The grace that heal'd a breach like mine,
  And put my foes to shame!

4 How oft did Satan's cruel boast
  My troubled soul affright!
He told me I was surely lost,
  And God had left me quite.

5 Guilt made me fear, lest all were true
  The lying tempter said;
But now the Lord appears in view—
  My enemy is fled.

6 My Saviour, by his powerful word,
　　Has turn'd my night to day ;
　And his salvation's joys restored
　　Which I had sinn'd away.

7 Dear Lord, I wonder and adore,
　　Thy grace is all divine ;
　Oh! keep me that I sin no more
　　Against such love as thine!

## 54.

### *Hear what He has done for my Soul!*

1 SAVED by blood, I live to tell
　What the love of Christ hath done ;
　He redeem'd my soul from hell,
　Of a rebel made a son :
　Oh! I tremble still to think
　How secure I lived in sin ;
　Sporting on destruction's brink,
　Yet preserved from falling in.

2 In his own appointed hour,
　To my heart the Saviour spoke ;
　Touch'd me by his Spirit's power,
　And my dang'rous slumber broke.
　Then I saw and own'd my guilt :
　Soon my gracious Lord replied,
　"Fear not, I my blood have spilt,
　'Twas for such as thee I died."

3 Shame and wonder, joy and love,
　All at once possess'd my heart ;
　Can I hope thy grace to prove
　After acting such a part?
　"Thou hast greatly sinn'd," he said,
　"But I freely all forgive ;
　I myself thy debt have paid,
　Now I bid thee rise and live."

4 Come, my fellow-sinners, try,
　Jesus' heart is full of love!
　Oh that you, as well as I,
　May his wondrous mercy prove!

He has sent me to declare,
All is ready, all is free :
Why should any soul despair,
When he saved a wretch like me?

## 55.

*Freedom from Care.*

1 WHILE I lived without the Lord,
(If I might be said to live,)
Nothing could relief afford,
Nothing satisfaction give.

2 Empty hopes and groundless fear
Moved by turn my anxious mind :
Like a feather in the air,
Made the sport of every wind.

3 Now I see, whate'er betide,
All is well, if Christ be mine ;
He has promised to provide,
I have only to resign.

4 When a sense of sin and thrall
Forced me to the sinner's Friend,
He engaged to manage all,
By the way, and to the end.

5 " Cast," he said, " on me thy care,
'Tis enough that I am nigh ;
I will all thy burdens bear,
I will all thy wants supply.

6 " Simply follow as I lead,
Do not reason, but believe ;
Call on me in time of need,
Thou shalt surely help receive."

7 Lord, I would, I do submit,
Gladly yield my all to thee ;
What thy wisdom sees most fit,
Must be surely best for me.

8 Only, when the way is rough,
  And the coward flesh would start,
Let thy promise !and thy love
  Cheer and animate my heart.

## 56.

*Humiliation and Praise.*

[IMITATED FROM THE GERMAN.]

1 WHEN the wounded spirit hears
    The voice of Jesus' blood,
  How the message stops the tears
    Which else in vain had flow'd!
  Pardon, grace, and peace proclaim'd,
  And the sinner call'd a child;
  Then the stubborn heart is tamed,
    Renew'd and reconciled.

2 Oh! 'twas grace indeed to spare
    And save a wretch like me!
  Men or angels could not bear
    What I have offer'd thee!
  Were thy bolts at their command,
  Hell ere now had been my place;
  Thou alone couldst silent stand
    And wait to show thy grace.

3 If, in one created mind,
    The tenderness and love
  Of thy saints on earth were join'd
    With all the hosts above;
  Still that love were weak and poor,
  If compared, my Lord, with thine;
  Far too scanty to endure
    A heart so vile as mine.

4 Wondrous mercy I have found,
    But, ah, how faint my praise!
  Must I be a cumber-ground,
    Unfruitful all my days?

Do I in thy garden grow,
Yet produce thee only leaves?
Lord, forbid it should be so!
    The thought my spirit grieves.

5 Heavy charges Satan brings
    To fill me with distress;
Let me hide beneath thy wings,
    And plead thy righteousness:
Lord, to thee for help I call:
'Tis thy promise bids me come;
Tell him thou hast paid for all,
    And that shall strike him dumb.

## 57.

*For the Poor.*   C.

1 WHEN Hagar found the bottle spent,
    And wept o'er Ishmael,
A message from the Lord was sent
    To guide her to a well.

2 Should not Elijah's cake and cruse
    Convince us at this day,
A gracious God will not refuse
    Provisions by the way?

3 His saints and servants shall be fed,
    The promise is secure:
" Bread shall be given them," as he said.
" Their water shall be sure."

4 Repasts far richer they shall prove,
    Than all earth's dainties are;
'Tis sweet to taste a Saviour's love,
    Though in the meanest fare.

5 To Jesus then your trouble bring,
    Nor murmur at your lot;
While you are poor, and he is King,
    You shall not be forgot.

## 58.

*Home in View.*

1 As when the weary trav'ler gains
  The height of some o'erlooking hill,
  His heart revives if, cross the plains,
  He eyes his home, though distant still.

2 While he surveys the much-loved spot,
  He slights the space that lies between;
  His past fatigues are now forgot,
  Because his journey's end is seen.

3 Thus when the Christian pilgrim views
  By faith his mansion in the skies,
  The sight his fainting strength renews,
  And wings his speed to reach the prize.

4 The thought of home his spirit cheers,
  No more he grieves for troubles past,
  Nor any future trial fears,
  So he may safe arrive at last.

5 'Tis there, he says, I am to dwell
  With Jesus in the realms of day;
  Then I shall bid my cares farewell,
  And he shall wipe my tears away.

6 Jesus, on thee our hope depends,
  To lead us on to thine abode:
  Assured our home will make amends
  For all our toil while on the road.

SIMILAR HYMNS.

Book i, Hymns 4, 7, 9, 11, 25, 35, 36, 39, 41, 46, 47, 48, 70,
   95, 128, 132.
Book ii, Hymns 45, 46, 47.

## V. DEDICATION AND SURRENDER.

### 59.

*Old Things are passed away.*

1 LET worldly minds the world pursue
   It has no charms for me;
   Once I admired its trifles too,
   But grace has set me free.

2 Its pleasures now no longer please,
   No more content afford;
   Far from my heart be joys like these,
   Now I have seen the Lord.

3 As by the light of op'ning day
   The stars are all conceal'd;
   So earthly pleasures fade away
   When Jesus is reveal'd.

4 Creatures no more divide my choice,
   I bid them all depart;
   His name and love and gracious voice
   Have fix'd my roving heart.

5 Now, Lord, I would be thine alone,
   And wholly live to thee;
   But may I hope that thou wilt own
   A worthless worm like me?

6 Yes! though of sinners I'm the worst,
   I cannot doubt thy will;
   For if thou hadst not loved me first,
   I had refused thee still.

### 60.

*The Power of Grace.*

1 HAPPY the birth where grace presides.
   To form the future life!
   In wisdom's path the soul she guides,
   Remote from noise and strife.

2 Since I have known the Saviour's name,
    And what for me he bore;
  No more I toil for empty fame,
    I thirst for gold no more.

3 Placed by his hand in this retreat,
    I make his love my theme,
  And see that all the world calls great
    Is but a waking dream.

4 Since he has rank'd my worthless name
    Amongst his favour'd few,
  Let the mad world, who scoff at *them*,
    Revile and hate *me* too.

5 O thou whose voice the dead can raise,
    And soften hearts of stone,
  And teach the dumb to sing thy praise,
    This work is all thine own!

6 Thy wond'ring saints rejoice to see
    A wretch like me restored,
  And point and say—" How changed is he
    Who once defied the Lord!"

7 Grace bid me live, and taught my tongue
    To aim at notes divine;
  And grace accepts my feeble song—
    The glory, Lord, be thine!

## 61.

*My soul thirsteth for God.*   C.

1 I THIRST, but not as once I did,
    The vain delights of earth to share;
  Thy wounds, Emmanuel, all forbid
    That I should seek my pleasures there.

2 It was the sight of thy dear cross
    First wean'd my soul from earthly things,
  And taught me to esteem as dross
    The mirth of fools and pomp of kings.

3 I want that grace that springs from thee,
    That quickens all things where it flows,

And makes a wretched thorn like me
Bloom as the myrtle or the rose.

4 Dear fountain of delight unknown!
No longer sink below the brim;
But overflow, and pour me down
A living and life-giving stream!

5 For sure, of all the plants that share
The notice of thy Father's eye,
None proves less grateful to his care,
Or yields him meaner fruit than I.

## 62.

*Love constraining to Obedience.*    C.

1 No strength of nature can suffice
To serve the Lord aright;
And what she has she misapplies,
For want of clearer light.

2 How long beneath the law I lay
In bondage and distress!
I toil'd the precept to obey,
But toil'd without success.

3 Then to abstain from outward sin
Was more than I could do:
Now, if I feel its power within,
I feel I hate it too.

4 Then all my servile works were done
A righteousness to raise;
Now freely chosen in the Son,
I freely choose his ways.

5 What shall I do, was then the word,
That I may worthier grow?
What shall I render to the Lord?
Is my inquiry now.

6 To see the law by Christ fulfill'd,
And hear his pard'ning voice,
Changes a slave into a child,
And duty into choice.

## 63.

*The Heart healed and changed by Mercy.*    C.

1 SIN enslaved me many years,
   And led me bound and blind,
Till at length a thousand fears
   Came swarming o'er my mind.
Where, said I, in deep distress,
Will these sinful pleasures end?
How shall I secure my peace,
   And make the Lord my friend?

2 Friends and ministers said much,
   The gospel to enforce;
But my blindness still was such
   I chose a legal course:
Much I fasted, watch'd, and strove,
Scarce would show my face abroad,
Fear'd almost to speak or move,
   A stranger still to God.

3 Thus afraid to trust his grace,
   Long time did I rebel,
Till, despairing of my case,
   Down at his feet I fell:
Then my stubborn heart he broke,
And subdued me to his sway,
By a simple word he spoke,
   "Thy sins are done away."

## 64.

*Hatred of Sin.*    C.

1 HOLY Lord God! I love thy truth,
   Nor dare thy least commandments slight;
Yet pierced by sin, the serpent's tooth,
   I mourn the anguish of the bite.

2 But though the poison lurks within,
   Hope bids me still with patience wait;

Till death shall set me free from sin,
Free from the only thing I hate.

3 Had I a throne above the rest,
Where angels and archangels dwell,
One sin, unslain, within my breast,
Would make that heav'n as dark as hell.

4 The pris'ner, sent to breathe fresh air,
And bless'd with liberty again,
Would mourn were he condemn'd to wear
One link of all his former chain.

5 But oh! no foe invades the bliss
When glory crowns the Christian's head:
One view of Jesus as he is
Will strike all sin for ever dead.

## 65.

### *The Child.*

1 Quiet, Lord, my froward heart,
Make me teachable and mild,
Upright, simple, free from art,
Make me as a weaned child:
From distrust and envy free,
Pleased with all that pleases thee.

2 What thou shalt to-day provide,
Let me as a child receive;
What to-morrow may betide,
Calmly to thy wisdom leave:
'Tis enough that thou wilt care,
Why should I the burden bear?

3 As a little child relies
On a care beyond his own;
Knows he's neither strong nor wise,
Fears to stir a step alone:
Let me thus with thee abide,
As my Father, Guard, and Guide,

4 Thus preserved from Satan's wiles,
Safe from dangers, free from fears,

May I live upon thy smiles,
Till the promised hour appears,
When the sons of God shall prove
All their Father's boundless love.

## 66.

### *True Happiness.*

1 FIX my heart and eyes on thine!
What are other objects worth?
But to see thy glory shine
Is a heaven begun on earth:
Trifles can no longer move, —
Oh, I tread on all beside
When I feel my Saviour's love,
And remember how he died!

2 Now my search is at an end,
Now my wishes rove no more!
Thus my moments I would spend,
Love and wonder and adore:
Jesus, source of excellence!
All thy glorious love reveal;
Kingdoms shall not bribe me hence
While this happiness I feel.

3 Take my heart, 'tis all thine own,
To thy will my spirit frame;
Thou shalt reign, and thou alone,
Over all I have or am:
If a foolish thought shall dare
To rebel against thy word,
Slay it, Lord, and do not spare,
Let it feel thy Spirit's sword.

4 Making thus the Lord my choice,
I have nothing more to choose
But to listen to thy voice,
And my will in thine to lose:
Thus, whatever may betide,
I shall safe and happy be;
Still content and satisfied,
Having all in having thee.

P

## 67.

*The happy Debtor.*

1 Ten thousand talents once I owed,
   And nothing had to pay;
But Jesus freed me from the load,
   And wash'd my debt away.

2 Yet since the Lord forgave my sin,
   And blotted out my score,
Much more indebted I have been
   Than e'er I was before.

3 My guilt is cancel'd quite, I know,
   And satisfaction made;
But the vast debt of love I owe
   Can never be repaid.

4 The love I owe for sin forgiven,
   For power to believe,
For present peace and promised heaven,
   No angel can conceive.

5 That love of thine, thou sinner's Friend!
   Witness thy bleeding heart!
My little all can ne'er extend
   To pay a thousandth part.

6 Nay, more; the poor returns I make,
   I first from thee obtain;
And 'tis of grace that thou wilt take
   Such poor returns again.

7 'Tis well—it shall my glory be,
   (Let who will boast their store,)
In time and to eternity,
   To owe thee more and more.

SIMILAR HYMNS.

Book I. Hymns 27, 50, 70, 93, 122.
Book II. Hymns 23, 90.

## VI. CAUTIONS.

### 68.

*The New Convert.*   C.

1  THE new-born child of gospel grace,
   Like some fair tree when summer's nigh,
   Beneath Emmanuel's shining face,
   Lifts up his blooming branch on high.

2  No fears he feels, he sees no foes.
   No conflict yet his faith employs,
   Nor has he learn'd to whom he owes
   The strength and peace his soul enjoys.

3  But sin soon darts its cruel sting,
   And comforts sinking day by day;
   What seem'd his own, a self-fed spring,
   Proves but a brook that glides away.

4  When Gideon arm'd his num'rous host,
   The Lord soon made his numbers less;
   And said, " Lest Isr'el vainly boast,
   ' My arm procured me this success.' "

5  Thus will he bring our spirits down,
   And draw our ebbing comforts low,
   That, saved by grace, but not our own,
   We may not claim the praise we owe.

### 69.

*True and False Comforts.*   C.

1  O GOD, whose favourable eye
     The sin-sick soul revives,
   Holy and heav'nly is the joy
     Thy shining presence gives.

2  Not such as hypocrites suppose,
     Who, with a graceless heart,
   Taste not of thee, but drink a dose
     Prepared by Satan's art.

3 Intoxicating joys are theirs,
    Who, while they boast their light,
And seem to soar above the stars,
    Are plunging into night.

4 Lull'd in a soft and fatal sleep,
    They sin and yet rejoice:
Were they indeed the Saviour's sheep,
    Would they not hear his voice?

5 Be mine the comforts that reclaim
    The soul from Satan's pow'r;
That make me blush for what I am,
    And hate my sin the more.

6 'Tis joy enough, my All in All,
    At thy dear feet to lie;
Thou wilt not let me lower fall,
    And none can higher fly.

## 70.

### *True and False Zeal.*

1 ZEAL is that pure and heav'nly flame
    The fire of love supplies;
While that which often bears the name
    Is self in a disguise.

2 True zeal is merciful and mild,
    Can pity and forbear;
The false is headstrong, fierce, and wild,
    And breathes revenge and war.

3 While zeal for truth the Christian warms,
    He knows the worth of peace;
But self contends for names and forms,
    Its party to increase.

4 Zeal has attain'd its highest aim,
    Its end is satisfied,
If sinners love the Saviour's name,
    Nor seeks it aught beside.

5 But self, however well employ'd,
    Has its own ends in view;

And says, as boasting Jehu cried,—
 "Come, see what I can do."

6 Self may its poor reward obtain,
 And be applauded here;
But zeal the best applause will gain,
 When Jesus shall appear.

7 Dear Lord! the idol self dethrone,
 And from our hearts remove;
And let no zeal by us be shown
 But that which springs from love.

## 71.

### *A Living and a Dead Faith.* C.

1 THE Lord receives his highest praise
 From humble minds and hearts sincere;
While all the loud professor says
 Offends the righteous Judge's ear.

2 To walk as children of the day,
 To mark the precept's holy light,
To wage the warfare, watch, and pray,
 Show who are pleasing in his sight.

3 Not words alone it cost the Lord
 To purchase pardon for his own;
Nor will a soul by grace restored
 Return the Saviour words alone.

4 With golden bells the priestly vest,
 And rich pomegranates border'd round,
The need of holiness express'd,
 And call'd for fruit as well as sound.

5 Easy, indeed, it were to reach
 A mansion in the courts above,
If swelling words and fluent speech
 Might serve instead of faith and love.

6 But none shall gain the blissful place
 Or God's unclouded glory see,
Who talks of free and sov'reign grace,
 Unless that grace has made him free!

## 72.

*Abuse of the Gospel.*   C.

1 Too many, Lord, abuse thy grace,
    In this licentious day;
And while they boast they see thy face,
    They turn their own away.

2 Thy book displays a gracious light.
    That can the blind restore;
But these are dazzled by the sight,
    And blinded still the more.

3 The pardon such presume upon,
    They do not beg but steal;
And when they plead it at thy throne.
    Oh! where's the Spirit's seal?

4 Was it for this, ye lawless tribe,
    The dear Redeemer bled?
Is this the grace the saints imbibe
    From Christ the living head?

5 Ah, Lord! we know thy chosen few
    Are fed with heavenly fare;
But these, the wretched husks they chew
    Proclaim them what they are.

6 The liberty our hearts implore,
    Is not to live in sin;
But still to wait at Wisdom's door,
    Till Mercy calls us in.

## 73.

*The Narrow Way.*   C.

1 WHAT thousands never knew the road!
What thousands hate it when 'tis known!
None but the chosen tribes of God
Will seek or choose it for their own.

2 A thousand ways in ruin end,
One only leads to joys on high;
By that my willing steps ascend,
Pleased with a journey to the sky.

3 No more I ask or hope to find
  Delight or happiness below;
  Sorrow may well possess the mind
  That feeds where thorns and thistles grow.

4 The joy that fades is not for me,
  I seek immortal joys above;
  There glory without end shall be
  The bright reward of faith and love.

5 Cleave to the world, ye sordid worms,
  Contented lick your native dust;
  But God shall fight with all his storms,
  Against the idol of your trust.

## 74.

*Dependence.*   C.

1  To keep the lamp alive,
     With oil we fill the bowl;
   'Tis water makes the willow thrive,
     And grace that feeds the soul.

2  The Lord's unsparing hand
     Supplies the living stream;
   It is not at our own command,
     But still derived from him.

3  Beware of Peter's word,
     Nor confidently say,
   "I never *will* deny thee, Lord,'
     But grant I never may.

4  Man's wisdom is to seek
     His strength in God alone;
   And even an angel would be weak
     Who trusted in his own.

5  Retreat beneath his wings,
     And in his grace confide;
   This more exalts the King of kings
     Than all your works beside.

6  In Jesus is our store,
     Grace issues from his throne;
   Whoever says, "I want no more,"
     Confesses he has none.

## 75.

*Not of Works.*  C.

1 GRACE, triumphant in the throne,
Scorns a rival, reigns alone;
Come and bow beneath her sway,
Cast your idol-works away.
Works of man, when made his plea,
Never shall accepted be;
Fruits of pride (vain-glorious worm)
Are the best he can perform.

2 Self, the god his soul adores,
Influences all his pow'rs;
Jesus is a slighted name,
Self-advancement all his aim:
But when God the Judge shall come,
To pronounce the final doom,
Then for rocks and hills to hide
All his works and all his pride!

3 Still the boasting heart replies,
What, the worthy and the wise,
Friends to temperance and peace,
Have not these a righteousness?
Banish every vain pretence
Built on human excellence;
Perish every thing in man,
But the grace that never can.

## 76.

*Sin's Deceit.*

1 SIN, when view'd by Scripture light,
Is a horrid, hateful sight;
But when seen in Satan's glass,
Then it wears a pleasing face.

2 When the gospel-trumpet sounds,
When I think how grace abounds,
When I feel sweet peace within,
Then I'd rather die than sin.

3 When the cross I view by faith,
  Sin is madness, poison, death:
  Tempt me not, 'tis all in vain,
  Sure I ne'er can yield again.

4 Satan for a while debarr'd,
  When he finds me off my guard,
  Puts his glass before my eyes,
  Quickly other thoughts arise.

5 What before excited fears,
  Rather pleasing now appears;
  If I sin, it seems so small,
  Or perhaps no sin at all.

6 Often thus through sin's deceit,
  Grief and shame and loss I meet;
  Like a fish, my soul mistook,
  Saw the bait, but not the hook.

7 O my Lord, what shall I say?
  How can I presume to pray?
  Not a word have I to plead,
  Sins like mine are black indeed.

8 Made by past experience wise,
  Let me learn thy word to prize;
  Taught by what I've felt before,
  Let me Satan's glass abhor.

## 77.

*Are there few that shall be saved?*

1 DESTRUCTION's dangerous road
    What multitudes pursue,
  While that which leads the soul to God
    Is known or sought by few.

2 Believers enter in
    By Christ, the living gate;
  But they who will not leave their sin,
    Complain it is too strait.

3 If self must be denied,
    And sin forsaken quite,

P 2

They rather choose the way that's wide,
And strive to think it right.

4   Encompass'd by a throng,
On numbers they depend ;
So many surely can't be wrong,
And miss a happy end.

5   But numbers are no mark
That men will right be found ;
A few were saved in Noah's ark,
For many millions drown'd.

6   Obey the gospel call,
And enter while you may,
The flock of Christ is always small,
And none are safe but they.

7   Lord, open sinners' eyes
Their awful state to see ;
And make them, ere the storm arise,
To thee for safety flee.

## 78.

### *The Sluggard.*

1   The wishes that the sluggard frames,
Of course must fruitless prove ;
With folded arms he stands and dreams,
But has no heart to move.

2   His field from others may be known,—
The fence is broken through,
The ground with weeds is overgrown,
And no good crop in view.

3   No hardship he or toil can bear,
No difficulty meet ;
He wastes his hours at home, for fear
Of lions in the street.

4   What wonder then, if sloth and sleep
Distress and famine bring,
Can he in harvest hope to reap,
Who will not sow in spring ?

5 'Tis often thus in soul concerns
  We gospel sluggards see ;
Who, if a wish would serve their turns,
  Might true believers be.

6 But when the preacher bids them watch,
  And seek and strive and pray,
At every poor excuse they catch—
  A lion in the way.

7 To use the means of grace how loath!
  We call them still in vain ;
They yield to their beloved sloth,
  And fold their arms again.

8 Dear Saviour, let thy pow'r appear,
  The outward call to aid.
These drowsy souls can only hear
  The voice that wakes the dead.

## 79.

### *Not in Word, but in Power.*

1 How soon the Saviour's gracious call
  Disarm'd the rage of bloody Saul.
Jesus, the knowledge of thy name
  Changes the lion to a lamb.

2 Zaccheus, when he knew the Lord,
  What he had gain'd by wrong restored ;
And of the wealth he prized before,
  He gave the half to feed the poor.

3 The woman who so vile had been,
  When brought to weep o'er pardon'd sin,
Was from her evil ways estranged,
  And show'd that grace her heart had changed.

4 And can we think the power of grace
  Is lost by change of time and place ?
Then it was mighty, all allow,
  And is it but a notion now ?

5 Can they whom pride and passion sway,
  Who mammon and the world obey,

In envy or contention live,
Presume that they indeed believe?

6  True faith unites to Christ the root,
By him producing holy fruit;
And they who no such fruit can show,
Still on the stock of nature grow.

7  Lord, let thy word effectual prove
To work in us obedient love!
And may each one who hears it, dread
A name to live, and yet be dead.

SIMILAR HYMNS.

Book I.   Hymns 8, 20, 85, 87, 91, 104, 12 , 139, 14
Book II.  Hymns 34, 49, 86, 91, 99.

## VII. PRAISE.

### 80.

*Praise for Faith.*   C.

1  OF all the gifts thine hand bestows,
Thou Giver of all good!
Not heaven itself a richer knows,
Than my Redeemer's blood.

2  Faith too, the blood-receiving grace
From the same hand we gain;
Else, sweetly as it suits our case,
That gift had been in vain.

3  Till thou thy teaching power apply,
Our hearts refuse to see,
And, weak as a distemper'd eye,
Shut out the view of thee.

4  Blind to the merits of thy Son,
What misery we endure!
Yet fly that hand from which alone
We could expect a cure.

5 We praise thee, and would praise thee more;
　　To thee our all we owe,—
　The precious Saviour, and the power
　　That makes him precious too.

## 81.

*Grace and Providence.*   C.

1 ALMIGHTY King! whose wondrous hand
　Supports the weight of sea and land,
　Whose grace is such a boundless store
　No heart shall break that sighs for more,

2 Thy providence supplies my food,
　And 'tis thy blessing makes it good;
　My soul is nourish'd by thy word—
　Let soul and body praise the Lord.

3 My streams of outward comfort came
　From him, who built this earthly frame;
　Whate'er I want his bounty gives,
　By whom my soul for ever lives.

4 Either his hand preserves from pain,
　Or, if I feel it, heals again;
　From Satan's malice shields my breast,
　Or over-rules it for the best.

5 Forgive the song that falls so low
　Beneath the gratitude I owe!
　It means thy praise, however poor,—
　An angel's song can do no more.

## 82.

*Praise for redeeming Love.*

1 LET us *love* and *sing* and *wonder*,
　　Let us *praise* the Saviour's name!
　He has hush'd the Law's loud thunder,
　　He has quench'd mount Sinai's flame:
　　He has wash'd us with his blood,
　　He has brought us nigh to God.

2 Let us *love* the Lord who bought us,
　　Pitied us when enemies,

Call'd us by his grace, and taught us,
  Gave us ears, and gave us eyes:
He has wash'd us with his blood,
He presents our souls to God.

3 Let us *sing*, though fierce temptation
    Threaten hard to bear us down!
  For the Lord, our strong salvation,
    Holds in view the conq'ror's crown:
  He, who wash'd us with his blood,
  Soon will bring us home to God.

4 Let us *wonder*, grace and justice
    Join, and point to mercy's store :
  When through grace in Christ our trust is,
    Justice smiles, and asks no more:
  He who wash'd us with his blood
  Has secured our way to God.

5 Let us *praise*, and join the chorus
    Of the saints enthroned on high;
  Here they trusted him before us,
    Now their praises fill the sky:
  "Thou hast wash'd us with thy blood,
  Thou art worthy, Lamb of God!"

6 Hark! the name of Jesus sounded
    Loud from golden harps above!
  Lord, we blush, and are confounded,
    Faint our praises, cold our love!
  Wash our souls and songs with blood,
  For by thee we come to God.

## 83.

*I will praise the Lord at all times.*   C.

1 WINTER has a joy for me
  While the Saviour's charms I read,
  Lowly, meek, from blemish free,
  In the snow-drop's pensive head.

2 Spring returns, and brings along
  Life-invigorating suns:
  Hark! the turtle's plaintive song
  Seems to speak his dying groans!

3 Summer has a thousand charms,
    All expressive of his worth        ;
    'Tis his sun that lights and warms,
    His the air that cools the earth.

4 What! has autumn left to say
    Nothing of a Saviour's grace?
    Yes, the beams of milder day
    Tell me of his smiling face.

5 Light appears with early dawn;
    While the sun makes haste to rise,
    See his bleeding beauties drawn
    On the blushes of the skies.

6 Evening, with a silent pace,
    Slowly moving in the west,
    Shows an emblem of his grace,
    Points to an eternal rest.

## 84.

### *Perseverance.*

1 REJOICE, believer, in the Lord,
    Who makes your cause his own;
    The hope that's built upon his word
    Can ne'er be overthrown.

2 Though many foes beset your road,
    And feeble is your arm,
    Your life is hid with Christ in God,
    Beyond the reach of harm.

3 Weak as you are, you shall not faint,
    Or fainting shall not die;
    Jesus, the strength of every saint,
    Will aid you from on high.

4 Though sometimes unperceived by sense,
    Faith sees him always near,
    A guide, a glory, a defence;
    Then what have you to fear?

5 As surely as he overcame
    And triumph'd once for you;

So surely you that love his name
Shall triumph in him too.

## 85.

### Salvation.

1  SALVATION! what a glorious plan!
    How suited to our need!
  The grace that raises fallen man
    Is wonderful indeed!

2  'Twas Wisdom form'd the vast design,
    To ransom us when lost;
  And Love's unfathomable mine
    Provided all the cost.

3  Strict Justice, with approving look,
    The holy cov'nant seal'd;
  And Truth and Power undertook
    The whole should be fulfill'd.

4  Truth, Wisdom, Justice, Pow'r, and Love,
    In all their glory shone
  When Jesus left the courts above,
    And died to save his own.

5  Truth, Wisdom, Justice, Pow'r, and Love,
    Are equally displayed,
  Now Jesus reigns enthroned above,
    Our Advocate and Head.

6  Now sin appears deserving death,
    Most hateful and abhorr'd;
  And yet the sinner lives by faith,
    And dares approach the Lord.

## 86.

### Reigning Grace.

1  Now may the Lord reveal his face,
    And teach our stamm'ring tongues
  To make his sovereign, reigning grace,
    The subject of our songs!
  No sweeter subject can invite
    A sinner's heart to sing;

Or more display the glorious right
   Of our exalted King.

2 This subject fills the starry plains
   With wonder, joy, and love;
And furnishes the noblest strains
   For all the harps above :
While the redeem'd in praise combine
   To grace upon the throne,
Angels in solemn chorus join,
   And make the theme their own.

3 Grace reigns, to pardon crimson sins,
   To melt the hardest hearts;
And from the work it once begins
   It never more departs :
The world and Satan strive in vain
   Against the chosen few;
Secured by grace's conq'ring reign,
   They all shall conquer too.

4 Grace tills the soil, and sows the seeds,
   Provides the sun and rain,
Till from the tender blade proceeds
   The ripen'd harvest grain.
'Tis grace that call'd our souls at first,
   By grace thus far we're come,
And grace will help us through the worst,
   And lead us safely home.

5 Lord, when this changing life is past,
   If we may see thy face,
How shall we praise and love at last,
   And sing the reign of grace.
Yet let us aim, while here below,
   Thy mercy to display;
And own at least the debt we owe,
   Although we cannot pay.

## 87.

*Praise to the Redeemer.*

1 PREPARE a thankful song
   To the Redeemer's name!

His praises should employ each tongue,
  And every heart inflame!

2  He laid his glory by,
    And dreadful pains endured,
  That rebels such as you and I
    From wrath might be secured.

3  Upon the cross he died,
    Our debt of sin to pay;
  The blood and water from his side
    Wash guilt and filth away.

4  And now he pleading stands
    For us, before the throne,
  And answers all the Law's demands,
    With what himself hath done.

5  He sees us willing slaves
    To sin and Satan's power;
  But with an outstretch'd arm he saves
    In his appointed hour.

6  The Holy Ghost he sends
    Our stubborn souls to move;
  To make his enemies his friends,
    And conquer them by love.

7  The love of sin departs,
    The life of grace takes place,
  Soon as his voice invites our hearts
    To rise and seek his face.

8  The world and Satan rage,
    But he their power controls;
  His wisdom, love, and truth, engage
    Protection for our souls.

9  Though press'd, we will not yield,
    But shall prevail at length,
  For Jesus is our sun and shield,
    Our righteousness and strength.

10  Assured that Christ our King
    Will put our foes to flight,
  We on the field of battle sing,
    And triumph while we fight.

## 88.

*Man by Nature, Grace, and Glory.*

1 Lord, what is man? extremes how wide
In this mysterious nature join!
The flesh to worms and dust allied,
The soul immortal and divine!

2 Divine at first, a holy flame
Kindled by the Almighty's breath;
Till, stain'd by sin, it soon became
The seat of darkness, strife, and death.

3 But Jesus, O amazing grace!
Assumed our nature as his own,
Obey'd and suffer'd in our place,
Then took it with him to his throne.

4 Now what is man, when grace reveals
The virtue of a Saviour's blood?
Again a life divine he feels,
Despises earth and walks with God.

5 And what, in yonder realms above,
Is ransom'd man ordain'd to be?
With honour, holiness, and love,
No seraph more adorn'd than he.

6 Nearest the throne, and first in song,
Man shall his hallelujahs raise;
While wond'ring angels round him throng,
And swell the chorus of his praise.

SIMILAR HYMNS.

Book I. Hymns 57, 58, 59, 79, 80.
Book II. Hymns 37, 38, 39, 41, 42.

## VIII. SHORT HYMNS,

### BEFORE SERMON.

### 89.

Confirm the hope thy word allows,
Behold us waiting to be fed ;
Bless the provisions of thy house,
And satisfy thy poor with bread :
Drawn by thine invitation Lord,
Thirsty and hungry we are come !
Now from the fulness of thy word,
Feast us, and send us thankful home.

### 90.

1 Now, Lord, inspire the preacher's heart,
    And teach his tongue to speak ;
Food to the hungry soul impart,
    And cordials to the weak.

2 Furnish us all with light and pow'rs
    To walk in wisdom's ways ;
So shall the benefit be ours,
    And thou shalt have the praise.

### 91.

1 Thy promise, Lord, and thy command,
    Have brought us here to-day ;
And now, we humbly waiting stand
    To hear what thou wilt say.

2 Meet us, we pray, with words of peace,
    And fill our hearts with love ;
That from our follies we may cease,
    And henceforth faithful prove.

## 92.

1 HUNGRY and faint and poor,
  Behold us, Lord, again
Assembled at thy mercy's door,
  Thy bounty to obtain.

2 Thy word invites us nigh,
  Or we must starve indeed ;
For we no money have to buy,
  No righteousness to plead.

3 The food our spirits want
  Thy hand alone can give;
Oh! hear the pray'r of faith, and grant
  That we may eat and live.

## 93.

### Psalm cvi, 4, 5.

1 REMEMBER us, we pray thee, Lord,
  With those who love thy gracious name;
And to our souls that good afford
  Thy promise has prepared for them.

2 To us thy great salvation show,
  Give us a taste of love divine ;
That we thy people's joy may know,
  And in their holy triumph join.

## 94.

1 NOT to Sinai's dreadful blaze,
  But to Zion's throne of grace,
By a way mark'd out with blood,
  Sinners now approach to God.

2 Not to hear the fiery law,
  But with humble joy to draw
Water, by that well supplied
  Jesus open'd when he died.

3 Lord, there are no streams but thine
  Can assuage a thirst like mine ;
'Tis a thirst thyself didst give,
  Let me therefore drink and live.

## 95.

1 OFTEN thy public means of grace,
  Thy thirsty people's wat'ring-place,
    The archers have beset;
  Attack'd them in thy house of pray'r,
  To prison dragg'd, or to the bar,
    When thus together met.

2 But we from such assaults are freed,
  Can pray and sing and hear and read,
    And meet and part in peace:
  May we our privileges prize,
  In their improvement make us wise,
    And bless us with increase.

3 Unless thy presence thou afford,
  Unless thy blessing clothe the word,
    In vain our liberty!
  What would it profit to maintain
  A name for life, should we remain
    Formal and dead to thee?

AFTER SERMON.

## 96.

Deut. xxxiii, 26, 29.

1 WITH Isr'el's God who can compare?
  Or who like Isr'el happy are?
  O people saved by the Lord,
  He is thy shield and great reward!

2 Upheld by everlasting arms,
  Thou art secured from foes and harms:
  In vain their plots, and false their boasts,
  Our refuge is the Lord of Hosts.

## 97.

### Habakkuk, iii, 17, 18.

JESUS is mine! I'm now prepared
To meet with what I thought most hard!
Yes, let the winds of trouble blow,
And comforts melt away like snow;
No blasted trees or failing crops
Can hinder my eternal hopes:
Though creatures change, the Lord's the same;
Then let me triumph in his name.

## 98.

WE seek a rest beyond the skies,
  In everlasting day;
Through floods and flames the passage lies,
  But Jesus guards the way:
The swelling flood and raging flame
  Hear and obey his word;
Then let us triumph in his name,
  Our Saviour is the Lord.

## 99.

### Deut. xxxii, 9, 10.

1 THE saints Emmanuel's portion are,
Redeem'd by price, reclaim'd by power;
His special choice, and tender care,
Owns them and guards them every hour.

2 He finds them in a barren land,
Beset with sins and fears and woes;
He leads and guides them by his hand,
And bears them safe from all their foes.

## 100.

### Hebrews, xiii, 20, 22.

1 Now may He who from the dead
Brought the Shepherd of the sheep,

Jesus Christ, our King and Head,
All our souls in safety keep!

2 May he teach us to fulfill
What is pleasing in his sight;
Perfect us in all his will,
And preserve us day and night!

3 To that dear Redeemer's praise,
Who the cov'nant seal'd with blood,
Let our hearts and voices raise
Loud thanksgivings to our God.

## 101.

### 2 Corinthians, xiii, 14.

MAY the grace of Christ our Saviour,
And the Father's boundless love,
With the Holy Spirit's favour,
Rest upon us from above!
Thus may we abide in union
With each other and the Lord;
And possess in sweet communion,
Joys which earth cannot afford.

## 102.

THE peace which God alone reveals,
And by his word of grace imparts.
Which only the believer feels,
Direct and keep and cheer your hearts:
And may the Holy Three in One,
The Father, Word, and Comforter,
Pour an abundant blessing down
On every soul assembled here.

## 103.

1 To thee our wants are known,
From thee are all our pow'rs;
Accept what is thine own,
And pardon what is ours:
Our praises, Lord, and pray'rs receive.
And to thy word a blessing give.

2 O grant that each of us,
  Now met before thee here,
  May meet together thus
  When thou and thine appear,
And follow thee to heaven our home!
Even so, Amen, Lord Jesus, come.


GLORIA PATRI.

## 104.

1  THE Father we adore,
   And everlasting Son,
The Spirit of his love and pow'r,
The glorious Three in One!

2  At the creation's birth
   This song was sung on high,
Shall sound through every age on earth,
   And through eternity.

## 105.

1 FATHER of angels and of men,
   Saviour, who hast us bought,
  Spirit, by whom we're born again,
   And sanctified and taught!

2 Thy glory, holy Three in One,
   Thy people's song shall be,
Long as the wheels of time shall run,
   And to eternity.

## 106.

1 GLORY to God the Father's name,
  To Jesus, who for sinners died;
The Holy Spirit claims the same,
By whom our souls are sanctified.

Q                              46

2 Thy praise was sung when time began,
 By angels, through the starry spheres :
 And shall, as now, be sung by man
 Through vast eternity's long years.

## 107.

YE saints on earth, ascribe, with heav'n's high host,
 Glory and honour to the One in Three :
To God the Father, Son, and Holy Ghost,
 As was, and is, and evermore shall be.

# POEMS.

———

My waking dreams are best conceal'd;
Much folly, little good they yield;
But now and then I gain, when sleeping,
A friendly hint, that's worth the keeping;
Lately I dream'd of one who cried,
" Beware of self, beware of pride;
When you are prone to build a Babel,
Recall to mind this little fable."

———

ONCE on a time a paper kite
Was mounted to a wondrous height,
Where, giddy with its elevation,
It thus express'd self-admiration:
" See how yon crowds of gazing people
Admire my flight above the steeple;
How would they wonder if they knew
All that a kite like me can do?
Were I but free, I'd take a flight,
And pierce the clouds beyond their sight;
But, ah! like a poor pris'ner bound,
My string confines me near the ground:
I'd brave the eagle's towering wing
Might I but fly without a string."
It tugg'd and pull'd, while thus it spoke,
To break the string—at last it broke.
Deprived at once of all its stay,
In vain it tried to soar away;
Unable its own weight to bear,
It flutter'd downward through the air:
Unable its own course to guide,
The winds soon plunged it in the tide.

Ah! foolish kite, thou hadst no wing,
How couldst thou fly without a string?
　My heart replied, "O Lord, I see
How much this kite resembles me!
Forgetful that by thee I stand,
Impatient of thy ruling hand;
How oft I've wish'd to break the lines
Thy wisdom for my lot assigns!
How oft indulged a vain desire
For something more, or something higher!
And, but for grace and love divine,
A fall thus dreadful had been mine."

## A THOUGHT ON THE SEA-SHORE.

1 In every object here I see
Something, O Lord, that leads to thee:
Firm as the rocks thy promise stands,
Thy mercies countless as the sands,
Thy love a sea immensely wide,
Thy grace an ever-flowing tide.

2 In every object here I see
Something, my heart, that points at thee:
Hard as the rocks that bound the strand,
Unfruitful as the barren sand,
Deep and deceitful as the ocean,
And, like the tides, in constant motion.

## THE SPIDER AND TOAD.

Some author (no great matter who,
Provided what he says be true,)
Relates he saw, with hostile rage,
A spider and a toad engage:
For though with poison both are stored,
Each by the other is abhorr'd;
It seems as if their common venom
Provoked an enmity between 'em.

Implacable, malicious, cruel,
Like modern hero in a duel,
The spider darted on his foe,
Infixing death at every blow.
The toad by ready instinct taught,
An antidote, when wounded, sought
From the herb plaintain, growing near,
Well known to toads its virtues rare,
The spider's poison to repel;
It cropp'd the leaf, and soon was well.
This remedy it often tried,
And all the spider's rage defied.
The person who the contest view'd,
While yet the battle doubtful stood,
Removed the healing plant away—
And thus the spider gain'd the day;
For when the toad return'd once more
Wounded, as it had done before,
To seek relief, and found it not,
It swell'd and died upon the spot.
    In every circumstance but one
(Could that hold too I were undone)
No glass can represent my face
More justly than this tale my case.
The toad's an emblem of my heart,
And Satan acts the spider's part.
Envenom'd by his poison, I
Am often at the point to die;
But He who hung upon the tree,
From guilt and woe to set me free,
Is like the plaintain leaf to me.
To him my wounded soul repairs,
He knows my pain and hears my pray'rs;
From him I virtue draw by faith,
Which saves me from the jaws of death;
From him fresh life and strength I gain,
And Satan spends his rage in vain.
No secret arts or open force
Can rob me of this sure resource;
Though banish'd to some distant land,
My med'cine would be still at hand;

Q 2

Though foolish men its worth deny,
Experience gives them all the lie;
Though Deists and Socinians join,
Jesus still lives, and still is mine.
'Tis here the happy diff'rence lies,
My Saviour reigns above the skies,
Yet to my soul is always near,
For he is God, and every where.
His blood a sov'reign balm is found
For every grief and every wound:
And sooner all the hills shall flee
And hide themselves beneath the sea,
Or ocean, starting from its bed,
Rush o'er the cloud-topt mountain's head,
The sun, exhausted of its light,
Become the source of endless night,
And ruin spread from pole to pole,
Than Jesus fail the tempted soul.

# TABLE TO THE HYMNS.

## BOOK I.

## BOOK II.

### I. SEASONS.

#### NEW-YEARS' HYMNS.

#### BEFORE ANNUAL SERMONS.

Glasgow: Printed by William Collins & Co.

LaVergne, TN USA
03 January 2011
210966LV00003B/15/A